BitTorrent™ For Dumm

CW00547041

How BitTorrent Works

1. **A user *seeds* (places) a torrent file into the BitTorrent network.**

   Some torrents are uploaded to a Web server; others are served off a local machine.

2. **You click a Web link to the torrent, telling your BitTorrent client to read the torrent file and begin downloading the media files you want.**

   The torrent keeps track of which pieces are needed to create a complete copy of the file(s). At the same time, the *tracker,* or Web server software, handles coordinating the *swarm* (group) of *peers* (those with the file) and *leechers* (those who want the file).

3. **As you start downloading, you immediately begin to upload as well, creating a continuous exchange of pieces throughout the network, as shown in this figure.**

   The more requests are made to the tracker, and the more peers that join the swarm of uploading and downloading, the faster the file distribution is.

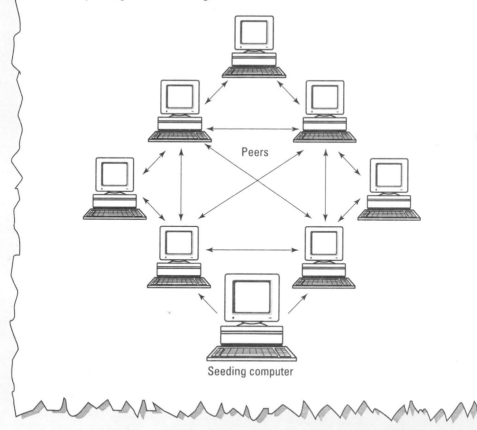

Peers

Seeding computer

BitTorrent™ For Dummies®

Cheat Sheet

Looking at the Official BitTorrent Client

You can download and install the Official BitTorrent client for free at www.bittorrent.com.

Torrent currently being downloaded.

Set the upload rate you want to use to send the files back into the network.

List of torrent files in the queue to be downloaded.

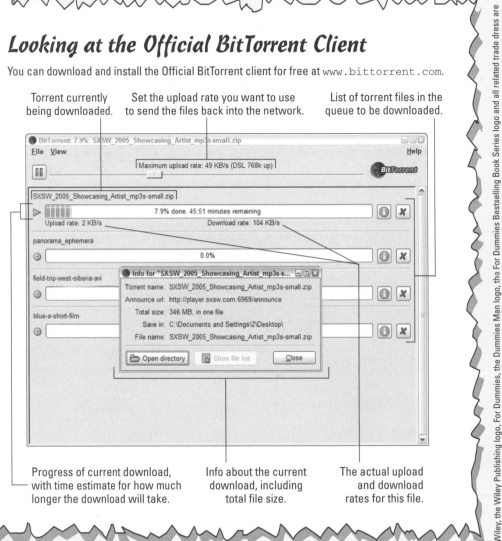

Progress of current download, with time estimate for how much longer the download will take.

Info about the current download, including total file size.

The actual upload and download rates for this file.

For Dummies: Bestselling Book Series for Beginners

BitTorrent™

FOR

DUMMIES®

by Susannah Gardner
Author of *Buzz Marketing with Blogs For Dummies*

and Kris Krug
Writer and technologist

WILEY

Wiley Publishing, Inc.

BitTorrent™ For Dummies®

Published by
Wiley Publishing, Inc.
111 River Street
Hoboken, NJ 07030-5774
www.wiley.com

WILEY

About the Authors

Susannah Gardner is the creative director of Hop Studios, a Web design company specializing in custom publishing solutions, and the author of *Buzz Marketing with Blogs For Dummies*. She has also worked for *The Los Angeles Times* Web site and taught online journalism for the University of Southern California.

Kris Krug is a writer, designer, photographer, and Web aficionado based in Vancouver, British Columbia.

Dedication

Susannah: The weekend of my final book deadline for *Buzz Marketing with Blogs For Dummies* my much-loved cat Lukaska died. Although it was too late to dedicate that book to her, I can make up for that here. This book is for Lukaska, a cat whose personality was matched only by her beauty. She kept me company while I wrote my first solo book, and was much missed while I wrote this one.

Authors' Acknowledgments

Susannah: I owe a great deal to my husband, Travis, for supporting me on this project even though he thought I was crazy to take on another book before the last was even in bookstores. His quiet strength by my side is something I rely on every day.

Very special thanks are due to my wonderful co-author, Kris Krug, who is responsible for much of the expertise and knowledge this book contains. His clear explanations of technology kept the book from spinning off into technical mumbo-jumbo, and his dedication to this project in the face of other deadlines and pressures was outstanding.

Thanks also to Michael Overing, who wrote the legal chapter for this book and who generally helped us wade through some of the rather murky waters that surround file-sharing these days. His insight and quick grasp of the essential technical issues involved were crucial.

As always, I want to extend a special hug to Janine Warner, the friend who got me started working on books. She continues to be an important source of information and inspiration as I work on books of my own.

We had two editors on this book. Beth Taylor started us off on the right foot and then left to have her first child. She was ably succeeded by Nicole Haims, whose relaxed handling of crises and missing screenshots will not be forgotten. Nicole was also the copy editor on this book and kept things spelled right and grammatically functional. Cameo Wood technical-edited her way to making the book understandable — thanks, Cameo! And special thanks go to the technically prescient Melody Layne, acquisitions editor at Wiley, and to everyone listed in the publisher's acknowledgments. I am grateful to all of you.

Thanks also to my parents, Jan and Phil Gardner, my brother Matt, my sister Debbie, my mother-in-law, Pat Smith, and my sister-in-law, Virginia Smith. Thanks also to Lance Watanabe, Jae and Karin Sung, Elaine Zinngrabe, Zipporah Lax, Jason and Noriko Manikel, Deborah Nathanson, Tracy Dominick, Robin Rauzi, Amy Leach, Dorothy Ingebretsen, and everyone in The Breakfast Club.

Thanks are also due to Bram Cohen, without whom there would be no need for this book, and to everyone else who has used or will use BitTorrent and keep the community alive.

And thanks to you, dear reader.

Kris: Writing a book is by no means a solo effort. This project was exceptionally smooth and a pleasure to work on from start to finish. *BitTorrent For Dummies* is my first book and I was lucky to write for such a professional and friendly team at Wiley. I'd like to thank Beth Taylor, Nicole Haims, Melody Layne, and Cameo Wood for all the guidance and direction they provided on this first project. You are a great team and it would be fun to work with you again.

Susie, thank you so much for taking me under your wing and showing me the "Wiley Way." You have been a great friend and mentor, and really this book should be dedicated to you. Thank you also to Travis, who kept us well fed and also made sure we were up on the latest BitTorrent news and headlines via IM and e-mail.

There were lots of other folks in my camp on this project who deserve mentioning, most notably Shane Birley. Thanks, Shane, for all the research, writing, beer, and friendship you provided throughout this project. Somebody should get this guy the next book deal!

Melissa, Sierra, and Judah who sacrificed evenings and weekends with Daddy so that I could get this thing done; thank you so much. Thank you for supporting me and loving me. The summer is young and we have a lot of time to make it up. Bring on Paris!

Boris, Roland, Richard, the RainCity crew, Sxates Christine Vandebeek, VanDigiCam, Chris Pirillo, and all my other friends who let me put things on hold for a while when deadline weekends drew near — thank you so much. Lastly, thanks to Bram Cohen and the rest of the BitTorrent community for furthering technology that truly gives normal people the power of mass distribution through independent online publishing.

Publisher's Acknowledgments

We're proud of this book; please send us your comments through our online registration form located at www.dummies.com/register/.

Some of the people who helped bring this book to market include the following:

Acquisitions, Editorial, and Media Development

Project Editors: Nicole Haims, Beth Taylor

Acquisitions Editor: Melody Layne

Technical Editor: Cameo Wood

Editorial Managers: Carol Sheehan, Jodi Jensen

Media Development Manager: Laura VanWinkle

Media Development Supervisor: Richard Graves

Editorial Assistant: Amanda Foxworth

Cartoons: Rich Tennant (www.the5thwave.com)

Composition Services

Project Coordinator: Maridee Ennis

Layout and Graphics: Carl Byers, Andrea Dahl, Denny Hager, Joyce Haughey

Proofreaders: Leeann Harney, Carl William Pierce, Dwight Ramsey, TECHBOOKS Production Services

Indexer: TECHBOOKS Production Services

Publishing and Editorial for Technology Dummies

 Richard Swadley, Vice President and Executive Group Publisher

 Andy Cummings, Vice President and Publisher

 Mary Bednarek, Executive Acquisitions Director

 Mary C. Corder, Editorial Director

Publishing for Consumer Dummies

 Diane Graves Steele, Vice President and Publisher

 Joyce Pepple, Acquisitions Director

Composition Services

 Gerry Fahey, Vice President of Production Services

 Debbie Stailey, Director of Composition Services

Contents at a Glance

Table of Contents

Introduction

Welcome to *BitTorrent For Dummies!* I hope you're as excited about this technology as I am. BitTorrent is a great tool for sharing content with people — your friends and family, and even people you've never met around the world. This book is designed to walk you through using BitTorrent from start to finish, from choosing and installing a BitTorrent client to finding content to download and authoring and sharing your own multimedia.

Because file sharing can be a legally troublesome area, I also spend some time outlining just the risks of downloading pirated material like television shows and movies are. Ultimately, you're the one who makes the final choice in what you download, but you should understand the risks involved when you download copyrighted material using BitTorrent.

I've purposely written this book with beginners in mind, people who have welcomed computers into their homes and are adventurous about trying new technologies, but who may want a friend to help them along. More experienced computer users who are new to BitTorrent will still find this book useful.

About This Book

BitTorrent downloads account for about a third of all Internet traffic right now, and that figure is rising. I'm betting that means you bought this book hoping to start using the technology right away — so I've written it to facilitate just that. Don't feel that you need to start with Chapter 1 and work your way to the end. Use the detailed Table of Contents to hop straight to the chapters and sections containing the answers you need first, and come back to the others later. Each chapter is designed to give you easy answers and guidance, accompanied by step-by-step instructions for specific tasks.

In fact, if you want to find out how to start downloading content right away, the first three chapters may be all you need! Chapters 1 through 3 are designed to plunge you right into the nuts and bolts of *torrenting,* with software recommendations and help handling what you download. Don't forget to review the chapter on using BitTorrent without violating copyright, though!

Although you can use BitTorrent strictly to download content, this book contains plenty of information for the creative and business-minded folks among you who want to share content quickly and to a large audience. As this technology grows and changes it will become more and more exciting and dynamic to use. I congratulate you on taking the plunge into a young technology with such great potential.

Conventions Used in This Book

Keeping things consistent makes them easier to understand. In this book, those consistent elements are *conventions*. Notice how the word *conventions* is in italics? That's a convention I use throughout the book. New terms are in italics, and are typically followed by a definition immediately afterward or within a few sentences.

I include many Web addresses, or URLs, in the book. Throughout, they look like this: www.bittorrentfordummies.com. Occasionally, you may find a Web address set off on a separate line, like this:

```
www.bittorrentfordummies.com
```

I never include the http:// that is part of Web addresses in the text — but not simply because I get tired of typing that particular set of letters! Most browsers don't need you to include them when you enter a URL. Very old browsers are the rare exception to that rule, and if you find yourself having to type in the http://, consider upgrading your browser! The Mozilla Firefox browser is terrific (www.getfirefox.com).

Sets of features and lists of related items are set in bullets. When you see a numbered list, that's your cue to read from the top of the list from beginning to end. The steps in a numbered list outline tasks that must be done in order.

What You're Not to Read

This book is comprehensive on the subject of installing a BitTorrent client, downloading content, handling it after you download it, creating your own BitTorrent content, and serving it to the world. I've even included some extras to help you promote and protect your content, and to protect yourself from pirated material. What all that means is that you may not need to read every single chapter. Feel free to skip directly to what interests you most. Skip whole sections if you like; it'll be there for you later if you need it.

Foolish Assumptions

When I was writing this book and told people the topic, I got a lot of blank looks. BitTorrent is a new technology for a lot of people! If you're reading this book, you know enough to be interested, but that doesn't mean I expect you to be an expert. That's my job, after all!

At the same time, realize that using BitTorrent can be very technical and tough for beginners. Don't be too hard on yourself while you're figuring out how to make things work. This idea of the *For Dummies* series isn't that you are a dummy at all. The whole idea is that this reference is an easy-to-use guide designed for readers with all kinds of technical experience. All you really need to bring to these pages is a willingness to figure things out and try new things. Oh, and having a computer is also pretty essential!

In fact, one assumption I make is that you have a computer with enough hard drive space to store big files. Ideally, you have a high-speed Internet connection that enables your computer to stay online all day and all night. A DSL or cable modem connection is especially important if you plan to download or share very large files.

If you're new to BitTorrent, this book gets you started and walks you step-by-step through all the skills and elements you need to have a successful BitTorrent experience. If you've been using BitTorrent for some time now, *BitTorrent For Dummies* can help you round out those areas that are a little shaky, or answer those niggling questions you've had about how this all works.

How This Book Is Organized

To make things as clear and logical as possible, I've written *BitTorrent For Dummies* to be a comprehensive resource. This next section breaks down each part of the book and outlines what you can find in them. The chapters themselves are designed to deal with a single task or concept, covering it completely before you move on to the next.

Part 1: Getting Started with BitTorrent

Part I is the crucial one — the one that gets you using BitTorrent in a hurry. Spend some time in Chapter 1 to find out a little bit about what makes this technology tick, and what makes it so unique among peer-to-peer file-sharing technologies. In fact, reading this chapter and seeing how BitTorrent puts the bits and pieces together may help you understand why you need to take certain actions in order to make BitTorrent function at its best!

In Chapter 2, I give you a survey of some good BitTorrent clients, and show you how to download and install one. There's some special — and technical — information here on getting your Internet connection configured properly to get the most out of your download times, which is very important when you are downloading large data files!

While reading Chapter 3, you find out what to do with the data you download. After you have a file on your desktop, it can be a little confusing to figure out how to get at the good part, especially when it has been compressed into an archive format. I tell you about some good audio and video players as well, and how to go about getting them onto your computer if you don't have one already.

Part II: Managing BitTorrent Content

Part II is the unsexy part of BitTorrent — keeping your files organized, knowing what to delete, and when. Part II is also where you find out all about BitTorrent and the law. In Chapter 4, you can have some fun using the Internet search engines and public *tracker* sites to find torrents to download.

Use Chapter 5 to discover how to manage all this data. Some of these files can be pretty big. Is your computer up to storing all of them? I talk in this chapter about how to back up what you download or store it in sensible ways that enable you find it when you need it.

It's important to remember that not everything you find available to download is actually safe to download. A lot of the TV shows and movies you come across are there because someone *pirated* them — copied them and put them on the Web. In Chapter 6, I help you understand how to know when material you download can get you in trouble, and what the penalties are if you do decide to download the latest Hollywood release.

Part III: Creating BitTorrent Content

I think one of the most exciting parts of BitTorrent is that it makes it possible for any of us to become a broadcaster, to have a radio show, or to publish a book. If you are a budding cinematographer, BitTorrent provides a way to distribute your film without taking out a small business loan. All of Part III is dedicated to getting some of the skills you need to create audio and video content in your hands.

In Chapter 7, I spend some time outlining good recording techniques, and give you concrete suggestions that can help you make the most of your recording. As well, you find out about some of the audio editing software on the market, from free packages to the high-end editors.

In Chapter 8, I walk you through the basics of choosing video equipment, whether you plan to tape in your living room or on the street. The chapter also talks you through how to get a good shot, right down to what kind of tape you need to keep your cables from tripping people!

Chapter 9 walks you through taking your new video footage off the camera and onto the computer so that you can edit it, add sound and special effects, and then turn it into a file you can actually distribute to Internet users. There's a lot to be learned about video editing, but this chapter gets you started.

Part IV: Delivering BitTorrent Content

In Part IV, you find a series of chapters that help you get your media ready to go using BitTorrent. Here are the essentials to taking your film or radio show and getting it out to the millions who are clamoring for it!

Chapter 10 gets the process started by helping you to create a torrent file, the little table of contents that lets the network know all about your data. Then you discover how to release it to a *tracker,* the software that actually coordinates all the uploading and downloading that is part of the BitTorrent file-sharing process. This step isn't for the technically timid, but when you reach the end you'll have a firm grasp of the issues and how to address them successfully.

In Chapter 11, you find out how to take the torrent and seed it so that others can find and download it. Plus, I include some torrent best practices that help you make files that can be easily organized and understood by those who download them.

In Chapter 12, you get to use your budding marketing skills to promote what you have created. I give you some specific strategies for letting people know about your documentary, book, or photo collection, so that they know how to download it. It's hard to say which of these three chapters is the single most important for enabling you to distribute your content to the BitTorrent world. Frankly, you can't skip any of them!

Part V: Getting More out of BitTorrent

So you're a pro now, are you? Great! Part V is for you. Here are the extras that help you dress up your content and add some copyright protection. In Chapter 13, you get a comprehensive overview of the resources available to you, from stock photography to public domain material. You can find a surprising array of reasonably priced media out there that you can use to fill out your own material when you need that shot of a volcano and can't find one locally.

Chapter 14 tells you how to protect what you've created. Every creator should know how to protect his material with copyright, even if you want it to be freely downloadable using BitTorrent.

In Chapter 15, I take some time to look at a few of the growing number of business that have discovered that they can use BitTorrent to cut costs and deliver media easily.

Part VI: The Part of Tens

Ah, the Part of Tens. All good things come in tens, don't they? They do in this book!

Chapter 16 walks you through all the possible file types you can run across as you start to download BitTorrent content, from strange image formats to compressed files that you have to figure out in order to even get at what you're really interested in.

Because using the Internet and downloading material from strangers can be a little hazardous, I spend some time in Chapter 17 discussing how you can protect yourself, your computer, and your data from spyware, viruses, and worms. Better safe than sorry!

And, for the final treat, in Chapter 18 you get ten fun freely downloadable files that you can download using BitTorrent. Get a taste of the rich array of audio, video, text, eBooks, images, and more that you can find online and download using BitTorrent.

Icons Used in This Book

This icon points you toward valuable resources on the Web.

This icon reminds you of an important concept or procedure that you'll want to store away in your memory bank for future use.

This icon signals technical stuff that you may find informative and interesting but isn't essential for you to know. Feel free to skip over these sections if you don't like the techy stuff.

This icon indicates a tip or technique that can save you time and money — and a headache.

This icon warns you of any potential pitfalls — and gives you the all-important information on how to avoid them.

Where to Go from Here

When I read books, I like to start with Chapter 1, and that's what I suggest you do now. I wrote Chapter 1 to walk you through the BitTorrent technology, giving you a brief taste of what is discussed in depth later in the book. If you're new to BitTorrent, start with Chapter 1 and then go right on to Chapters 2 and 3 where you get right down to brass tacks: installing a BitTorrent client and downloading content.

Another place you can go from here is straight to the Web. I've created a Web site to help you keep track on the confusing world of BitTorrent news, including legal developments that could affect the BitTorrent community. Visit `www.bittorrentfordummies.com` to get the latest news and information about BitTorrent. At this site, I also note exciting new files that are available via BitTorrent that you can download.

If you're a content developer, visit www.bittorrentfordummies.com to let me know about media you create that you want to share with other BitTorrent users. I'll create a directory of content created by readers of this book so that we can all benefit from the imaginative and exciting digital media you can distribute via BitTorrent. (Although it goes without saying, I will say it anyway: In order to be part of the directory your files must be available via BitTorrent and legally distributable.)

Part I
Getting Started with BitTorrent

"I don't mean to hinder your quest for knowledge; however, it's not generally a good idea to try and download the entire Internet."

In this part . . .

Chapters 1, 2, and 3 may be all you need to read in this book. After all, they get the job done, from helping you understand how BitTorrent works to showing you how to go about actually downloading content using a BitTorrent client. In Chapter 1, I spend time talking about what makes BitTorrent an exciting technology to use, and why it is so good at handling very large files. From there, jump right into using BitTorrent by reading about how to install a BitTorrent client in Chapter 2, and how to download and consume files in Chapter 3. This part gets you up and running with BitTorrent quickly and easily — no muss, no fuss.

Chapter 1

Cluing In to BitTorrent

*F*ile sharing isn't a new concept — we all remember the heady days of Napster downloading. Since Napster was shut down, new file-sharing technologies have been created and used — KaZaA, LimeWire, and others — in addition to traditional data transfer technologies like e-mail, FTP, and other services.

BitTorrent isn't the newest of the *peer-to-peer* (often abbreviated as P2P) file-sharing technologies, but it is one with a major difference. (Peer-to-peer file sharing describes the process of sharing data between computer users, rather than using a Web server to host the content.) BitTorrent was designed to distribute the downloading load among many users of a file. The result is a technology that is ideal for sharing very large files. How large? Think *gigabytes*. Think movies, TV shows, large software applications, entire databases, complete inventory lists, scanned document collections, and more, all quickly and easily transferred across the Internet, many in their original, uncompressed format.

The implications of BitTorrent are immense for individual home users, creators of movies and other material, and businesses. In fact, a study by CacheLogic, a British peer-to-peer consulting company, shows that BitTorrent was *already* responsible for 25 to 35 percent of all Internet traffic by the spring of 2005 — including e-mail, Web surfing, and traditional file downloading — and that figure is growing.

This chapter brings you up-to-date on the state of BitTorrent today, and gives you some feel for how BitTorrent is already being used. I talk about how you can make use of BitTorrent yourself to obtain media files, or share your own files with others, and I show you what you need to know about copyright law before you get started.

Reviewing P2P Flaws

What's ground-breaking about BitTorrent, and what makes it fundamentally different from previous file-sharing technologies, is that every time a user downloads a file, that user also automatically distributes the file to other users. This twist in the technology means that every downloader receives the file quicker, but the original source bears much less of the bandwidth burden, even if many people are downloading.

This technology stands in stark contrast to the traditional P2P file-sharing model, which is outlined and evaluated in the following sections.

Overviewing old-school file-sharing processes

File-sharing technologies have generally worked this way:

1. **You connect to the network of users of the file-sharing software.**

   The network enables you to search other members' computers for files you're interested in having.

2. **You locate the file or files you want to download.**

3. **After you find a file you want, you connect to the computer that has the file saved on it so that you can download it.**

4. **You download 'til you drop.**

   This process ties up *bandwidth* — Internet connectivity — on your computer and on the computer of the person who is sharing the file during the transfer. If two people want to download the file at the same time, each person only gets half the bandwidth available.

Evaluating the holes in old-school file-sharing processes

The traditional P2P file-sharing model works just hunky-dory for small files that can be transferred across the Internet in a few seconds, or for unpopular files that are rarely requested. But as soon as you enter the realm of multi-media, you know that huge files often require gigs and gigs of bandwidth to transfer online. Here's an overview of the issues that arise when you try to upload and download big media files:

- ✔ When Internet activity is high, traffic gets jammed.

- ✔ You generally have better download speeds than upload speeds, so the person uploading files usually has the smaller pipe, which determines the speed of the entire transaction.

- ✔ If the person who is sharing the file shuts down his or her computer and goes to bed in the middle of your download, your download is interrupted, and can't be resumed until the user turns on the computer again.

Introducing the Magic that Is BitTorrent

BitTorrent changes the traditional P2P model significantly by *distributing* the file-sharing process. Here's how it works:

1. **While surfing the Web, you come across a link to a BitTorrent file, called a *torrent*, and click it.**

   A torrent is a very small file you download that contains a sort of table of contents to the actual file you want.

   If you were using another P2P file-sharing system, you would start to download the actual file at this point.

2. **You open the torrent in a BitTorrent software client.**

   The client connects to a Web site running tracker software that keeps tabs on who else is also downloading that main file. Your client downloads small pieces of the file from all those users who have a copy of it, keeping the file-sharing load from being borne by a single user.

3. **As you download pieces of the file, the BitTorrent software client assembles the pieces using the table of contents in the torrent.**

   The software also begins to share those pieces you've received with other people who are also trying to download the file. By downloading, you're also helping to make parts of the file available. Without even trying. You're such a giver.

The result is a speedier process for everyone, and one in which the distributor of the data isn't hit with huge bandwidth problems. In fact, the more popular a file is, the faster you can obtain it, because more pieces of it are available; the only limit on the download is the speed of your own connection.

Getting an Idea of What You Can Do with BitTorrent

All kinds of people and businesses are using BitTorrent to distribute large data files. For example, BitTorrent has found popularity among those people sharing versions of the Linux operating system, and that's just the beginning; there are many more examples of businesses and individuals taking advantage of this technology. Here are just a few ways that individuals, groups, and businesses are using BitTorrent:

- **Distribute computer operating systems:** The Linux operating system, created by Linus Torvalds, is an open-source operating system available for free. In fact, it is the main alternative for computer users who don't want to be tied to Microsoft Windows or the Macintosh OS. Because of the way Torvalds licensed Linux, any developer can download and alter it, so many versions are available. As you can imagine, an entire operating system can be quite large. BitTorrent has become a favorite method for distributing Linux. The Linux Mirror Project (www.tlm-project.org) actually has torrents for most Linux versions, as shown in Figure 1-1. (A mirror Web site is one that duplicates another Web site, so in this case The Linux Mirror Project is bringing together files available elsewhere in one location.)

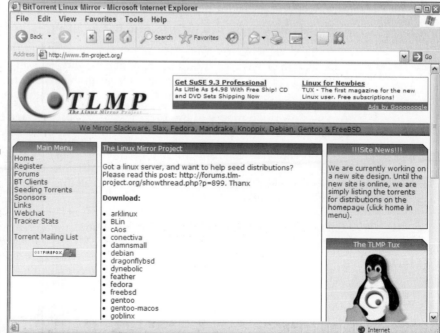

Figure 1-1:
The Linux
Mirror
Project
provides
versions of
the Linux
operating
systems
using
BitTorrent.

- ✔ **Distribute your film to create buzz:** Filmmaker Rick Prelinger is one of those who has used BitTorrent to do something he has never been able to do before. Prelinger used clips of publicly available industrial, educational, advertising, and amateur footage from 1940 to 1980 to create the documentary collage, *Panorama Ephemera*. Using BitTorrent, several thousand people have been able to download the film (which Prelinger has licensed for reuse and viewing). For Prelinger, BitTorrent made distribution easy — and inexpensive, which film distribution traditionally isn't.

- ✔ **Distribute your book:** Author and Stanford University professor Lawrence Lessig used BitTorrent to make his book *Free Culture* available for download. (You can also find and download an audio version of the book, created by volunteers who each read a chapter of the book.)

You can download both *Panorama Ephemera* and *Free Culture* from LegalTorrents (`www.legaltorrents.com`), a Web site that lists legally downloadable torrents that are licensed for public use or viewing.

- ✔ **Distribute musical recordings:** Rock groups Phish and the Grateful Dead encourage concert-goers to make recordings of their performances; those large digital files are shared by fans using BitTorrent.

The Web site Etree.org is a community BitTorrent tracker for sharing live concert recordings of artists that permit their performances to be recorded. You can find recordings of Phish, the Black Crowes, Blues Traveler, the Grateful Dead, Radiohead, and many others through Etree. Etree is shown in Figure 1-2, and is online at `bt.etree.org`.

- ✔ **Distribute beta software:** The game World of Warcraft, a multiplayer online role-playing game created by Blizzard Entertainment, was released in November 2004. Prior to its release, however, Blizzard provided beta versions of the game to its testers using BitTorrent, eliminating shipping and production costs for software that would be patched on a nearly daily basis.

- ✔ **Today, software, tomorrow the world:** Even the BBC is getting in on the action. Although it doesn't use the BitTorrent format, the BBC is investigating the use of a very similar peer-to-peer technology to provide TV shows to consumers for up to seven days after they are broadcast. The BBC ran a trial in late 2005 and used the interactive Media Player to deliver digital rights managed TV shows and radio programs to 5,000 participants.

Of course, plenty of people are sharing content they shouldn't. Let me be clear, here. When I say they shouldn't, I mean that sharing copyrighted content is a crime. For more on this topic, jump to the "Pinpointing Legal Issues" section at the end of this chapter.

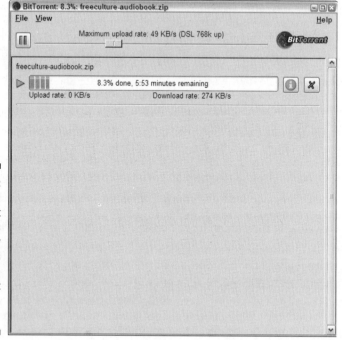

Figure 1-2:
You can find
live concert
recordings
of many
artists
available
legally at
`bt.etree`
`.org.`

Understanding the advantages of BitTorrent

The advantages of BitTorrent are pretty exciting:

- The more popular a file is — the more people want a copy of it — the faster it can be downloaded, because there are more places to get pieces of it. Whereas with traditional P2P file-sharing applications popular files are more difficult to download, with BitTorrent, popularity becomes a good thing.

- Distributors of content formerly had to have the bandwidth to deliver a large file to hundreds of individual users (this is no small feat). BitTorrent enables distributors to share the distribution load with all the people who get a copy of it, reducing the bandwidth burden on the distributor.

- BitTorrent requires that users share files back with the community, so no one can get files without also giving files — this level of reciprocity makes the system stronger and faster.

BitTorrent was created in 2001 by programmer Bram Cohen. (You can read more about Bram Cohen in the sidebar, "A short bio of Bram Cohen," in this chapter.)

A short bio of Bram Cohen

Programmer Bram Cohen is best known for creating BitTorrent. After dropping out of State University of New York in the midst of the dot-com boom, Cohen worked his way through a number of technical jobs relating to the Internet, the now-defunct MojoNation among them. (MojoNation enabled simultaneous distribution and acquisition of encrypted data across several computers at a time. It no longer has a Web presence.)

Cohen left MojoNation in 2001 to work on BitTorrent. To get help testing the technology, and to ensure that it was used, Cohen collected free pornography and distributed it using BitTorrent. Linux developers who were sharing versions of the Linux operating system also picked up and began using the tool.

When asked about the legality of the software he created, Cohen usually notes that BitTorrent is independent of copyright issues but that he nonetheless believes current media distribution methods are outdated and in trouble. Because he wants to protect BitTorrent (and himself) from legal action, Cohen says he has never used BitTorrent to download illegally available copyrighted material.

Cohen now lives in Bellevue, Washington.

Getting more information about how BitTorrent works

Generally speaking, using BitTorrent is free. For example, there is no charge to download and use the Official BitTorrent client, written by Bram Cohen, although you may want to make a donation to Cohen if you find the program useful. The Official BitTorrent client Web site is at www.bittorrent.com, and is shown in Figure 1-3.

There are other BitTorrent clients available — you can read more about those in Chapter 2. Some providers of torrent files may charge for their content.

Some less savory individuals sell copies of the Official BitTorrent client, or offer versions of it that include spyware. To avoid versions that have been altered, be sure to download your BitTorrent software only from the creator's Web site. Before downloading new software, it never hurts to do a quick search on Google (a search for *software name problems* works) to see whether you find references to problems with it. Read what you find with a grain of salt and be sure to pay attention to the source of the information. After all, the Internet is largely unmoderated.

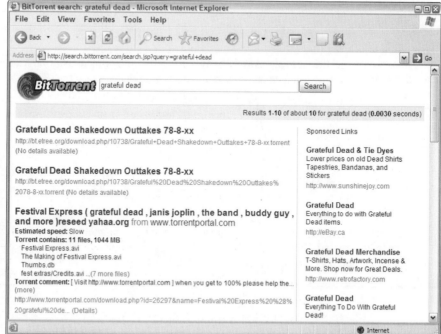

Figure 1-3:
Bram Cohen
created
BitTorrent
and
maintains
the Official
BitTorrent
client
Web site.

Keeping Tabs on BitTorrent Jargon

Like so many technologies, BitTorrent uses a fair amount of jargon. As you explore, getting a working understanding of terms is important (you need to know the terminology in order to make best use of future chapters of this book, as well!)

Here are a few terms you should know:

- **Leecher:** A person or computer that is in the process of acquiring a file using BitTorrent; a leecher doesn't have the whole file yet. In some contexts, leechers are people who fail to upload as much information as they download, and so aren't carrying their fair portion of the bandwidth load. In a more general sense, a leecher is just a label for anyone without the whole file.

- **Peer:** A somewhat more polite way to refer to a person or computer that is acquiring a file via BitTorrent and who hasn't got all the pieces of it yet.

- **Peer to peer (P2P):** Peer-to-peer distribution occurs when users of a network share files with each other across the network. Each peer, or computer, both distributes and acquires files, as opposed to a more typical *client-server* relationship, in which a single server distributes files to multiple computers, none of which can share content with each other.

✔ **Reseeding:** Reintroducing a file to the network. If no one is currently sharing (or *seeding*) a file, it must be reintroduced the network by someone who has a complete copy of the file.

✔ **Seed** or **seeder:** A person or computer that has a complete copy of a data file and is actively sharing it.

✔ **Share ratio:** The amount of a file that you've downloaded to your computer divided by the amount of data you've uploaded. As you use BitTorrent, you share the content you download back into the network. A share ratio of 1.0 means you've uploaded just as much of the file as you've downloaded.

Good BitTorrent etiquette means you should continue to share a file until your share ratio reaches 1.0, even if that means leaving the torrent running after you've downloaded the whole thing.

✔ **Swarm:** The whole collection of people and computers involved in seeding and leeching a file. You can see swarm information in Figure 1-4, a screenshot taken during a BitTorrent download using the BitTornado BitTorrent client. See Chapter 2 for more about various BitTorrent clients.

Figure 1-4:
The BitTorrent client BitTornado displays information about the peers and seeders engaged in sharing and distributing a torrent.

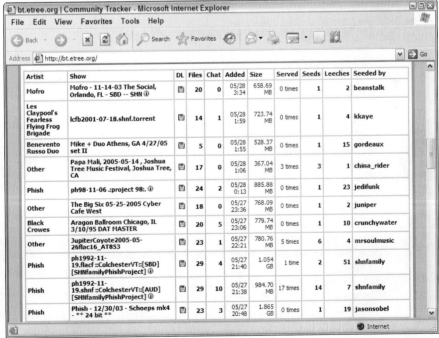

- ✔ **Torrent:** A pointer, or table of contents, of the data file. During transfer, the torrent file is used to map and assemble the pieces of the data.

  Although every transfer involves two files (the torrent and the file you actually want to share), users of BitTorrent generally don't make a distinction between the torrent file and the data file; in BitTorrent parlance, everything is called a torrent.

- ✔ **Tracker:** An application that monitors which computers have a copy of the data file being shared, pointing the BitTorrent client software to locations where it can find pieces of the file.

Downloading Files Using BitTorrent

Getting started using BitTorrent requires a bit of technical know-how and fiddling with your computer, but never fear — you've got a book that helps you figure all that out. Read through the following sections to get a view from 20,000 feet of the setup process, as well as the basics of finding and downloading content.

Getting a BitTorrent client

Downloading and installing a BitTorrent client is quite simple, especially if you've downloaded an application from the Web before. Start by downloading the Official BitTorrent client, available at www.bittorrent.com.

This client was created and is maintained by Bram Cohen, the creator of the BitTorrent technology. Its simple interface is great for beginners who are trying BitTorrent for the first time. You can take a peek at the Official BitTorrent client, which is used in how-to demonstrations throughout this book, in Figure 1-5.

Because BitTorrent is an evolving technology, you may find that the provider of your BitTorrent client offers a *beta* version and a *release* version of the client. A beta version is one that is in development, and possibly buggy. Unless you're an experienced computer user, you're usually in better shoes if you use the release version of the software. A release software version is one that the software developer has decided is good enough to provide to users; it is more stable than beta software.

Chapter 2 contains detailed, step-by-step instructions on downloading and installing a BitTorrent client, as well as a list of some of the various BitTorrent applications available to you.

Figure 1-5:
The Official BitTorrent client is a good client to download when you're getting started with BitTorrent.

Configuring your computer

Getting your computer and Internet connection set up to handle BitTorrent traffic is a little more complex, but fortunately you probably only have to do it once. Essentially, if you use a router when you connect to the Internet, you must set it up to allow the use of certain ports, or locations, for BitTorrent traffic. BitTorrent uses separate ports from those that your computer uses for e-mail, Web traffic, and so on. Get some good step-by-step instructions for doing this configuration in Chapter 2.

Finding torrents to download

When you have a BitTorrent client on your computer, and configure your computer correctly, you're ready to jump into the BitTorrent ocean! Finding torrents to download is as simple — and as difficult — as using a search engine. Fire up your Web browser and type the name of the content you're looking for, followed by the word *torrent,* into any search engine Web site. For example, if you want to see what kinds of Linux files are online, type **linux torrent** into a search engine such as Google.

Better yet, visit the BitTorrent Search Engine site created by Bram Cohen. The BitTorrent Search Engine lists only torrent files, so you won't have to wade through other Web content in your search results. You can find the search engine online at `search.bittorrent.com`, and shown in Figure 1-6.

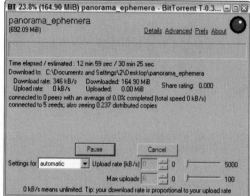

Figure 1-6:
Finding
torrents to
download is
pretty easy
when you
use the
BitTorrent
Search
Engine.

For detailed information on finding torrent files, read Chapter 4.

Be aware that much of the content you find to download is being shared illegally. Some files are of dubious quality, or even malicious. That's right; the torrent of *Star Wars Episode III: Revenge of the Sith* you found really is too good to be true. See the section, "Pinpointing Legal Issues," at the end of this chapter to find out more about the legal issues surrounding the downloading of copyrighted material. I cover some good strategies for protecting yourself from viruses in Chapters 5 and 17.

Decompressing archived files

Having downloaded a file using BitTorrent is only half the battle. Many torrent files are compressed, or archived, to make them as small as possible.

In order to actually get at the data you have downloaded, you need to decompress the file or files. There are several good utilities for handling these types of files, and you can download and install free or trial versions quite quickly. WinZip and WinRAR are two good programs to use on a PC, and StuffIt Expander is a good Macintosh utility.

Archived files often have file extensions like `.zip`, `.rar`, or `.sit`. If a file that you download using BitTorrent has one of these extensions, you definitely need to use WinZip, WinRAR, or StuffIt Expander before you can use the files — they are all capable of handling each file type, even those created by other platforms.

Read Chapter 3 for good information on downloading, installing, and running these compression and expansion utilities.

Watching, listening, reading . . .

Download, decompress — and then consume! The last step in using the files you download with BitTorrent is figuring out what application to use to watch them, listen to them, view them, or read them.

Depending on what you've downloaded, you may need to obtain a program that plays video and audio files, or that displays images and text. Most modern computers come with applications that can handle these files automatically (for example, if you use Windows XP, Windows Media Player is built in), but you can find lots of information in Chapter 3 on choosing, downloading, and installing one of these applications.

Sharing Content Using BitTorrent

When Bram Cohen created BitTorrent, the world at large was granted the ability to create and distribute large files with ease. Are you a budding broadcaster? The creator of a documentary? A musician? A photographer? In the past, sharing video and audio content, and even large text and image files, over the Internet was a limited endeavor, and one that was usually expensive.

The way it was

Filmmakers have long been able to produce a digital film on their computers, and can convert films into one of the Web video streaming formats for Windows Media Player or Real Player with the click of a mouse. But distributing these files via the usual means is traditionally pricey for most individuals. Many Web hosting providers don't offer video streaming services, and even among those that do, the costs can add up quickly. The lucky documentary creator whose film becomes popular quickly runs into server load and bandwidth issues, incurring yet more technical headaches and additional fees.

And forget about trying to distribute your multimedia content via more traditional methods — on television, or by creating DVDs, or trying to get your content played on the radio. These methods are nearly impossible for unknown artists with no money.

The way it is

BitTorrent has changed the traditional distribution process for electronic media. Now, the creator of a film can produce a high-quality video file in any popular digital video format (or multiple copies, each in a different format), create a torrent file, and seed the file herself. The peer-to-peer network does the work of distributing the video for the filmmaker.

Preparing your files

A good portion of this book is designed to put the tools for creating your own multimedia content into your hands. Chapter 7 walks you through the tools and methods for creating high-quality audio presentations, and is a must-read for musicians and would-be audio broadcasters. Chapters 8 and 9 are all about getting equipped for shooting video and editing it on your computer.

After you create the content, you want to distribute with BitTorrent, so you need to get your files ready to go. This involves saving them as a commonly accessible file format so that most users will be able to open them after you download them. For example:

- ✔ Format your video files as QuickTime, a format that can be read easily by both the PC and the Macintosh.

- ✔ Save your audio files as MP3s, a format most computer users are familiar with and that can be played back by almost any media player.

- ✔ Save your text in the RTF (Rich Text Format), a format that can be opened by most text editors. Or generate PDF files that can be opened on any computer that has the free Adobe Reader software.

- ✔ Save your images as JPEG files. JPEGs can be opened by any operating system.

Creating a torrent

A torrent file is the table of contents for the files you are sharing. It breaks up the files into pieces and lets BitTorrent clients who are downloading it know how many pieces are left before the file is complete.

Many BitTorrent clients include the ability to create torrents. You can read more about creating a torrent in Chapter 10.

Identifying a tracker

The next step to sharing your content is to identify a tracker you can use. A *tracker* is a piece of software that sits on a Web server and coordinates communication between seeds and peers for all the torrents you create. This coordination is crucial to the whole process. You can:

- ✔ Set up a tracker on your own Web site.
- ✔ Use the tracker on some of the public tracker Web sites.
- ✔ Use a BitTorrent client that offers trackerless sharing.
- ✔ You can read more about setting up and using a tracker in Chapter 11.

Seeding your torrent

Seeding a torrent is a process that tells the tracker software you're using about your torrent and your data. After you notify your tracker, you must keep your files (or *seeds*) available for as long as possible to ensure good distribution to others. At the very least, don't stop seeding until at least two other full copies of the file appear on other computers. The more popular your file is the longer it stays available. If you want your file to stay in distribution, check periodically to see if it is still available. If it isn't, reseed using the same process you used to seed your file.

Seeding is accomplished by running your BitTorrent client and pointing it to the torrent you created, whether online or on your computer. Of course, the data files must also be available! There is more information about seeding in Chapter 11.

Pinpointing Legal Issues

In this section, I talk about using BitTorrent to download large multimedia files like videos and TV shows, and I know some of you are wondering — is this legal? The answer is pretty simple. Using BitTorrent is legal. Using BitTorrent to acquire copyrighted material like TV shows and movies *isn't*.

Poke around BitTorrent Web sites and you find any number of movies and television shows available. *The Matrix Reloaded* hit the network a few days after it could be seen in theaters. *Star Wars Episode III: Revenge of the Sith* was available hours *before* the film was released. You can see one pirate torrent site advertising the availability of the Star Wars torrent in Figure 1-7.

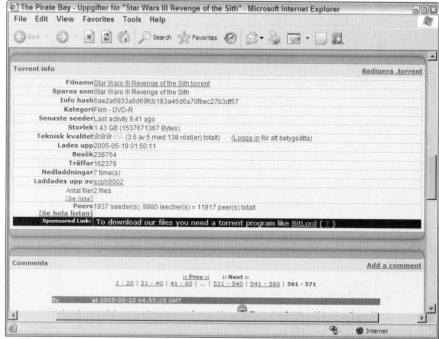

Figure 1-7:
Finding copyrighted material that's distributed illegally is easy, but you should never download this kind of content.

Think about it this way: VCR tapes are legal to buy and for personal use. But you can't legally make copies of someone else's movie on VCR tapes and start handing them out to all your friends, let alone sell them.

You should know about some inherent dangers to using BitTorrent to download movies and TV shows. Organizations like the Recording Industry Association of America (RIAA) and the Motion Picture Association of America (MPAA) actively prosecute people and companies that are engaged in making copyrighted content available to others illegally. Internationally, the laws are even more complex.

You are not anonymous when you use BitTorrent, because the process itself involves sharing of identifying information about your computer. This lack of anonymity puts you at risk if you use BitTorrent or other file-sharing technologies to download or share music, movies, TV shows, and other content.

In Chapter 6, I outline the ways in which you might be at risk if you choose to use BitTorrent to download or distribute copyrighted material.

Chapter 2

Downloading BitTorrent Files

*F*inding and downloading music, movies, TV shows, computer games, and software from the Internet using BitTorrent is surprisingly easy. It's fast, relatively simple, and, best of all, you don't need to spend any money or buy any new hardware to get started. You can download and install one of the many free BitTorrent software clients online, and most BitTorrent content is freely available.

In this chapter, I show you the basics of working with BitTorrent files by going through the steps necessary to get your computer ready to handle BitTorrent downloads. Then I show you how to download and install the BitTorrent client on your computer so that you can access torrent files.

Finally, I show you how to share the files you download with other BitTorrent users.

Downloading and Installing the BitTorrent Client

The first step in the process of setting up your computer to download and view BitTorrent content is to install a BitTorrent client. The BitTorrent client is simply a software program that your computer associates with torrent files.

Torrent files use the `.torrent` file extension. A torrent file is the small file you download that provides BitTorrent with information it needs to obtain all the pieces of the file. After installing the client, when you click a torrent file to begin the download, your computer launches BitTorrent to handle the request and manage the transmission of data.

You can find several freely available BitTorrent clients out there, but a good one to start with is the Official BitTorrent client, available from the official BitTorrent Web site at www.bittorrent.com. The Official BitTorrent client was developed by the creator of the BitTorrent technology, Bram Cohen, and is the basis for many of the more fully featured clients that are also available online.

The Official BitTorrent client is free, simple to use, but doesn't have some of the bells and whistles you may desire after you become more familiar with BitTorrent and peer-to-peer file sharing.

Follow these steps to download and install the Official BitTorrent client:

1. **Open Internet Explorer or your favorite Web browser and go to:** www.bittorrent.com, **shown in Figure 2-1.**

2. **Locate the Download BitTorrent heading and choose the operating system you use by clicking the appropriate link.**

   The browser opens a page listing Web sites on which the BitTorrent client is available. All the files available are identical.

Figure 2-1:
The Official
BitTorrent
client is
available
online at
www.bit
torrent
.com.

3. **Select the location from which you want to download the BitTorrent installer.**

   You can choose any location you want. After you click the appropriate link, your browser begins the download and may ask you where you want to save the file.

4. **Save the application to your desktop.**

   The browser finishes downloading the file.

5. **Double-click the `BitTorrent.exe` file on your desktop to start the installation.**

   After the BitTorrent client is finished installing, you receive a confirmation message.

6. **Click OK to complete the installation.**

   You can delete the `installation.exe` file from your desktop.

The BitTorrent client is now installed on your computer and can handle torrent files whenever you attempt to download one.

BitTorrent is not like other file-sharing applications you may be familiar with. After the Official BitTorrent client software is installed it waits invisibly on your system until you attempt to download a torrent file. As soon as you open a torrent file, the client springs to life to handle the downloading process.

The BitTorrent client you've downloaded and installed is not intended to help you find torrents to download. To get more information about finding torrents to download, jump to Chapter 4.

Introducing Other BitTorrent Clients

In addition to the Official BitTorrent client, there are several other excellent BitTorrent clients available for the PC, Macintosh, and Linux machines. Because BitTorrent is based on an open-source protocol, developers are free to build their own version of a BitTorrent client using the freely distributed source code. The result is that there are many different clients with different features, varying stability, and documentation. Because these clients are mainly developed by individuals, rather than corporations, extensive support and technical help is generally unavailable.

You can find a bunch of BitTorrent flavors out there; each is designed to work best for different kinds of users. For instance, those with very friendly graphical user interfaces are great for beginners, and others appeal more to the geeks in the crowd.

Some of the more elaborate functionalities available in other clients include

- ✔ **Traffic shaping:** The ability to control upload and download rates for each torrent. The Azureus client offers this feature.

- ✔ **Getting hard-to-find pieces first:** The ability to look first for the pieces of the file that are least distributed so that you get those before they get any harder to find. The Bits on Wheels client offers this feature.

- ✔ **Metadata about torrents:** The ability to track information about how the file is being shared now, and how it has been shared in the past. The BitTornado client shares this kind of information.

Not all clients are created equal. Some are freeware or shareware and are supported (minimally) and documented (in obscure language) by the developer of the software. Check to make sure the client you download is supported before you decide to install it.

Getting to know Azureus

Azureus, shown in Figure 2-2, is a cross-platform torrent client built in Java. Cross platform? Oh, yes, this BitTorrent client can do everything a good client can do, and also runs on multiple operating systems. It has excellent basic functionality, including resuming interrupted downloads and traffic shaping plug-ins; it even has a non-centralized torrent file database that may replace BitTorrent trackers as the standard way of organizing a swarm.

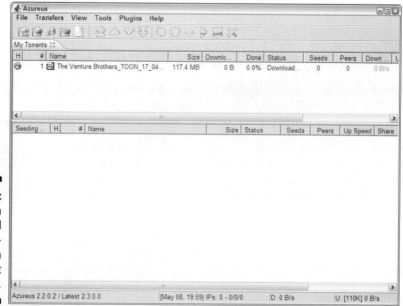

Figure 2-2:
Azureus is a powerful cross-platform BitTorrent client.

To run this client, you need to install Sun Microsystems Java client. You can get both the client and the Java download at `azrueus.sourceforge.net`.

Meeting BitTornado

BitTornado, shown in Figure 2-3, is one of the most popular clients out there, and is a good starting place if you want to try something other than the Official BitTorrent client.

The client is based on the code of the Official BitTorrent client, and has a very similar feel to it — but adds in a few extra features many people find handy. For instance, you can limit the upload rate of particular torrents so that you get better performance. BitTornado also displays your *share ratio* (the ratio of uploaded content to downloaded content) in the main download window so that you know exactly how much content you've seeded back to the peer-to-peer community. BitTornado also offers several other configuration options, such as the ability to change the port used by BitTorrent traffic. Its handy status lights visually indicate the health of your downloads.

You can download BitTornado at `www.bittornado.com`.

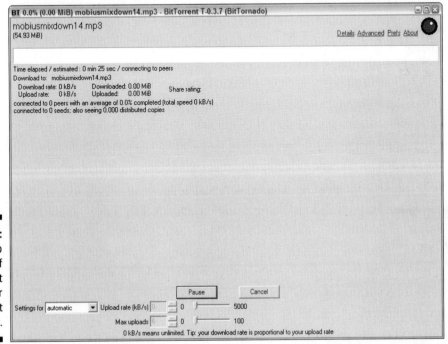

Figure 2-3: BitTornado is one of the most popular BitTorrent clients.

ABC: Yet Another BitTorrent Client

Yet Another BitTorrent Client, shown in Figure 2-4, is excellent for beginning users, and has many of the features that BitTornado and Azureus offer. This client also features a great queue system that enables you to prioritize and control the order of your downloads. You can pause, restart, and resume downloads, as well. Unlike some BitTorrent clients, ABC enables you to control many downloads from a single window. It also supports the automatic seeding of files after the download ends; it can be configured to auto-seed torrents upon startup.

This client is for the PC and Linux platforms. You can download ABC at `ping pong-abc.sourceforge.net`.

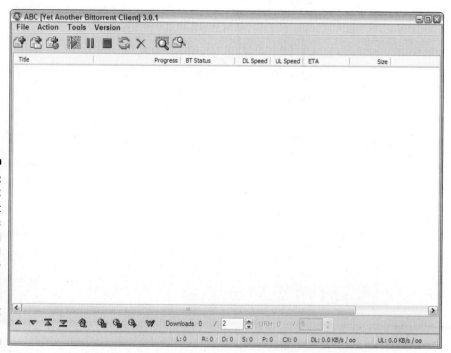

Figure 2-4:
The ABC
BitTorrent
Client offers
several
useful
features for
working
with
BitTorrent
files.

Bits on Wheels

For those using the Macintosh platform, Bits on Wheels (shown in Figure 2-5) is one of the best — maybe even *the* best — BitTorrent clients out there. It is extremely popular and works like other clients — but with a twist. Bits on Wheels has a unique 3D graphical interface that allows you to visualize the *swarm* (the collection of those who are sharing the file) that you're connected to. As you download pieces of a file, you can view the computers on the network.

Bits on Wheels also has some great features for organizing torrent files. For example, you can assign priority to the files you want to download first, and you can allocate your bandwidth for sharing.

This client is definitely for more experienced users, but is also worth trying if you're a beginner who wants to see what's possible when you share torrents.

To use this client, you must be running Mac OS X. You can download Bits on Wheels at www.bitsonwheels.com.

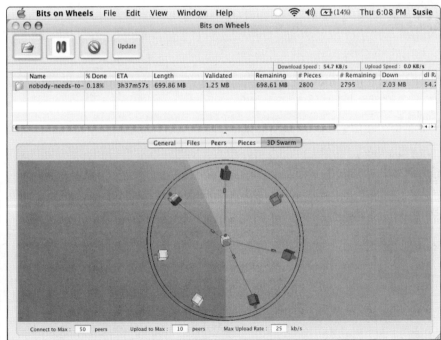

Figure 2-5:
Bits on
Wheels is
the best
Macintosh
BitTorrent
client
currently
available.

Setting Up Your Firewall

I know that setting up your firewall to accommodate BitTorrent traffic doesn't sound like fun, but bear with me. This process only needs to be done once, and then you can move on to downloading.

Getting your firewall configured properly to permit BitTorrent traffic to move freely across your local network is a key piece of the setup — and it is often overlooked. The consequence of skipping these important steps are not fun:

- ✔ Slow downloads
- ✔ Failed downloads
- ✔ A generally frustrating experience

The following sections walk you through this setup process so that you can quickly move on to less annoying tasks. Getting things set up properly takes only a few minutes.

If you have a firewall installed on your computer, your download speed is much faster if you provide BitTorrent an open pathway for file transfers. Because firewalls protect your system from intruders by allowing only authorized access to your computer's *ports,* clearing the way for BitTorrent traffic simply means opening up a port specifically for BitTorrent.

Think of a port as a channel, or a way for data to flow to and from your computer. Each port on your computer has a unique number to identify it and is associated with a specific type of communication. For example, standard Web surfing traffic uses the port numbered 80. The default ports assigned to BitTorrent are 6881 through 6889. After your BitTorrent ports are configured, your firewall sends all BitTorrent upload and download traffic across these points, leaving other Internet communication like Web browsing and e-mail to other ports.

A firewall acts to block all unwanted entry from outside your network, so it stands to reason that the ports BitTorrent uses are blocked by your firewall by default; hence, you need to authorize your firewall to open them up to handle BitTorrent traffic. Opening up ports on your firewall may lead you to think that you're opening your computer to hackers. Although this may be true in rare cases, common sense saves the day. When you're done using your BitTorrent client, close the ports on your firewall. You can always open them again later. Closing unused ports is always a good plan for keeping your computer and network safe.

Because of the way BitTorrent works, you may also need to set up your firewall to identify your computer to other BitTorrent peers who are trying to obtain content from you. This function is called *port forwarding,* and means that your firewall can recognize incoming BitTorrent requests and forward them to ports 6881 through 6889.

A *firewall* is software that works to prevent unauthorized traffic from accessing your computer by using your Internet connection. A *router* is used by people who have two or more networked computers that share the same Internet connection; routers frequently come with firewall features. If you are using a router, you need to run your port configuration in the router interface.

Figuring out your IP address

In order to configure your firewall properly, you need to know what your internal IP address is. PC users can follow these steps to find out what that IP address is:

1. **Select Start⇨Run from the Start menu.**

   The Run dialog box opens.

2. **Type** CMD **and click OK.**

   A DOS command prompt window opens. (Bet you haven't seen one of these in a while!)

3. **At the C:\ prompt type** IPCONFIG **and press Enter.**

   The IPCONFIG function runs, and your internal IP address appears, as shown in Figure 2-6.

```
Command Prompt                                              _ □ ×
Microsoft Windows XP [Version 5.1.2600]
(C) Copyright 1985-2001 Microsoft Corp.

Windows IP Configuration

Ethernet adapter Local Area Connection:

        Connection-specific DNS Suffix  . :
        IP Address. . . . . . . . . . . . : 192.168.1.105
        Subnet Mask . . . . . . . . . . . : 255.255.255.0
        Default Gateway . . . . . . . . . : 192.168.1.1

C:\Documents and Settings\2>_
```

Figure 2-6:
Run
IPCONFIG
from the
DOS
command
prompt to
determine
your internal
IP address.

Configuring the Windows Firewall

The Windows Firewall is a fairly robust firewall that comes packaged with all Windows XP machines that were manufactured after the release of Service Pack 2. If the only firewall you have is the Windows Firewall, here's how you can make exclusions to the firewall setup and allow BitTorrent data to flow freely.

1. **Choose Start⇨Control Panel.**

   Windows opens the Control Panel folder.

2. **Double-click the Windows Firewall icon.**

   Windows opens the Windows Firewall dialog box.

3. **Select the Exceptions tab.**

4. **Click the Add Program button.**

   The Add a Program dialog box opens.

5. **Select the BitTorrent client you installed and click OK.**

   Windows adds the program to the Windows Firewall exception list.

6. **Click OK to close the window.**

   Don't forget, after you finish using your BitTorrent client, you must turn off the exception to your client and close that hole in your Windows Firewall.

For most BitTorrent clients, simply adding it to the Windows Firewall exception list allows it to use the ports it needs. However, if you continue to have problems, you can also configure a specific port for the use of the client. Refer to your client documentation to find out how to do this.

Configuring a Linksys router

After you know your internal IP address, you can use these steps to walk through configuring the router or firewall for your PC. The following steps run you through the process using a Linksys router, but the general routine is relatively similar for the firewall or router you use:

1. **Access your router's Admin screen by opening a Web browser and typing your IP address into the address bar. Then click Enter.**

   For example, I would type **192.168.1.1**. The browser opens a Login/Password dialog box.

   Alternatively, you can access the Admin screen by using the instructions provided with your router.

2. **Enter your username and password and click OK.**

   The default Linksys username and password for most consumer routers is `admin`, and the password box is left blank.

   The browser opens the Linksys Admin screen.

3. **Click the Advanced tab.**

   The browser displays the Filters page of the Admin interface.

4. **Click the Forwarding tab.**

   The browser displays the Port Range Forwarding page of the Admin interface.

5. **In the topmost empty row of the form, type the name of the type of traffic** (BitTorrent) **and the port range you want to open** (6881-6889).

6. **Click to add a checkmark to the TCP box and to the UDP box.**

7. **Enter your IP address.**

8. **Click to add a check mark to the Enable box.**

9. **Click Apply to save the changes, as shown in Figure 2-7.**

Because every firewall product is unique, you should check the documentation or product Web site for your firewall/router for help in configuring your own system correctly. The tasks outlined above stay the same, even if specific menu names and techniques for making changes differ.

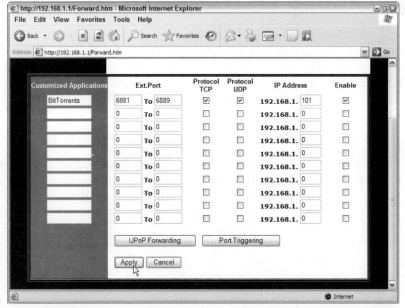

Figure 2-7: You need to configure your router in order to optimize BitTorrent transfers.

Finding a File

You won't find a single repository of BitTorrent content on the Web. This reality is both the beauty and the bane of finding BitTorrent files. Historically, locating torrents using search engines and traditional searching techniques has been tough. This difficulty is part of why BitTorrent has a reputation for being inaccessible to non-geek users. However, BitTorrent files *are* all over the Web, and many sites that operate as *trackers,* or search engines, designed to point you to torrent files you can download.

BitTorrent search engines and tracker Web sites are often shut down, frequently as the result of legal action (currently on the rise in the United States) from organizations like the Recording Industry Association of American (RIAA) or Motion Picture Association of America (MPAA), which are attempting to prevent the unauthorized distribution of copyrighted movies, music, and television shows. New search engines and trackers quickly spring up to take the place of those that are shut down, but the here-today-gone-tomorrow factor does make the hunt for torrents seem like a wild goose chase sometimes. If you're new to using BitTorrent, keeping up is tough. After a while, though, the hunt gets easier.

For extensive information on searching for torrent files to download, jump to Chapter 4. For information on the legal issues surrounding unauthorized copyrighted material obtainable using BitTorrent, read Chapter 6.

Downloading BitTorrent Content

When you download a torrent file, what you're actually downloading is a small file that contains a sort of table of contents to the real content you're downloading. That table of contents file tends to be quite small, so it downloads quickly. The file must be opened with a BitTorrent client in order for the actual data to be downloaded. This is the point at which the large file downloading happens.

Using the Official BitTorrent client, follow these steps to download your first BitTorrent file from the LegalTorrents Web site:

1. **Run Internet Explorer or the Web browser of your choice by opening the program from the Start menu of your computer.**

2. **Visit the LegalTorrents Web site** (www.legaltorrents.com).

   The browser goes to the Web page shown in Figure 2-8.

3. **Look over the available list of torrents (everything here is guaranteed to be legally available) and click the name of the file you are interested in to begin downloading the torrent.**

   The browser opens a Save As window.

4. **Navigate to the location you would like to save the torrent file. Click Save.**

   The file is saved to the location you specified. For this set of instructions, I saved the torrent on the desktop.

5. **When the download is complete, double-click the torrent file.**

   The torrent file opens in BitTorrent and begins to download, as shown in Figure 2-9. Large files may take a long time to download.

Depending on how you have configured your browser, and which BitTorrent client you install, you may experience some variations in these steps. The basic progression, however, is the same for all users.

The more popular a torrent file is the more people will be sharing pieces of the file that you need. In short, popularity makes the download faster. Look for torrents with many seeders and downloaders for the fastest experience in obtaining files.

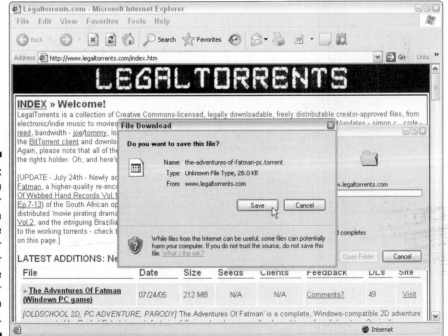

Figure 2-8: You can open or save a torrent file to your computer after the browser begins to download it.

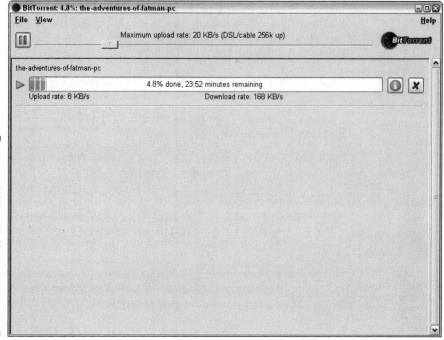

Figure 2-9:
After you double-click a torrent file, the BitTorrent client begins to download the complete file.

Working around disconnections

BitTorrent is unique because it allows people to share huge files without using any particular user's bandwidth. (Downloading a large file from a single user is extremely slow, and ends as soon as the other computer is shut down — even if the download isn't complete.)

If you get disconnected from the Internet while your file is downloading, or if you have to pause the transfer and go offline, reconnecting to the torrent when you are ready to resume the process is simple. The partial file you downloaded remains intact on your hard drive in the location you specified when you paused or canceled the download. When you're ready to reconnect to the file, double-click the same torrent file. Your BitTorrent client scans the file on your computer, recognizes it as a partially downloaded file, and resumes the transfer.

Managing disk space

Before you get too carried away downloading torrents, make sure you have enough disk space. BitTorrent is used especially for sharing large files. If you're downloading multimedia content, the files are commonly 1GB, 2GB, or even larger! Ensure that you have enough hard drive space on your computer to store an entire file — with room to spare.

Follow these instructions to see how much available space remains on your hard drive:

1. **Click the Windows Start button and select My Computer from the menu that appears.**

   A list of the disk drives and folders at the root level of your computer appears.

2. **Right-click on your hard drive (usually, the** `C:` **drive) and select Properties from the context-sensitive menu that appears.**

   The drive might be listed as `Local Disk`, or simply as `Drive_C`.

   If you have multiple hard drives, right-click on the appropriate hard drive.

   A Properties window appears.

3. **Click the General tab if it isn't already active.**

4. **Look at the amount of free space available on your hard drive.**

   This data is graphically represented in a pie graph, as you can see in Figure 2-10, alongside a numerical listing of the amount of free and used disk space.

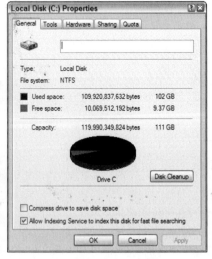

Figure 2-10: Check your available hard drive space before download-ing large BitTorrent files.

As long as the total file size of the BitTorrent content you want to download is smaller than the amount of remaining disk space available, you're going to be fine and can proceed with the download of your content. Having said that, if you fill up your hard drive until you have only a few megabytes of space left your computer won't be happy. Leave yourself at least 1GB of free space at all times.

As you download from BitTorrent more frequently, you quickly discover that you need a lot of free space on your hard drive to accommodate the large files and new data you collect. Many BitTorrent power users buy external hard drives to store and archive content. You can find more information on options and strategies for managing and archiving your data in Chapter 5.

Seeding a Torrent File

When a torrent is done downloading, a message appears that notifies you that the download is none. In fact, the message looks like this: `Done, share ratio 0%, will seed indefinitely.` (See Figure 2-11.) Because you have the entire file, you can now send pieces of the file out to other BitTorrent clients trying to download it.

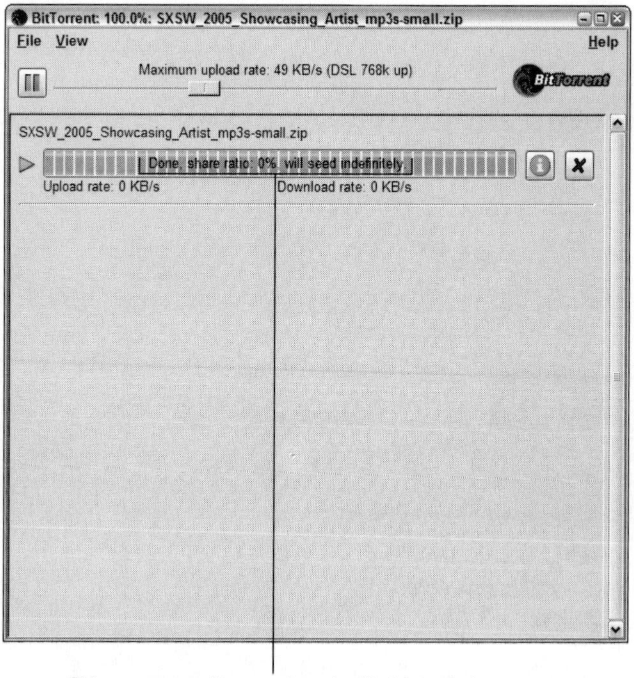

Figure 2-11:
When a file finishes downloading, keep the BitTorrent client open and connected to the swarm in order to become a seed and share the file.

> 🖥️ BitTorrent: 100.0%: SXSW_2005_Showcasing_Artist_mp3s-small.zip
> File View   Help
> ❚❚   Maximum upload rate: 49 KB/s (DSL 768k up)   *BitTorrent*
>
> SXSW_2005_Showcasing_Artist_mp3s-small.zip
> ▷ ▨▨▨▨▨▨▨| Done, share ratio: 0%, will seed indefinitely. |▨▨▨▨▨▨▨   🛈 ✗
> Upload rate: 0 KB/s   Download rate: 0 KB/s

This message tells you when the file is seeded.

Good BitTorrent etiquette is to leave this window open so that you can share the file with others. Keep the window open on-screen for at least a few hours; this is called _seeding_. A _seed_ is a client on the network that is in possession of the entire file. When you leave your BitTorrent client running after it finishes downloading, you are _seeding_ the file back onto the Internet.

It is considered good _netiquette_ to continue to seed until the ratio of data downloaded from the network and the ratio of data uploaded to the network is at least 1:1. This is your chance to give back to the peer-to-peer file-sharing community. After all, the more good seeders there are out there, the more, faster downloads available for everyone.

You can become a seeder in one of two ways:

- ✔ **Leave your download window open after the file is finished downloading.** This method is the easiest, and it keeps your machine connected to the torrent and continuing to share the file until you close the window.

- ✔ **Open a saved torrent file or click a Web site link for a torrent you already have.** BitTorrent then scans the file, recognizes that it's complete, and then connects to a tracker that points other BitTorrent clients to it. This method works fine, but it does require you to remember to follow the extra step; make a point of following the first option every time you download a file.

Does your Internet service provider charge you for uploads? In some rare cases, your ISP may limit or charge you for the transmission of upstream data (uploads). Look into your ISP's uploading policy before sharing torrent files to ensure you don't get a surprise bill from your ISP at the end of the month.

Chapter 3

Playing BitTorrent Files

· ·

In This Chapter

▶ Dealing with archived and compressed files

▶ Opening compressed BitTorrent media files

▶ Playing audio and video easily

▶ Understanding video codecs

· ·

*I*n Chapter 2, I show you how to download a torrent. Maybe now you're ready to open it up and sit back with a bag of popcorn. Although I hope enjoying the multimedia file you've just downloaded is a matter of double-clicking the file and putting the popcorn in the microwave, it's entirely possible that your computer won't recognize the file; even if your computer does recognize the file, you may have to expand, or *decompress,* it before you can get to snacking.

Unfortunately, these aren't the only two possible glitches. If your computer automatically launches a media player application like Windows Media Player, you may see the dreaded message `Codec Not Found`.

Never fear. This chapter helps you deal with all three possible issues. Becoming a master of file sharing and BitTorrent requires a working understanding of your file types and a handful of media playing applications — and a little patience.

In this chapter you get a grip on using decompression software, CD/DVD emulators, codecs, and media players. You figure out what you need to download, and how to use these programs so that you can focus on the fun stuff — finding and consuming great content.

I include a comprehensive list of possible file types you may encounter using BitTorrent in Chapter 16 — there are enough file types to fill an entire chapter on their own!

Understanding Archive File Types

BitTorrent users encounter different media formats all the time. When you download a torrent, you may download an audio format you're not familiar with, or a file that uses proprietary format that requires a media player you don't have. And if that's not confusing enough, how do you tell all the file formats apart? Which files play in what player? How do you access the media?

As a consumer of media via BitTorrent, you generally don't have a choice about the file format the audio or video comes in. The maker of the media makes the decision and you live with it.

But before you get to the files themselves, you have to get past the file compression format. Most BitTorrent content is downloaded in a *compressed,* or *archived,* format. Compressing a file is just like it sounds — making it smaller than the original. Compressing or archiving content that consists of multiple files is useful, as well, because then you can transfer the whole lot of files as a single file — quickly. After you download compressed files, you must *decompress,* or *expand* them before you can access the media.

Introducing the major archive file applications

The many formats used to compress files can be daunting to the new BitTorrent user, but you only need to deal with a few applications to handle the bulk of these files. You can quickly become familiar with these apps, and in fact you probably only need to install a single application to begin with (if you don't already have one installed on your computer).

Take a look at these three possibilities to find one that suits your operating system:

- **WinZip ($29):** WinZip, shown in Figure 3-1, is a common file compression application you can use to decompress files you download via BitTorrent. WinZip is most frequently associated with the `.zip` file extension, but it can open most files created with standard archiving formats. WinZip software often comes preinstalled on standard Windows PCs. You can download and use a 21-day evaluation version, after which you are prompted with messages to purchase the software. WinZip is available for Windows users.

  Files compressed using WinZip usually have `.zip` file extension. Download WinZip from `www.winzip.com`.

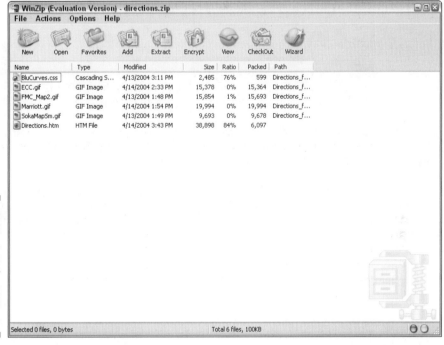

Figure 3-1:
WinZip is a
popular,
inexpensive
solution for
opening
archived
content.

✔ **WinRAR ($29):** WinRAR, shown in Figure 3-2, is used to manage large
series of files and is popular among hardcore BitTorrent users because
of its raw compression power. (It has the ability to compress a 1GB file
into 600MB or smaller.) The program can also break up one large file into
many small pieces for ease of transmission. As with WinZip, you can use
WinRAR to open a wide variety of archive file types. WinRAR is free to
evaluate for 40 days. WinRAR is available for Windows, Macintosh,
Linux, and several other computing platforms.

Files compressed using WinRAR usually have a `.rar` file extension.
Download WinRAR from `www.rarlab.com`.

✔ **StuffIt Expander (Free):** StuffIt Expander, developed by Allume Systems
and shown in Figure 3-3, is a shareware application for working with
compressed files. StuffIt comes preinstalled on most modern Apple computers. It is the default compression and archiving software for the Mac
platform and is likely already associated with archived files on your Mac.
StuffIt Expander can open more than 25 archive formats, and versions of
StuffIt Expander are available for the Windows and Linux operating systems, as well. *Note:* Expander is free to use for opening archived files,
but that StuffIt Standard Edition ($24.99) is required if you want to create
compressed files yourself.

Files compressed using StuffIt usually have a `.sit` file extension. You
can download StuffIt at `www.stuffit.com`.

Figure 3-2:
WinRAR is a powerful tool for compressing files and decompressing archived content.

Figure 3-3:
Using StuffIt Expander to open archived files couldn't be easier.

Seeing your filename extensions, even when Windows doesn't want you to

Unfortunately, most Windows operating systems these days make file extensions invisible by default. You can look up the file extension for an individual file by right-clicking on the file it and choosing Properties from the menu that appears. Or, you can make filename extensions visible for all files on your computer by following these steps:

1. **Click the Windows Start button and select My Computer from the menu that appears.**

   An Explorer window opens showing your hard drives.

2. **Choose Tools⇨Folder Options.**

   The Folder Options window opens.

3. **Click the View tab.**

4. **Uncheck the Hide Extensions for Known File Types check box, and click Apply to save and apply the changes, as shown in the following figure.**

From this point on, the files on your computer will have visible file extensions.

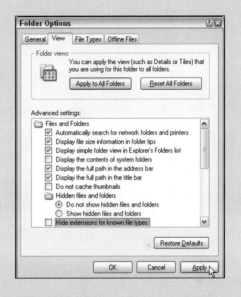

The process of downloading and installing these simple programs is quite easy, and each Web site includes installation instructions you can refer to.

Download a few torrents and you may be faced with an array of new data files on your computer that you can't identify. To figure out whether these files need to be decompressed (and which software to use for the decompression), check out the file extensions (.rar, .zip, and .sit).

Decompressing BitTorrent Files

In this section, I walk you through the process of expanding a compressed file using the WinZip program. To get started, first download a torrent using your BitTorrent client. For a sample torrent, visit

```
www.bittorrentfordummies.com/torrents/btfd.torrent
```

If you don't already have WinZip loaded on your computer, visit www.winzip.com and install the trial version of the WinZip utility before you complete the following steps.

Follow these directions to open the archive:

1. **Double-click the file to open it.**

   If the trial WinZip software is installed on your computer, a window appears, asking you to agree to the terms of use.

2. **Click I Agree.**

   WinZip opens completely, showing you the content contained in the archive.

3. **Click the Extract button at the top of the window.**

   Don't click any of the files listed before you click the Extract button.

   The WinZip Extract dialog box opens and suggests a location to save the files.

4. **Use the Folders/Drives box to select a location to save the files and then click the Extract button.**

   In Figure 3-4, I saved my files to the desktop.

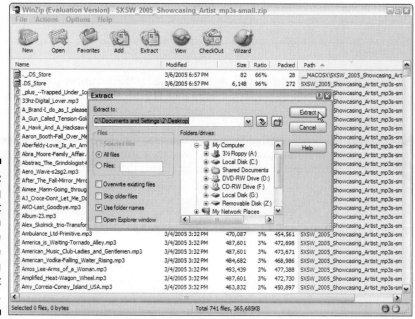

Figure 3-4:
Extracting content from an archived file is as simple as clicking the Extract button.

WinZip runs the extraction process that decompresses the files and saves them to the location you specified.

Be patient! Large files can take some time to finish.

5. Close WinZip.

The files are now decompressed. You can access the files and open them in a media player.

You may notice that some large torrent files, like movies, show up as a folder of multiple compressed files. These files are often named sequentially — for example, `moviename.rar`, `moviename.r01`, `moviename.r02`, and so on. To open this archive of multiple files, double-click the file that ends in the `.rar` (or `.zip`, or `.sit`) extension. The single file with a `.rar` extension is the only file you need to double-click to initiate the expansion process. The `.rar` file has a map of how to reconstruct a single large file for playback from the sum of all the files in the folder.

Playing Audio Files

Playing audio files that you download from peer-to-peer file-sharing networks is generally much less frustrating and more straightforward than playing video content, mainly because you have fewer possible file formats and encoding methods to deal with. Therefore, you have just a few standard players to choose from.

You can find several popular media players to download and install to handle your audio files. They vary based on features and functions, user interface, and manufacturer, but generally all do the same thing: They play digital music files.

You can install and run more than one of these on your system with impunity. Because the applications are small in size and free to download, nothing's stopping you from testing each of them to find the one you like best. If you are a PC user, you already have Windows Media Player installed on your computer by default. Macintosh computers often already have iTunes installed as part of the operating system. (Versions of both these programs are available for the other platform.)

Each of the following audio players can handle the common types of music and audio file formats.

WinAmp

WinAmp, from Nullsoft, is a great audio player that you can set up to handle all kinds of digital audio file types, including MP3, WAV, CDA, and more. Here are some other great WinAmp features:

- ✔ WinAmp can automatically connect you to dozens of Internet radio stations.

- ✔ You can customize the program by picking one of the many different *skins,* or looks, from the WinAmp skin library.

- ✔ If skins don't offer enough visual stimulation for you, you can run one of the excellent music visualizers. (Groovy, man!)

The program has great documentation in case you need help using it. And if you're a junior programmer and artist, you can even develop your own custom skins and plug-ins. In fact, WinAmp is completely *extensible,* so you can find a wide variety of plug-ins and skins written by others to increase the functionality of the original program. It is available for free online at www.winamp.com.

If you choose to purchase the souped-up version of the player, WinAmp Pro, you can rip MP3s from your music CDs and burn playlists from the application onto your own CDs.

iTunes

iTunes, shown in Figure 3-5, has quickly taken over the audio player market and is one of the most user-friendly and enjoyable audio applications out there. iTunes pushes the envelope with cool new features like the following:

- ✔ You can share your music library locally with other users on your home network.

- ✔ You can create smart playlists that keep track of songs that you listen to a lot or haven't heard in a while.

- ✔ You can let iTunes look up the artist and album information for files when you play them in iTunes.

Developed by Apple and first intended for use with the Apple iPod, iTunes is available for both Macs and Windows and doesn't require that you own or use an iPod or shop at the Apple iTunes Music Store, though these are additional features that may prove useful. You can play AAC, AIFF, audio CD, MP3 and MP4, WAV, and several other files in iTunes. Download iTunes from www.apple.com/itunes.

Figure 3-5:
The iTunes audio player is available for both Mac and Windows computers.

Windows Media Player

Windows Media Player is the default audio and video handler on Windows PCs. If you own a PC, your computer came to you with some version of this software running on it. Windows Media Player is a powerful application that can handle the audio and video content on your computer, and you can use it as a centralized jukebox for burning CDs and organizing multimedia content. Like WinAmp, Windows Media Player has great visualizations. Like iTunes, Windows Media Player offers the following features:

✔ Looks up album information for you upon request.

✔ Allows you the synch up playlists and files with a portable media player.

✔ Creates automatic playlists to help you manage songs you listen to frequently or haven't heard for a while.

Although Windows Media Player can handle most files, some files, such as .wma and .asx, won't play on any other player. To hear them, you must use Windows Media Player.

If you don't have Windows Media Player, or want to find out more about it, visit www.microsoft.com/windows/windowsmedia/default.aspx.

Playing Video

If you've downloaded and installed a BitTorrent client, downloaded a torrent file, and decompressed the torrent, if necessary, using WinZip, WinRAR, or StuffIt Expander, you've done your share of work. Now you're ready to get down to the business of watching the video you have downloaded.

Much of the time, playing a video file is as simple as double-clicking the decompressed video files (usually in `.avi`, `.mpeg`, or `.dat` format). Your computer responds by opening the default media player in order to play the file. On a PC, this is usually Windows Media Player.

Some of the video files you download may be in `.cue`, `.bin`, or `.dat` files. Frequently, these formats are associated with CDs, DVDS, TV shows, or movies that have had their encryption cracked and have been illegally distributed via BitTorrent. Unless you use special software, your computer won't recognize these files or play them.

Besides the default video players that come installed on your operating system, you can download and install others. The following programs can be used to play video on your computer.

Windows Media Player

For Windows users, the powerful Windows Media Player fills the bill for most types of video files. It can handle most video file types. If you do run across a video file Windows Media Player can't handle, chances are you can download additional video codecs to fix the problem, thus expanding the playing ability of Windows Media Player. The software can play DVDs, video files of most types, and it can also burn music to CD. Customize the look of the program with a new skin (that's the graphical look). Windows Media Player comes pre-installed on Windows machines, and is also available for Macintosh computers.

To get more information about Windows Media Player, go to `www.microsoft.com/windows/windowsmedia/default.aspx`.

QuickTime

QuickTime is Apple's custom player for the Macintosh operating system, and comes pre-installed on all Mac computers. This player is geared to work specifically with QuickTime video files, but can also handle a limited number of other video file types.

The free version of QuickTime is excellent, but its features are limited when compared to what you get for a reasonable price. For a slight fee, you can upgrade to QuickTime Pro. The professional version adds some basic video-editing tools to the program. The program is also available for PC computers, but is not as flexible as the Macintosh version. The QuickTime movie format is known for high-quality visual images.

To download the free version or purchase the Pro version, go to `www.apple.com/quicktime`.

VLC Media Player

VLC Media Player is the secret weapon for digital media files. VLC, shown in Figure 3-6, stands for VideoLAN Client (LAN stands for *local area network*), and it's a great free, open-source, multiformat and multiplatform media player. You can use it to play DVDs, MP3s, DivX files, and almost any other type of media file, including audio files. (DivX is a type of video file.) Although you can't customize the look of VLC as you can with Windows Media Player, VLC more than compensates for its lack of style with its simple effectiveness.

The developers of VLC set out to create a player that's easy to use and can play anything. Available for almost every computing platform, you can use VLC on your Macintosh or PC. This is a player worth checking out, and a must-add to your collection.

For more information and to download VLC, visit `www.videolan.org/vlc`.

Figure 3-6:
VLC is an
excellent
media
player
available
for many
computing
platforms.

Figuring Out Codecs

Even after you get a selection of video players installed on your system, you may find the occasional video file you can't play. When this happens, the fault frequently lies in the realm of video *codecs*.

If your video player occasionally indicates that it can't play a file because it is missing the correct codec, don't freak out too much. Although codecs were once headaches that only videophiles needed to worry about, with the right information you can deal with them just fine.

A *codec* is a piece of computer code that *co*mpresses and *dec*ompresses digital data (get it?). Because most digital video is eventually compressed in some way, media players have to be able to understand what kind of computer algorithm, or calculation, was used to compress the file in order to play it correctly. Sounds simple, right? If your player doesn't have the right codec, you just need to go get it, right? Well, yes, essentially.

You rarely encounter a need for codecs that aren't already part of a media player, because most of the media on the Internet is created to be accessible to as many applications as possible. Video files tend to be made for common players like Windows Media Player. Audio files tend to be made into MP3s, which can be played by virtually every player available. But sometimes media creators do choose to create media using unusual codecs, usually because of some factor specific to the file itself and much too esoteric to get into here.

Getting codec help with VideoInspector

If your player asks for a codec you don't already have, figure out what to download and then run a quick search on the Internet to find it.

If that doesn't sound like the simplest advice, luckily, a codec utility is available to help you figure out what codec you're missing so that you can install it and play your mysterious media file.

KC Softwares has an application called VideoInspector, shown in Figure 3-7. This is a regularly updated commercial product that you can use to diagnose your codec problem. Your video has no sound? It doesn't play correctly or at all? VideoInspector is designed to figure out the issue.

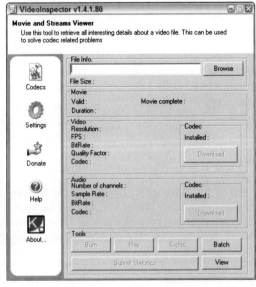

Figure 3-7:
If your video player is missing a codec, use Video-Inspector to find out how to fix the problem.

You can also use VideoInspector to get a list of all the codecs that are already installed on your computer. A free trial version is available, and the software maker suggests a donation after a period of use. It is available for Windows 95/98/Me/NT/2000 and XP. You can download VideoInspector from `www.kcsoftwares.com/index.php?vtb`.

Being wary of dream solutions to codec problems

Don't worry unnecessarily about codecs. A time is likely to come when you need to think about them and deal with them, but you don't need to cross that bridge until you get to it. That said, when the time comes (as it must), don't get suckered into downloading a *codec-specific* player (one built just to handle a single type of multimedia file).

If you're trying to find the Holy Grail combination of video players, audio players, and utilities, you really won't find a perfect multimedia beast. Sure, some programs aren't half bad, but your search for the impossible may bring you more headaches than you ever dreamed of — *data mining*.

Many software packages out there promise all kinds of solutions for some very basic problems (like having to deal with codecs!), but some of them charge a high price in return; they may try to steal your data and sell it for a profit. Read the Terms of Use for some of these applications and you discover that companies can

- ✔ Exploit your e-mail address by "sharing it with partners" (that means "selling it to spammers").
- ✔ Collect data about your Web surfing habits, all the better to serve you with annoying pop-up ads.

Installing a program with a crummy Terms of Use policy ends up adding more spam into your e-mail box and spyware to your computer — and it may not solve your codec problem.

The best solution is to set up your favorite player with the appropriate codecs. If you can get the appropriate codecs for your already useful and familiar player by visiting the product Web site or contacting technical support, why not do so? In fact, if you have Windows Media Player and Apple QuickTime, you're well covered.

You can find the QuickTime codec page at `www.apple.com/quicktime/resources/components.html`. Find out more about Windows Media Player codecs at `www.microsoft.com/windows/windowsmedia/9series/codecs.aspx`.

Dealing with Corrupted Files

Sometimes your attempts to play video files still fail, even after trying all the media players and codecs described in this chapter. Here are a couple of common issues that may be the culprit:

- ✔ **The file or archive you've downloaded is corrupted or was not fully downloaded.** If you believe this is the case, try deleting the file, reconnecting to the torrent, and downloading the file again. If the original file wasn't corrupted, the new download should play properly.

- ✔ **The file is compressed using an extremely rare or proprietary codec, media compression software, or a more current version of software you have installed.** A bit of troubleshooting of your system's video players and codecs may be required. If everything you have installed seems to be working and up to date and you still have trouble, you may consider enlisting the help of the person who shared the original file, or contacting the tracker site that's hosting the file. If you can't figure out who provided the file from the Web site where you found the torrent, you may still be able to let the tracker site know that there is a problem with the file.

- ✔ Alternatively, look for another source for a torrent of the content.

Part II
Managing
BitTorrent Content

The 5th Wave   By Rich Tennant

"Poor guy's still doing P2P filesharing."

In this part . . .

*A*ll those pesky folders and files must be piling up on your desktop by now. And how is it that you found the latest Hollywood release before it was even in your local theater, anyway? In Part II, I answer your questions about what to do with all the new media files you, no doubt, have collected, and I show you exactly what you shouldn't be downloading if you have concerns about the long arm of the law. In Chapter 4, I help you find some good BitTorrent content to download. Chapter 5 helps you organize all these new files, from setting up a sensible set of folders to backing up and storing what you've downloaded. Finally, in Chapter 6 you find out what risks you run if you decide to download pirated material.

Chapter 4

Finding BitTorrent Content

● ●

In This Chapter

▶ Knowing where to look for torrents

▶ Discovering how to make the most of search engine searches

▶ Using new tools and technologies to get torrents

● ●

*F*inding BitTorrent files to download can be a bit of a challenge — but not more of a challenge than finding Web content can be. You can look in so many different places for torrent files that getting lost in the Internet torrent fluff or being sidetracked by constant technological details and updates is always a danger.

However, I have a few tricks that I'm happy to share so that you can find the torrents you want to investigate and download. There are about as many ways to search out torrents as there are to post and share your own. In fact, many Web sites are dedicated to keeping track of torrent files; and some sites specialize in only one kind or genre of torrent. You may find the quantity of files so overwhelming that you're tempted to download everything — or nothing.

In this chapter, you find out how to use common search techniques to make effective use of search engines and torrent sites. You may even find what you discover here useful when you search for other kinds of Internet content!

Looking at Torrent Availability

When you search for BitTorrent content, you really need to know what you want. You won't find a single central repository of BitTorrent information to search, and those sites that attempt to achieve such a lofty goal are far from fully reliable.

This fact makes life harder for BitTorrent users, but is also part of the beauty of the BitTorrent system: The availability of a torrent is a direct reflection of its popularity. The more people want a file, the larger the swarm of seeds and peers. But, if no one's interested in a torrent file, it gradually dies out of availability and completely disappears. Any Web site that tries to track torrent availability faces a huge task in staying current on what is available. As with all thing Web- and network-related, change is a constant with torrents.

Doing your part to keep torrents alive

The single most important factor that can help you find and download the torrents you want is *seeding*. A file may be visible or available online, but if no one's seeding it, the file might as well be in a vacuum. Click the link as many times as you like and you will never be able to download it. The older a torrent gets, and the less popular it is, the less likely it is that it is still being seeded into the network.

You may think I've gotten off the point of finding torrents to download, but the more strongly you associate searching and seeding, the better off the BitTorrent community will be. Keep seeding! The files that you seed into any BitTorrent system remain alive as long as they are maintained and seeded by the people who create them, or by others who have a copy of them. If you stop seeding your own torrents, or those you have downloaded through the network, you may prevent others from getting access to them.

Seeding files, and re-seeding them, are important aspects of being a member of the BitTorrent community, especially if you're using the network to distribute your own media. Say it with me: Keep seeding! After multiple seeders on the network take on the task with you, you can take a break, but even those seeders will disappear from time to time and not share your digital masterpieces. So don't forget to re-seed when that happens.

Getting search tips

If you do come across a search engine or tracker site with good listings, you can only consume so much content in an average day, so the next step to finding torrents is to be selective. Get picky about what you want to view or listen to. If you are the adventurous type, you can also just do a random search on any search engine to find torrent files, but you may be surprised what you get — and what you don't.

Here are some fairly simple rules that you can follow when attempting a search:

✔ **Research, research, research:** Watch for tracker sites that keep tabs on the particular kinds of files and genres you look for. Take note of what kinds of searches get you good results.

✔ **Choose appropriate keywords for genre choices:** Making sure you have a solid idea of the content you want to find helps you narrow down search result lists.

✔ **Share your downloads:** When you share your downloads you also become a seeder and thus allow more people to search and find the content you enjoy. Seeding back into the network is the best possible method for ensuring availability of the content of you have, and you encourage others to do the same with their content. See "Doing your part to keep torrents alive" for more basic facts about this topic.

Also, torrent file searches turn up all kinds of surprising results. As the popularity of BitTorrent grows, content creators like bands and game companies are starting to release their content directly from their Web sites using BitTorrent. Some bands even use BitTorrent to broadcast their videos! You can't rely on search engines alone — visit the Web sites of musicians and artists you want to find.

In England, the BBC is even researching a peer-to-peer file-sharing system similar to BitTorrent that would allow television watchers to get programming via their computers. Such trends point to more content producers using BitTorrent, so be creative in your search for torrents.

A Note about Copyrighted Content

Many file-sharing networks and technologies are susceptible to use by those who share and acquire copyrighted material like movies, TV shows, and music. BitTorrent is no exception. Downloading some of the torrent files you find online is sometimes referred to as *digital piracy*. Whatever you call it, the bottom line is that you want to avoid copyright infringement.

Digital piracy exposes both the technology and the network to legal issues, hurting just about everyone:

✔ File-sharing developers, who are doing their best to advance technology

✔ Legitimate users of file-sharing technology, who aren't doing anything wrong

✔ Copyright owners, often artists and musicians, who just want to make a living doing what they love

To counteract this activity, more and more tracker sites are introducing monitoring filters to try to keep copyrighted material out of their listings. The situation is likely to get uglier before it gets better.

You should be careful about what you download, and what you share. The more content generated by the public and released using BitTorrent technology, the better chance BitTorrent has at continuing to be available. Legal usage will solidify this technology as being efficient and not the domain of those who wish to violate content copyright laws.

Getting educated about copyright issues

The BitTorrent situation is not a new one and should not surprise people using BitTorrent. In 1998, the United States presented a bill known as the Digital Millennium Copyright Act, which detailed the rights and freedoms of copyright holders and consumers in the digital medium. The bill was signed into law. I encourage you to find out more about copyright infringement in Chapter 6, and about the Digital Millennium Copyright Act at one of these Web sites:

- UCLA Online Institute for Cyberspace Law and Policy: `www.gseis.ucla.edu/iclp/dmca1.htm`
- Wikipedia entry on the Digital Millennium Copyright Act: `en.wikipedia.org/wiki/Digital_Millennium_Copyright_Act`
- Text of the Digital Millennium Copyright Act of 1998, in PDF format (shown in Figure 4-1): `www.copyright.gov/legislation/dmca.pdf`

In Chapter 6, you can read in more detail about how copyright works and find out more about the risks you run if you engage in digital piracy.

Educating others about the merits of BitTorrent

Many professional content makers paint BitTorrent with the same brush as the file-sharing networks that have become notorious for letting users infringe on copyright. Others are simply frightened off because it is a new and somewhat confusing technology. As a BitTorrent user, your mission (should you choose to accept it) is to let others see just how useful and important BitTorrent is.

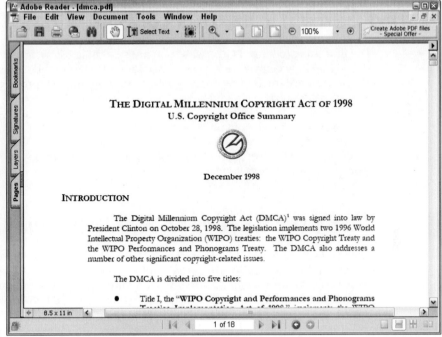

Figure 4-1:
The Digital
Millennium
Copyright
Act of 1998
specifically
addressed
some of the
copyright
issues as
they pertain
to digital
technology.

When you see content that could be delivered effectively using BitTorrent, write letters, send e-mail messages, or find some other way to start a buzz in your local community about BitTorrent. Here are just a few things you can do:

- ✔ E-mail your favorite artists and mention that they could use BitTorrent to release content quickly and inexpensively.

- ✔ Let your local cable company know that you want to download television programs to your computer.

- ✔ Because BitTorrent users are the ones seeding the network, the users, not the makers of the technology, have the power to make BitTorrent — or break it.

For more information on how BitTorrent is being used today by artists, businesses, and organizations, read Chapter 15.

Using Search Engines to Find Torrents

The first thing to know is just what you are searching for. What do you intend to find and how can you describe it? Because thousands and thousands of BitTorrent files are floating around out there, using the file format as your only search criteria isn't advisable.

Also, you have no way of knowing how someone has named a file that's been seeded using BitTorrent. If they're going to be found, content must be described with keywords, preferably keywords that are unique to the particular content you're searching for.

Using the BitTorrent Search Engine

The quickest route to finding torrents is to use the BitTorrent Search Engine, developed by Bram Cohen, the creator of BitTorrent. This search engine only returns results for torrent files — you won't find Web sites, news articles, images, or other Web materials with this engine. Visit the BitTorrent Search Engine at `search.bittorrent.com`.

What you find with the BitTorrent Search Engine may not be legally available. Because the status of torrents can change quickly based on how many seeds they have, some results you find may not be available on the BitTorrent network, even though they were available yesterday.

Searching using keywords

You can use the tips outlined here to find torrents on any search engine, from Google (`www.google.com`) or Ask Jeeves (`www.ask.com`):

1. **Research what you want so that you know how it is described online.**

   For example, if you're looking for NASA video footage, you might do some research on specific shuttle and astronaut names.

   The search results give you a hint as to the keywords you might use in a Web search. For example, my research led me to discover that *Challenger space ship* is often better described as *Challenger space shuttle*.

2. **Establish keywords for the content and enter them into a search engine.**

   Your search terms should be as unique as possible, and they should match the content very closely. See Figure 4-2.

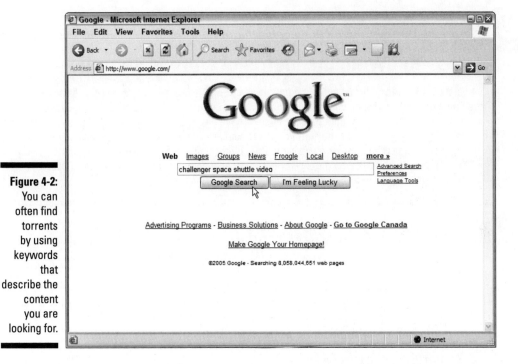

Figure 4-2:
You can
often find
torrents
by using
keywords
that
describe the
content
you are
looking for.

Narrowing down a basic keyword search

The effectiveness of a keyword search has a lot to do with how specific the keywords are. For instance, using a keyword like a band name brings back a listing for every Web page that mentions the band, whether it's a music review, a fan Web site, or a discography. You need more specific keywords to get better results.

Searching for the band 8BitPeoples (a musical collective that freely distributes its music), yields around 7,360 results. That's a lot to sort through if I'm only looking for a torrent of the group's music.

The addition of more keywords can help to bring the results you want to the top of the results list. For example, my results are narrowed to about 5,070 when I search for

```
8BitPeoples music
```

When you search on multiple keywords, search engines such as Google automatically link them together with an AND.

Knowing the merits of a broad search

When you search for a broad subject (such as the name of a music group), you will, no doubt, get a lot of results. Many people prefer to use broad search terms so that they don't miss anything, and so that they can browse through all kinds of results and see what new discoveries they might make along the way. Cruising through very general search results opens you up to associations and links you may not have expected, and potentially to new content makers that are interesting to hear or view. You might find a fan Web site, or a group that has been inspired by the one you looked up.

The result is a list of Web sites that use both the first term AND the second, and none that include only one keyword or the other.

You can also try to search based on the type of content you are looking for. If you use Google or Ask Jeeves, try searching for a keyword and adding the word *torrent* to the search expression. This technique often yields better results, but you may also get a lot of other torrent files or Web sites offering tracking services for torrent files that are totally unrelated to the band or artist you're looking for.

Those sites that use both keywords appear higher on the list of results, so you may be able to find what you're looking for, but it isn't the most efficient and quick way to finding specific content. Still, click through enough search result pages and you can find what you want.

I get 227 results when I search for

```
8BitPeoples torrent
```

Right now, using search engines is not the best way to find torrent files; but this situation will change (for the better) as BitTorrent is used by more and more content producers (like you) to release content. Still, much depends on Web sites using the word *torrent* in their descriptions of content, and not all content producers include this crucial word.

Using advanced search techniques

Most search engines work very similarly, largely because the content on the Web is all the same. The same keywords and data are available to each search engine, so the concepts in searching that content don't change all that much from search engine to search engine.

As a result, you can use the search techniques outlined in this chapter on many different search engines, from Google to Ask Jeeves to MSN Search, and the results you get back are largely the same. That said, however, you may notice small differences in how the search engines interpret what you enter into the search box, and how results are ranked, so don't expect a search on one to give you identical results on another.

In this section, I use Google to describe searching techniques. Google is one of the most popular search engines, and you're probably familiar with some of its basic search capabilities. I show you how to dig a little deeper using more specific search techniques.

How can you make your searches most efficient? Surprisingly, it is quite easy. By just adding a few different characters to a search query you can filter out a lot results that aren't exactly what you are looking for.

Using quotation marks to search for a phrase

Using quotations around keywords is a simple and useful technique. If a phrase is important to your search, using the quotation marks ensures that the whole phrase is searched as a single unit instead of as separate words on a Web page.

If you're searching for a piece of content that is named with more than two words, you can use quotation marks to make the search engine look for Web pages that use those words in the same order as you entered them.

Say you're looking for *Blue: A Short Film,* an animated film that's available for free on the Internet. You could try searching for

```
Blue short film
```

but this search produces roughly 5,930,000 results. If you use quotation marks, on the other hand, with a search query like

```
"Blue short film"
```

as shown in Figure 4-3, you get roughly 153 results — a much more reasonable proposition to sort through looking for the torrent of the film!

Using quotations is both more exact and a time saver. Your results will vary from search engine to search engine.

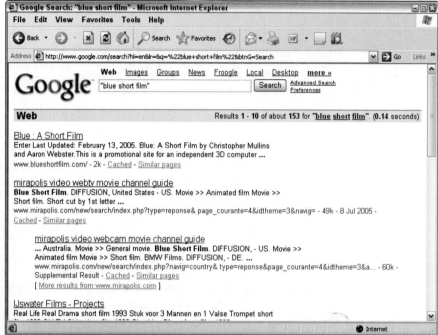

Figure 4-3:
Using
quotation
marks
around a
phrase
narrows
down the
results
returned by
the search
engine.

Using the plus sign

You can use the plus (+) sign with your keywords to include common words in your searches. Most search engines ignore common words like *the, and, a, an, where, how,* and so on; because these words appear in nearly every Web page, they would ruin search results if they were included. However, sometimes a common word is important to your search — in fact, impossible without it! For example, if you're searching for a file that has a particular name and really needs to include the term *the,* you can conduct your search like this:

```
heart +from
```

This ensures that the search engine returns a result that uses the keyword *heart* and also the word *from.* ("From the Heart" is an 8BitPeoples song.)

Sometimes you may need to search for a name or phrase that is commonly used in other ways. For example, many music groups out there (especially fledgling, unsigned acts) have the same name! In those cases, you need to search for your phrase and some additional descriptive keyword. Try using the plus sign to add the additional keyword. The results list includes listings with the keyword(s) you are looking for that also include the keyword that followed the plus sign. One way to narrow down a search might be to include a geographic identifier:

```
8BitPeoples +los angeles
```

For instance, suppose you are looking for a movie called *Cornbread* (there isn't actually a movie by this name, as far as I know). Obviously, several Web sites use the word *cornbread,* but only some of these will be about the movie. There will be Web sites with recipes, menus and so on.

Using the plus sign, you can tell the search engine that you want to find the movie name plus the keyword movie:

```
cornbread +movie
```

The search engine is then required to return results that include the word *cornbread,* but only if the Web page also uses the word *movie.* This combination definitely helps narrow your search.

Using the minus sign

You can use the minus sign (–) to exclude certain words from your search. In the previous section, I show you how to employ the plus sign (+) to search for a movie called *Cornbread* to only get results that also contain the word *movie.* The minus sign enables you to exclude words for your search. So, if you're looking for cornbread recipes, but you're not interested in the movie, you could conduct the following search:

```
cornbread -movie
```

This search turns up all the Web pages that use the word *cornbread,* and excludes those that also use the word *movie.* This is a useful tool to remove popular phrases and words that commonly go together and help get the number of results under control.

Using file type as a search criterion

One of the most interesting ways to find torrent files is to use a file type filter. By including file type in your search, you can narrow your search down to only results that include the keywords and are also the specified file format. For example, try a search like this:

```
blue short film filetype:torrent
```

The search engine filters out all results unless they make reference to or are a torrent file link to *Blue: A Short Film.* What a powerful way to search for torrent content.

Using advanced search features

Just about every search engine has an advanced search features. Usually, the main page has a descriptive link like Advanced Search, which leads you to a page filled with all kinds of ways to direct your searches so that they're more detailed and, thus, yield more detailed results. You can see Google's Advanced Search page in Figure 4-4.

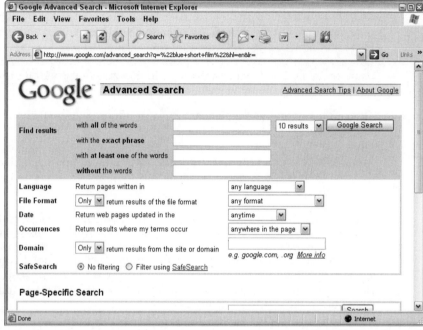

Figure 4-4:
Refine your
search
using the
Google
Advanced
Search
page.

Typical refinements of an advanced search page, as exemplified by Google's Advanced Search page, include the following:

- ✔ Limit the number of results that are returned.

- ✔ Carefully tailor the words chosen by including all, searching for an exact phrase, finding results that include at least one of your keywords, or search for results that exclude certain results.

- ✔ Limit the results to pages in certain languages.

- ✔ Limit the results to certain file types, or exclude certain file types.

- ✔ Determine results by where in the Web page your keywords appear.

- ✔ Limit results to only a certain domain or Web site.

Finding Torrents with New Tools

At times, you may find the pool of content you have to choose from is lacking in quality or quantity (or both). One of the facts you must realize about BitTorrent is that — through its very nature — some content may not be seeded at the time you want to download it. Torrents available last week may not be available this week, if the torrents' popularity has decreased to the point that BitTorrent users stopped seeding it.

Still, several trackers on the Internet attempt to ameliorate this problem. Each of them deals with monitoring and tracking of their torrent files a little differently. Most offer a search of listed torrent files, or make sure new torrents are identified. Some even offer *RSS* (Really Simple Syndication) feeds that allow you keep up to date on new torrent files as they are posted by users by using news reader software like Bloglines (www.bloglines.com).

Keeping up with RSS

BitTorrent enclosures are becoming popular. Web site trackers that accept submissions from content creators to point to torrent files are now beginning to provide torrent listings as an RSS feed.

With *RSS,* or Really Simple Syndication, a Web site or a blog can publish a *feed* of the latest updates to the site. That feed is picked up and read by news readers and news aggregators. Because many people who read a lot of blogs like to use a news reader to do so, RSS feeds keep users abreast of changes to the Web sites and blogs whose feeds they track. The result is that interested folks find out much faster when there is new content on a Web site, blog — or in this case, torrent tracker.

The TorrentSpy tracker site (www.torrentspy.com), shown in Figure 4-5, publishes an RSS feed of its latest torrents.

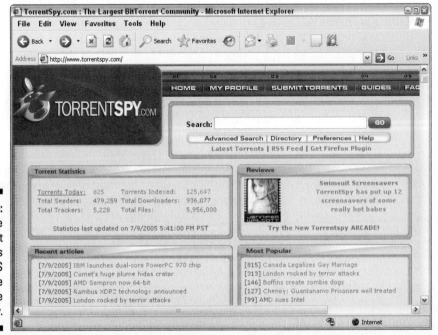

Figure 4-5: Get the latest updates via RSS from the tracker site TorrentSpy.

Broadcatching

Broadcatching is a recent trend in which trackers are combining the power of RSS feeds and torrent files to automate downloading of desired torrents. It works like this:

1. You subscribe to the RSS feed of a tracker Web site, which is updated as the tracker site adds new torrents.

2. You tell your BitTorrent client to watch the feed for certain torrents.

3. When a new torrent is added that you have identified as one you want, the BitTorrent client downloads it automatically.

The whole process is a lot like telling a personal video recorder device like Tivo to record certain TV shows — which it then does automatically without you having to tell the device when, and on what channel, the shows are on.

Broadcatching is quite an interesting idea for those who want to update song lists or video episodes of some publicly available program. With broadcasting in place, you won't have to search for torrents very often. You just set up your broadcatching software to watch for torrents on your favorite tracker RSS feed and get the files when they become available.

Making things easy with Exeem

Exeem is a newer peer-to-peer service that's based on BitTorrent technology and techniques. But this new system removes the requirement for a tracker to keep tabs on the hundreds of torrent links some of the busier trackers may take on every hour.

You can build your torrent files with Exeem and publish your home movies by placing them into a variety of categories. Searching for files in the Exeem system is also quite simple, and includes methods for sorting your results in different ways.

Currently, Exeem is still in early development, but it shows some promise by building upon the strengths of BitTorrent. The pool of content listed in the Exeem system is limited but grows daily. It will be interesting to see what happens to this product when it's fully developed.

You can download Exeem at www.exeem.com, shown in Figure 4-6.

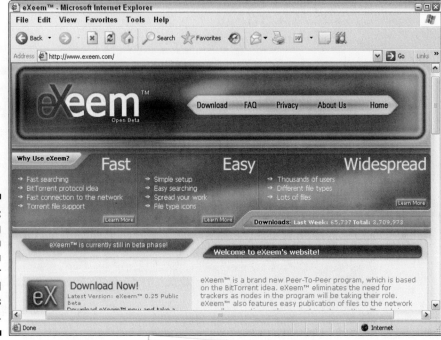

Figure 4-6:
Using
Exeem
helps you
share your
files and
find others
more easily.

Experimenting with Kedora TV

A fairly new project, Kedora is a BitTorrent-based system for distributing video programs. These programs are video shows created by users of the software and cover a variety of topics from hacking to games. Developed quite recently, Kedora is still in beta and best suited for hard-core techno-geeks. If you're not totally obsessed with technology, keep an eye on Kedora as it evolves, and maybe it'll be your cup of tea in the coming months.

Kedora is online at `www.kedora.net`, and shown in Figure 4-7.

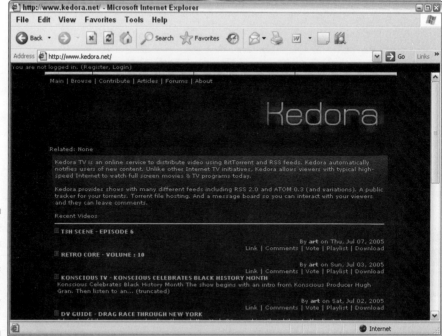

Figure 4-7:
Kedora is
distributing
torrents of
shows
using new
technology.

Chapter 5

Storing BitTorrent Content

- -

- -

*W*ith your newfound understanding of how to use BitTorrent to download all sorts of files comes a wealth of additional questions. You need answers if you want to enjoy and optimize your BitTorrent experience. And, you need a working knowledge of how to deal with the huge amount of new data on your computer.

In my first week of using BitTorrent alone, I downloaded more than 5GB (that's *gigabytes,* folks) of data of all sorts, including large audio and video files. I am not the exception; I'm the rule. After a few days of BitTorrent fun, you will quickly need to figure out ways to manage the unwieldy and ever-growing collection of files.

In this chapter, you discover the most efficient means of naming and organizing the files you download so that you can remember what they're called and where they live. I cover common tools used to index and sort your media collection for easy playback later.

The most important factor in how you organize your files it that the categorization means something to you and that you feel comfortable working with it.

In addition to naming and indexing, I discuss the various options out there for backing up, storing, and archiving the content you download using BitTorrent. This chapter gives you an overview of archiving data on internal and external hard drives as well as using CD and DVD burners to back up data. A big part of handling multimedia content is knowing which files you can get rid of, so don't miss the section in this chapter where I discuss what to delete, and how.

Setting Up Your Computer

Probably the most important thing to find out as you become a more frequent downloader is how to protect your system from the viruses, adware, spyware, and other harmful files floating around on the Internet. This section gives an introduction to these three risks, including a focus on the common tools used to keep your system safe so you don't have to worry about infecting or destroying your computer while using BitTorrent.

Blocking viruses

Downloading content from the Internet may be easy, but it isn't necessarily safe. Viruses come in many forms, some of which cause mere inconvenience and others quite lethal to your computer. Use your best judgment and common sense — and run, don't walk, to get yourself antivirus software.

The more questionable the origin of content is, the more likely it is to be infected with a virus. In other words, if you're considering downloading pirated content, you're putting your computer at considerable risk for viruses — and with the law.

One problem is that anyone can give any file any name and any description. As you search for torrents to download, remember that what you think you are downloading may not actually be what you are downloading. The title of the file and the description of the content aren't guaranteed to be accurate. You have no solid guarantees that what you want is really in the torrent file you request.

Antivirus software can protect your computer from the most malicious content by identifying viruses when you download infected files. Most good antivirus software alerts you to the presence of a bad file before it takes hold of your e-mail address book or hard drive. Antivirus software monitors your computer system and is programmed to recognize the particular behaviors of viruses, worms, Trojan horses, and other types of code designed to damage data, replicate e-mail, or collect personal data from your system.

Most computer manufacturers bundle antivirus software with new computers, or offer trial versions of antivirus software that work for 90 days before requiring users to purchase the complete program.

In addition to using antivirus software to check every new file you download, you should run regular scans of your system, as shown in Figure 5-1.

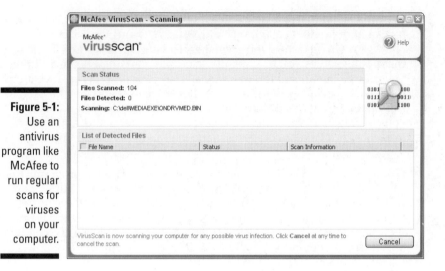

Figure 5-1:
Use an
antivirus
program like
McAfee to
run regular
scans for
viruses
on your
computer.

You're playing roulette by ignoring the risk of viruses, or putting off purchasing antivirus software because of the platform you use, the false assumption that antivirus software leads to a loss in performance, or because of the cost.

The best way to protect your computer from virus infections is quite easy — get antivirus software. Here are some of the more popular packages and a little bit about what they do.

- **Symantec Norton AntiVirus:** Symantec is the recognized leader in antivirus protection. Symantec's Norton AntiVirus program is designed to help individuals, small and mid-sized businesses, and large enterprises. Norton AntiVirus removes viruses automatically, blocks Internet worms, scans e-mail messages, detects spyware, examines compressed archive files before opening them, and enables you to download regular software updates so that you aren't susceptible to new viruses. This program is available for PCs and Macintosh computers for $50. If you need to protect a home network, you can get a package to protect multiple computers. Read more about Norton AntiVirus online at www.symantec.com/nav.

- **McAfee VirusScan:** McAfee is also a leader in antivirus protection. The company provides a variety of security products for both enterprise users and home users. VirusScan is McAfee's virus protection program. It checks for viruses in e-mail, downloaded files, files accessed during Web surfing, removes viruses from your system, prevents spyware, and automatically updates itself with the latest virus definitions. VirusScan is available for PCs, and an annual subscription costs $40. Find out more at www.mcafee.com.

✔ **Grisoft AVG Anti-Virus:** Grisoft is an antivirus program producer with a high-quality product called AVG Anti-Virus. AVG Anti-Virus scans e-mail, checks for viruses when you open files, isolates viruses when it finds them, and enables you to schedule scans of your computer. In addition, you get free updates to the software so that your protection stays up to date. This program is designed for the average user and may be used for free under certain conditions. The cost for this application is $33, and you can buy multiple licenses for several computers. AVG Anti-Virus is available for all major computer platforms, and is available online at www.grisoft.com.

✔ **ClamAV:** ClamAV is a free, open-source antivirus software program. You can use this very good product with almost any platform. ClamAV comes with a scheduling tool for virus scans, automatic updates to virus definitions, and e-mail scanning. This tool is currently a geek tool and is not recommended for use by average computer users. Keep a watch on this one; it will mature in the coming years. Read more about it and download it at www.clamav.net.

Avoiding adware and spyware

If you have ever had a pop-up window appear on your computer, you may recall that your first response was surprise — where in the *heck* did this thing come from? You can explain the origins of pop-up ads that you pick up when surfing the Web, but what about the time you were using your e-mail program or word processor and a pop-up appeared?

The most likely culprit of a pop-up ad that appears when you're checking your e-mail or innocently writing a memo in Microsoft Word is that an adware program has found its way onto your system, all the better for showing you some new commercial opportunity you probably don't need. *Adware* programs display advertisements on your desktop, but they also can upload information about your computer to the Mother Ship without your consent.

A note for users of the Big Mac

Many people believe that the Macintosh computer platform isn't affected by viruses. This belief is simply wrong. Although more viruses are geared toward PCs than to Macs, a few viruses out there affect Macintosh computers. Because the new Apple OS X is built on a BSD Unix platform, there are also Unix-based viruses to worry about. Some of these viruses can do a significant amount of damage.

Another thing to remember about the Mac and viruses: If your Mac isn't affected by a virus, that doesn't mean you can't transmit the virus. In fact, your Mac can show no signs of illness and still actively distribute the virus, just like healthy carriers sometimes infect other people with illnesses such as the flu. Antivirus software is as important for Macintosh users as it is for PC users.

Adware programs are mainly just annoying and intrusive rather than destructive. It's especially intrusive because you may not realize you've installed it; it is sometimes even packaged with tools you actually want.

Spyware is software that collects information about your computer, records data about how you use your computer, and sends the info to commercial entities and other organizations or individuals. It can also be used to take control of your computer for other uses. Spyware is capable of uploading data from your computer without your consent, keep tabs on your Web habits, and take control of your Web browser.

Spyware isn't always used for the *most* nefarious purposes; however, the line between nefarious and *merely* intrusive is often fuzzy. After all, the point of spyware is to invade your system without your knowledge. Whether the purpose is to hack your Web browser for kicks or to supply a company with information so that the company can bombard you with advertising and computer products, spyware is *bad*.

The best way to fight both adware and spyware is to install an adware and spyware blocker like SpyBot (`www.safer-networking.org`) or Ad-Aware (`www.lavasoftusa.com/software/adaware`). Then frequently scan your system with these products.

Keeping Track of Your Files

Being a BitTorrent user is kind of like being a kid in a candy store — you can find so much online (legally, of course). But keeping track of your huge and growing collection of media files can be a daunting task. Frequent users of BitTorrent and other file-sharing networks find that computer hard drives fill up quickly with new audio and video content files. Most of these new files use different and obscure file-naming conventions. Keeping track of all this content is a headache unless you take some steps to manage things for yourself.

Here are a few simple rules you can follow to make managing your file downloads more efficient:

1. **Choose one media player system.**

   Try the major players in the media management arena, choosing one, and then sticking with it. Because each media player uses its own system for tracking and naming files, trying to use more than one system can become a nightmare.

   A media player's primary function is to simply play music or video, but the latest and greatest versions of the popular players also help you organize and sort your ever-expanding collection of media. Digital audio and video can be a little bit unnerving when you're trying to sort through it (unless you only maintain a small media portfolio). Players have evolved into the best organizers to meet this demand.

Common examples of these tools are iTunes, RealPlayer, and Windows Media Player Jukebox.

2. **Rename your files.**

In order to manage your files efficiently, make sure you rename them in a logical way after you download them. People choose to name their video or audio files in different ways, and trying to keep tabs on all these methods can make you crazy. Make your file-naming scheme simple and logical, and include the information you find most important. Naming things yourself, and organizing them properly, helps you find the files later, and enables you to keep tabs on what you have.

3. **Use file identification tags.**

Every media file on a computer system in this day and age allows for *ID tagging*. For example, ID tagging records the album name, artist information, and media file details as part of each audio file on your computer. Editing or filling out this information is useful to media players and can help you both catalog and keep track of your files.

This information (artist name, song title, album name, and so on) is sometimes also called *metadata*.

4. **Use logical files and folders.**

Keeping audio and video files in their own directories is always a good idea for backup purposes and for organization. You can organize files in several ways, but knowing the files are in a single place is one easy shortcut. You can see an example of how I organize my content in Figure 5-2.

Use whatever organizational system works for you — as long as you use one! And in case you're wondering . . . keeping everything on your desktop is *not* an organizational system.

Organizing files with Windows Media Player

Users of Windows Media Player can sort files in a number of ways: by composer, album title, genre, and more. The library system in this player also includes a personal rating system that you can use to create playlists. For example, you can tell Windows Media Player to play all your top-rated songs. In Figure 5-3, you can see the Windows Media Player presentation of audio content.

Figure 5-2:
One method
to use in
organizing
your content
is by artist
name.

You can also sort video files by recording date, actor name, personal rating, date of purchase, and recorded date.

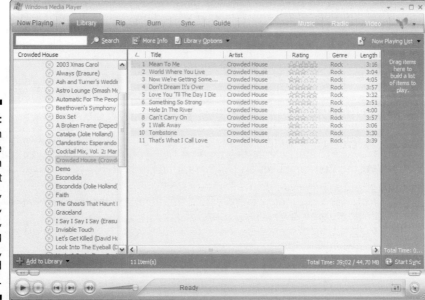

Figure 5-3:
You can
include
information
like artist
name,
album title,
song title,
your rating
of the piece,
genre, and
song length.

Using Windows Media Player playlists to your advantage

Windows Media Player takes playlists to a whole new level. This player can sort media by favorites, ratings, and other organizational features, but the one really worth mentioning is its Auto Playlist feature. By analyzing your playing habits, Windows Media player automatically creates playlists for (among other things)

✔ Tracks that have never been played (called *fresh tracks*)

✔ Tracks you play more often at night, during the day, or during the weekend

✔ Tracks you play frequently

✔ Tracks you haven't played lately

✔ Tracks recorded at better quality

Windows Media Player enables you to burn and synchronize media with other devices such as MP3 players. You can also access media information through the media information interface. You can add, or *rip* media, from your personal collection of CDs and DVDs, creating digital copies of your media collection on your computer.

Windows Media Player has all kinds of features for those who would like to view and organize their media in one simple tool. For example:

✔ You can quickly correct naming errors and typos by clicking and typing the correct information. If you correct the spelling of an album name that is already listed correctly, Windows Media recognizes the correction and places the tracks in the album list.

✔ You can choose to display the *metadata* (title, genre, actors, media type, rating, length, and so on) you find most valuable when viewing listings of your content. The range of metadata is huge, right down to identifying the content provider of the content or offering an episode description.

✔ You can *rip,* or digitally encode, your own music CDs to create a library of music and video on your computer. If you buy a portable MP3 player, you can then use Windows Media Player to move media between your player and your computer.

It comes pre-installed on computers using any current Windows platform and is ready to start cataloging the first time you run it. This player works well for the first-time user and allows for all kinds of flexibility. Download from www.microsoft.com/windows/windowsmedia.

Organizing files with iTunes

If you have an iPod or a new Apple computer, it is hard to avoid the iTunes software. (iTunes is also available for Windows computers, but it is *the* media player for Mac users.) iTunes is a simple, all-in-one, media library and player system.

Like the other major media players, you can use iTunes to organize, create playlists, burn CDs, and more. As well, iTunes has easy one-button access to the iTunes Music Store, where you can purchase high-quality music MP3s.

The player has all the typical functions: random play, shuffle play, cross-fading between tracks. But in additional to the usual tools, Apple offers the unusual: a powerful tool inside iTunes enables you to share music across a local network. For example, you can have multiple computers at home that all use the MP3 files on one computer, letting you listen to playlists and albums without having to rip your music CDs on each separate computer. This is a truly liberating feature!

You can import files as AAC, MP3 or WAV files. This functionality gives you the flexibility to use sounds in many different capacities from mixing music to throwing a party. You are able to add music to your playlists directly into your player. You can also synchronize with your iPod or other MP3 player device.

iTunes has all kinds of features for those who would like to view and organize their audio in one simple tool. For example:

- ✔ The program's simple Browse interface enables you to view your collection by genre, artist name, and album all at the same time, narrowing down your selection by selecting from each category.

- ✔ You can choose to display the *metadata* (title, genre, composer, personal rating, length, and so on) you find most valuable when viewing listings of your content. You can find metadata up the wazoo — even metadata that identifies the beats per minute of a song.

- ✔ Identify and eliminate duplicate songs in your collection. Choose Edit and select Show Duplicate Songs; then delete the extra copies.

- ✔ Manage music you purchase through the Apple Music Store via iTunes.

The iTunes player and organizer (shown in Figure 5-4) is for any user, from music addicts to the casual music listener — a little something for everyone. Download from `www.apple.com/ilife/itunes`.

Figure 5-4:
iTunes
displays
song name,
track length,
artist name,
album,
genre,
rating, and
album art
for each
song track.

Organizing files with RealPlayer

Once known as an innovative media player, today's Real Player — while still useful — is not as powerful as Windows Media Player or iTunes.

RealPlayer features include auto playlists, playlist customization, and burning and synchronization with player devices connected to your computer. This player, shown in Figure 5-5, has all the important features of good audio and video playback software, including a connection to online media purchases.

In large part, however, RealNetworks has hamstrung its player by urging signups for other products, hounding users to additional services, and drowning them in advertising messages. It frequently comes pre-installed on computers as part of manufacturer distribution deals, but you can also download it from www.real.com.

You can use RealPlayer to manage your files. For example:

- ✔ Use the program's Organizer interface to move files based on genres, albums, and other categories. After you move a file, RealPlayer automatically resets the listing, removing items that no longer contain content.

- ✔ Display the *metadata* (title, genre, composer, personal rating, length, and so on) for each type of content, creating a different set of data for music, video, playlists, purchased music, and search results.

- ✔ Update information for several files at a time selecting all of them and then right-clicking and choosing Edit Clip Info. If, for example, you change the album name once, the update is made for all the files you've selected.

- ✔ Locate media on your computer quickly by right-clicking on a file and selecting Locate File from the pop-up menu. The folder that contains the file immediately opens on your desktop.

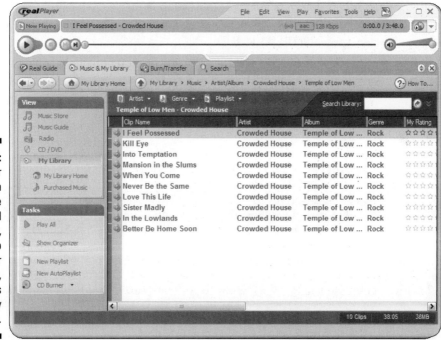

Figure 5-5:
RealPlayer can organize downloaded content, files you rip from your own CDs, and files that you buy online.

Knowing What to Delete

Downloading files from the BitTorrent network can fill up your hard drive with unwanted torrent files and compressed files you don't need, because you already consumed the content or because you decompressed an archived file and no longer need the archive. Keeping a solid handle on where the files live is always important in keeping track of everything.

Many files you download using BitTorrent are archived, or compressed. To get at the actual data, you must extract it from the archive file. (For a detailed walk-through of using file compression utilities, read Chapter 3.)

A typical process for torrent downloading goes like this:

1. You download the torrent, and the data file using a BitTorrent client.
2. You extract the data file from either a ZIP or RAR format.
3. You view, read, or listen to the media.
4. You move on with your life, neglecting to delete torrent and/or the compressed (ZIP, RAR) file.
5. The space on your hard drive fills up, and you cry aloud and curse your computer system for performing poorly.
6. You delete the offending, previously forgotten files, and return to Step 1.

Deleting old compressed files

Downloading archived or compressed files means that you are left with bunches of archive files lying around on your computer that you don't need and should delete.

A rule to remember is that after you extract audio or video content from its compressed file format you can (and should) discard the archive file, as shown in Figure 5-6. Simply select the files you want to get rid of and press the Delete or Backspace key on your keyboard; alternatively, you can drag the files to the Recycle Bin on your desktop.

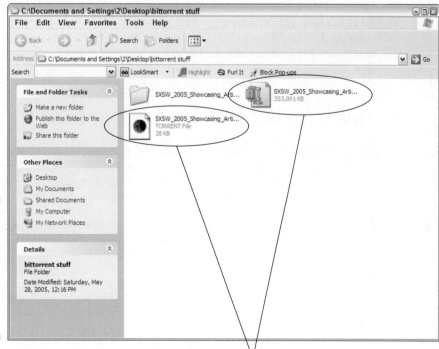

These files can be deleted.

Figure 5-6:
As soon as you extract and reseed archived files, delete those archives.

Don't delete archive files that you're still seeding back into the BitTorrent network. You may not need these files anymore, but you can't continue to share an archive if you delete it!

Sometimes you may attempt to delete a huge file and receive a message the file is too large for the Recycle Bin, as shown in Figure 5-7. Go ahead and click Yes; the file is removed from your system forever.

Figure 5-7:
You must delete very large files instead of placing them in the Recycle Bin.

When you delete a large amount of data from your system (more than a couple of gigabytes), you should empty your Recycle Bin to free up the space on your hard drive. Simply right-click on the Recycle Bin icon on your desktop and select the Empty Recycle Bin option from the context-sensitive menu that appears.

Deleting old torrents

After you're completely done downloading a file from the BitTorrent network and have finished seeding the file back to community it is okay to delete the original torrent file. This file is small and likely isn't taking up much of your computer's hard drive space, so deleting it won't free up a lot of room, but having a lot of old torrent files around can be messy and a little confusing. You may choose to keep the file on your system to seed the content back to the network at a later date.

Deleting the torrent file when you are finished downloading and seeding doesn't affect your ability to play back the file. If you delete data files, however, you must download them all over again in order to get them back onto your hard drive.

Media players tend to organize data in a virtual manner, meaning that when you delete a file from a playlist, you may not necessarily delete it from your computer hard drive. If you actually want to delete a file from your computer, you should locate the actual file and delete it instead of simply just removing it from the media player.

Archiving Files Hard Drives

If you're tired of hearing people remind you to back up, back up, back up data files, I'm right there with you. But no matter how annoying the mantra is, it's still true.

If you don't back up your files, chances are good that at some point down the road you will lose your data — forever. Backing up media files is just the same as backing up your Microsoft Word memos and Excel spreadsheets — but it tends to be quite a large job because media files are much larger than the average document.

After even a little time spent downloading torrent files, you may find yourself without any space left on your computer's hard drive. This occurrence is very common, and is something media collectors need to deal with.

Before you do any kind of a backup, delete the files you don't need. What's the point of backing up files you don't want around?

After you delete old files, you should assess your hard drive storage space situation. If you're planning on creating and trading many multimedia files and you're in a storage crunch, you should consider obtaining an additional hard drive. Unlike five years ago, storage space has become an affordable reality for most home users. You can get additional internal or external hard drives in sizes ranging from as low as 40GB to just over 300GB.

Of course, with all the additional options, buying a hard drive is not as simple as it once was. Discovering your best option depends on how you plan on using the drive, how much money you have to spend, and how much storage you need.

Deciding between an internal and an external hard drive

Your first consideration when looking at hard drives is whether or not you want to have an *internal* hard drive installed inside your computer system (which is not always possible) or whether you would like to have an *external* hard drive, located in a separate case. You plug in an external hard drive only when you require it. The rest of the time, you store it somewhere safe.

Internal drives are the most common. You simply purchase the drive, mount it in your computer case, and turn on your computer. The minute you turn on your computer, your computer recognizes it as new hardware. Point and click to install the drive.

Internal drives are connected via an *IDE connector* or an *SATA connector*. These cables are really not of too much concern, except that you need to make sure to purchase the correct drive for your computer system. Check your computer's manual or refer to your manufacturer's Web site to find out which kind of drive you need. The vast majority of PCs use IDE hard drive connectors.

When considering external hard drives, you have several off-the-shelf and simple, do-it-yourself solutions:

✔ **Off-the-shelf external hard drives:** These external hard drives come packaged with the cables you need to connect them to your computer. They are a little more expensive than do-it-yourself kits, but are the way to go to get hooked up quickly and with a minimum amount of hassle.

Off-the-shelf hard drives come with warranties and support services that you won't get if you build your own external hard drive.

✔ **Do-it-yourself external hard drives:** If you're handy, you can build your
     own external hard drive by buying an internal hard drive and an exter-
     nal hard drive case. The result looks and behaves much like an off-the-
     shelf hard drive, but is less expensive (up to half the price of an off-the-
     shelf drive).

     Mounting your internal hard drive in a case may void your warranty.

All major electronics retailers carry a wide variety of external drives, internal
drives, and cases.

Setting up your external drive

In terms of set up, off-the-shelf external hard drives are almost always easier
to set up than a do-it-yourself model — simply connect the USB or FireWire
cable to your computer and call it done. Your system recognizes the new
device and connects to it, often leading you through the installation process.

Expect to spend more time connecting and setting up a drive you have built
yourself. If you're handy with a screwdriver and like to figure things out —
this might be a fun Saturday night project!

Getting information about
hard drive speeds

The speed at which your hard drive spins is measured in *revolutions per
minute* (rpm). This number signifies how quickly your computer can write
data to, and read data from, the hard drive. The higher the number, the faster
the drive is.

Having a fast hard drive isn't all that important if all you intend to do is store
BitTorrent content on it. Having a fast primary hard drive is much more
important because you keep all your day-to-day data and applications,
including your operating system, on the primary drive.

Look for the best price and largest drive you can get, and don't worry about
speed when buying a hard drive to store BitTorrent data. A fast hard drive is
nice, but definitely a luxury.

Hard drives are getting cheaper. You can find drive sizes of 120GB and 200GB
for less than $150. These drives are huge and can store a lot of data.

If you aren't sure what to buy and need a recommendation, a good place to start is with a 200GB hard drive that has a speed of 7,200 rpm. I strongly recommend that you look for a hard drive that connects to your computer via FireWire to allow for speedy transfer of data from your computer to the drive.

Archiving Files to CD or DVD

Most of today's computers ship with CD and DVD burners installed, and these tools provide many BitTorrent users with a cheap and useful way to back up the media they download. Keeping media on your local hard drive that you rarely view doesn't make a whole lot of sense. However, you may not be ready to part with it completely. That's where CDs and DVDs come in handy!

Burning CDs and DVDs also creates a portable version of your files that you can use in a DVD player, or a CD player.

Using your CD burner

CD media can hold approximately 700MB (megabytes) of information. You can write data to a CD or create an audio compact disc that plays on a standard compact disc player.

CD burners on the market today burn at speeds of up to 52X, which means they transfer information 52 times faster than a regular compact disc player. The time it takes for the data to be burned to disc depends highly upon the speed of your computer's central processing unit (CPU).

If your computer doesn't have a CD burner and you want to install one, check out the drives manufactured by Iomega, HP, Plextor, and Samsung. These drives all come with software you can use to burn your CD. Alternatively, you can use the built-in utility that is part of modern computer operating systems; for example, Windows XP includes a CD burning utility, which is shown in Figure 5-8.

If you still need a software tool for creating CDs, I recommend Nero Ultra Edition (www.nero.com) or CDBurnerXP Pro (www.cdburnerxp.se), an open-source CD and DVD burning software.

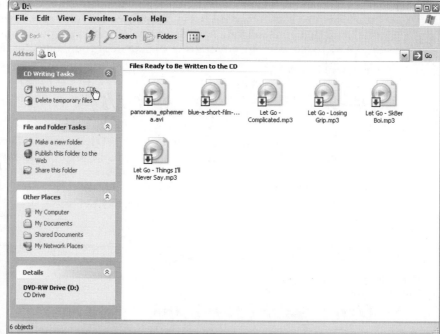

Figure 5-8:
Windows
has a
built-in
CD-burning
tool that
you can
use to
create
backups.

Using a DVD burner

DVD media can store approximately 4.7GB of data while newer dual-layer DVD media can store a little more than 9GB.

DVD burners have drastically dropped in price in the past couple of years, so you can purchase one cheaply. DVD burners are slowly replacing CD-only burners and, depending on the amount of data, can back up your data quickly and efficiently.

Don't have a DVD burner? Check out the drives from Sony, Iomega, Pacific Digital, HP, Plextor, and Samsung. Most DVD-burning drives come with software you can use to create DVDs, and today's computers all come with built-in utilities for burning DVDs. However, if you are looking for another program, consider purchasing Nero Ultra Edition (www.nero.com). This program has great tools for managing digital media and burning CDs and DVDs.

Chapter 6

Understanding BitTorrent and the Law

According to the Motion Picture Association of America (MPAA), $3 billion is lost annually because of *pirated* movies. (Pirated movies have been illegally copied and made available over the Internet, via street DVD sales, or through other underground distribution methods.) Similarly, according to the Recording Industry Association of America (RIAA), illegal copying of copyrighted music has been estimated to cost the music industry more than $4.5 billion each year. This loss of revenue has caused copyright holders to pursue copyright infringers very aggressively, even taking cases as far as the United States Supreme Court.

The distribution of illegally copied media files has been supported by file-sharing technologies and the Internet, and as a result, copyright holders have used a two-pronged strategy to go after copyright infringers: first, they have sued individuals who illegally download copyrighted materials; and second, they have sued the companies that make the software and computer networks that they say facilitate illegal downloading.

Although using BitTorrent itself is not an act of copyright infringement, what you choose to download can put you into the arena of *digital piracy,* because many users of BitTorrent — and, for that matter, all peer-to-peer file-sharing technologies — are sharing files that they don't have the right to distribute. So be careful: BitTorrent is a flexible and speedy means for downloading large data files, but not all those files are safe.

The MPAA, RIAA, and others are wary of BitTorrent and other peer-to-peer file-sharing technologies; infringers should expect to be prosecuted to the full extent of the law.

Understanding the Issues

Every day you seem to discover news of fresh frontal assaults on BitTorrent sites. Here are a few of the headlines plucked from the Internet:

- Lokitorrents versus MPAA
- MPAA Enters P2P Wars; Is BitTorrent in Trouble?
- Finnish BitTorrent Link Site Busted
- Australian Music Industry Cracks Down on BitTorrent Infringers
- Extinction Event for BitTorrent Web Sites

These headlines reflect a number of lawsuits and prosecutions underway. So what's the big deal? Why is everyone making such a fuss?

The U.S. federal government shut down the EliteTorrents Web site for trading illegal copies of *Star Wars Episode III: Revenge of the Sith*. EliteTorrents was a tracker site that became notorious for providing information about BitTorrent files that infringed copyright. When it was shut down in 2005 by the FBI and U.S. Immigration and Customs Enforcement Agency (ICE), government officials left a notice on the Web site that "Individuals involved in the operation and use of the EliteTorrents network are under investigation for criminal copyright infringement." You can see this warning in Figure 6-1.

The move against EliteTorrents was called Operation D-Elite by the federal government, which announced the action in a May 25, 2005, press release (shown in Figure 6-2). The press release clarifies the position of authorities:

> The theft of copyrighted material is far from a victimless crime. When thieves steal this data, they are taking jobs away from hard workers in industry, which adversely impacts the U.S. economy. The FBI remains committed to working with our partners in law enforcement at all levels and private industry to identify and take action against those responsible.

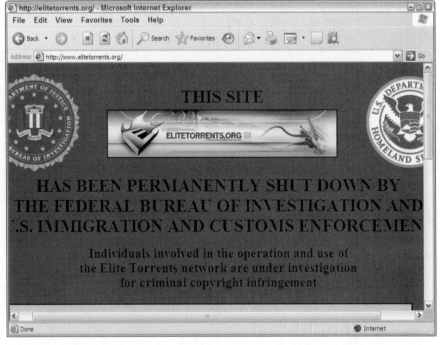

In other words, media piracy is a not-so-small monetary issue that trickles into several areas of the global economy. It affects

- Musicians, actors, writers, and artists the world over

- Agencies that sign and promote artists, selling albums, movies, and other media to domestic and international retailers and distributors

- Retailers that sell CDs, DVDs, and other products

- The manufacturers of CDs, DVDs, and other products used to legally distribute media

- The employees of all these businesses

- Advertisers that associate their products with media

In fact, at the same time as the EliteTorrents operation, the MPAA announced that it was filing six additional lawsuits against other highly trafficked BitTorrent sites that provided information about torrents that infringed upon copyright. In a May 12, 2005, press release (shown in Figure 6-3), the MPAA indicated that it was specifically targeting those who were pirating television shows.

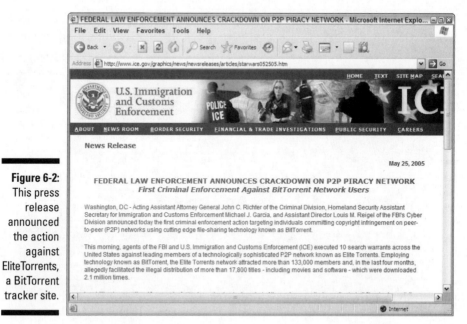

Figure 6-2:
This press release announced the action against EliteTorrents, a BitTorrent tracker site.

Using all the tools at their disposal, the MPAA, RIAA, and federal governments in the United States and Europe are prepared to take legal action against infringement.

Figure 6-3:
In May 2005, the MPAA filed lawsuits against Web sites contributing to copyright infringement of television shows.

TIP

Getting a legal definition of copyright infringement

Copyright infringement is stealing. If you use BitTorrent, or any other Internet technology, to download material that infringes on someone else's copyright and you get caught, you will be in serious trouble.

Copyright infringement occurs when you copy or distribute content that belongs to someone else, you don't have his or her permission, and you aren't creating the copy under a valid, permissible use authorized by law.

You must have explicit permission (usually written) from a copyright owner, or the content must

be free to copy and distribute (by law). Avoid downloading copyrighted material, unless you have the permission of the owner for the use you intend to make of the content.

Don't mistake permission from someone other than the copyright holder for real permission! It's easy to get confused about who has copyright and who is actually able to give legal permission for file distribution. Read licenses, ask questions, and when in doubt, don't download or share content if you aren't sure the copyright holder has permitted such use.

Knowing the Penalties for Copyright Infringement

Federal law permits severe civil and criminal penalties to punish and deter acts of copyright infringement. The U.S. Copyright Act authorizes the following provisions for acts of infringement:

- ✔ Section 502 authorizes *injunctions* (court orders) to prevent copyright infringement.

- ✔ Section 503 allows the court to impound and *destroy* computers or other equipment that is capable of being used to make illegal copies.

- ✔ Section 504 authorizes actual damages to be awarded against the infringer. If the infringement was *willful,* the court can impose damages up to $150,000.

- ✔ Section 505 allows the court to allow attorneys fees and costs in its reasonable discretion.

- ✔ Section 506 of the Act allows the U.S. Attorney's office to seek jail sentences of up to 10 years. These penalties are in addition to the civil sanctions identified in the previous bullets.

The penalties, shown in Figure 6-4, are identified in Chapter 5 of the Copyright Act on the Copyright Office Web site at www.copyright.gov.

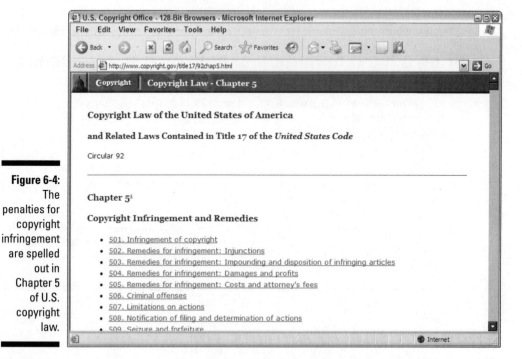

Figure 6-4:
The penalties for copyright infringement are spelled out in Chapter 5 of U.S. copyright law.

Many users of peer-to-peer technologies feel that they are anonymous. After all, you haven't filled out a form with your name in it, or provided a credit card number, right? So who's to know just what files you click late at night? Well, the very nature of BitTorrent means that identifying information about your computer is tracked, in order for the technology to function. If your computer can be identified, so can you. No matter how anonymous you feel when you use BitTorrent, you aren't.

Avoiding Copyright Infringement

You can find plenty of content available using BitTorrent that you can access, download, and share — safely. And remember, using BitTorrent isn't the problem. If you make intelligent choices about what you download, you won't have any problems. To help you use BitTorrent safely, here are a few things should understand about copyright:

- A copyright is the right to make a copy of something.

- Understand that making even *one* copy of a copyrighted work without permission is against the law.

- Copyright is automatically granted to the originators of any written or produced material, so unless a license specifically spelling out that distribution and download are allowed accompanies the file you're interested in, you should assume that it's protected by copyright.

- You can make a copy of a copyrighted work if you have the permission of the copyright holder.

The Copyright Act gives copyright holders certain exclusive legal rights — the rights to copy, distribute, and transmit. Under the Act, an owner has the *exclusive* right to control how work is copied, distributed, and transmitted. The copyright owner has a *monopoly* to exploit his or her content. Even if you can access it, view it, or even easily make a copy, you don't have those rights. See Chapter 14 for more information on the exclusive rights of copyright holders.

By the way, giving credit to a copyright holder when you make a copy of his or her work is very nice, but it doesn't change the fact that you're violating the law. For example, legally, you can't make a copy of a photograph taken by the local newspaper and put it on your Web site (even if the photo is of you, and even if you give the photographer credit) unless you get permission.

Getting Permission to Make Copies

Because copyright is exclusive to the owner, that owner gets to control how the work can be used. In other words, only uses that are authorized by the

Understanding the automatic part of copyright

The moment a movie, song, computer program, poem, or other tangible work is created, it already has copyright protection under the Copyright Act — nothing further is required! Protection is automatic. There is no need for notice, and the © symbol isn't necessary. The creator doesn't even need to bother with registration in order to obtain copyright protection. (Nevertheless, in Chapter 14 I provide you with some good reasons for content creators to complete the registration process.) The U.S. law applies regardless of the national origin of the originator.

owner (or by law) are permissible. You must obtain one of two forms of permission licenses and assignments:

✔ **Licensing:** A *license* is a contract that says what you can and cannot do with someone else's content. For example, an author gives a publisher the right to make 10,000 copies of a book; a songwriter allows a singer to perform a song live at a concert, but not to record it. In Figure 6-5 you can see the Creative Commons license used by the video blog Rocketboom (`creativecommons.org/licenses/by-nc-sa/1.0`); the Rocketboom license permits others to copy, distribute, display, perform, and make derivative works from the Rocketboom content under certain conditions.

Creative Commons (`www.creativecommons.org`) is a Web site dedicated to helping content creators set up licenses that permit their work to be distributed and reused by others. You can find out more about how Creative Commons works in Chapter 14.

Figure 6-5:
The Rocketboom video blog permits you to make copies of its content under certain conditions.

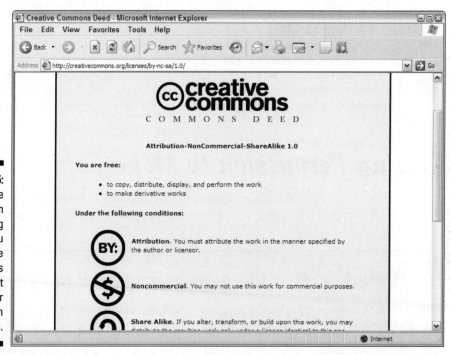

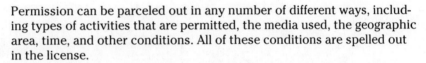

Permission can be parceled out in any number of different ways, including types of activities that are permitted, the media used, the geographic area, time, and other conditions. All of these conditions are spelled out in the license.

A license is a grant of permission that sets limits on what you can (and cannot) do with the copyrighted work. Under the law, any area *not* covered by the license is retained by the copyright holder.

✔ **Assignment:** An *assignment* is the broadest form of a license; it grants another person *all* the rights that the owner has to distribute, copy, perform, and display the work.

Whether a work is licensed or given over in an agreement, the person who wants to use a work that is owned by another person or company may have to pay a fee for use. Depending on the work, and how it will be used, the fees can be enormous.

Finding a copyright holder

If you want to obtain a license to make a copy of a work, you need to contact the copyright owner. Although many commercial Web sites have a license readily available for purchase, that may not always be the case. At times, obtaining a license of assignment may be more difficult than you expect. At others, it may simply be a matter of sending an e-mail and explaining what you want to do.

Because copyright protection is automatic, not all content creators register their copyright with the U.S. Copyright Office. However, you can find registered copyrights at the Copyright Office's database at www.copyright.gov/records. If the copyright has not been registered, you must trace the owner and seek permission directly.

Web sites and blogs often include copyright information at the bottom of the page, and sometimes also include a link to the content owners' terms and conditions. For example, many of the users of the photo-sharing service Flickr have created licenses for their work, which are linked to from the bottom of each photo page, as shown in Figure 6-6.

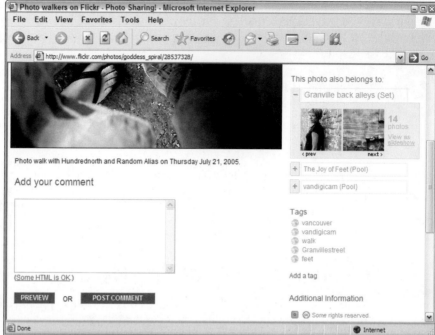

Asking permission for your use

After you locate the owner of a torrent, you need to determine what rights you need to secure. Your license needs to authorize every type of use that you intend to make of the copyrighted work. Do you intend to watch a video on your computer? Burn it to DVD? Show it to your friends? Seed it back into the BitTorrent network? For each case, a different license provision is required to avoid claims of infringement.

Aside from doing this work yourself, there are several rights clearance agencies that do the legwork for you — for a fee, of course. Depending upon the type of content you seek to use, you may want to contact a specialized rights clearance agency. Some clearance agencies specialize in specific areas — photography, video, cartoons, clip art, and music, and many clearance agencies are accessible online. Take a look at Copyright Clearinghouse (www. copyrightclearinghouse.com) for help with music licensing, or Creative Commons (www.creativecommons.org) for digital file formats.

Knowing when You Don't Need Permission

In a very few situations, you can use a copyrighted work without permission. This section discusses the three largest areas where permission is unnecessary. Be careful not to interpret the laws too loosely in a lazy attempt to get around getting permission for content, but do know these rules; they may save you some legwork.

Understanding fair use

You don't need a license to use copyrighted works if your use is a *fair use.* For example, if you're using a work for news reporting, quoting an excerpt for criticism, education, scholarship, or research purposes, your use of the content is covered by fair use provisions under the U.S. Copyright Act. You still have to give credit to the originator of the work, however.

Before you get too excited, you should know that it is definitely not considered fair use to copy an entire article, movie, song, or television broadcast.

There is a four-factor test for determining whether using part of a copyrighted work without permission is fair use:

- ✔ **The purpose and character of the use:** *Purpose and character* refer to whether the use is of a commercial nature or is for nonprofit educational purposes. The more you change the nature of the original or the more educational your purpose, the more likely a court is to find your use is a fair use; conversely, the more commercial your use, the more likely that a court will find that the use is not a fair one.

- ✔ **The nature of the copyrighted work:** Here, the court is concerned with whether the work is published or not, and whether it is informational or creative. Although every case is different and I can think of several exceptions to this statement, *in general,* a court is more likely to find a fair use when copying a factual work than copying a movie or fictional account.

- ✔ **The amount and substantiality of the portion used in relation to the copyrighted work as a whole:** This factor is concerned with how much of the originator's work you want to use. The less used, the more likely the use is a fair one.

This loophole doesn't mean that if you're a musician you can *sample* another musician's song and get away with it, however. Sampling is a somewhat complicated legal issue. If you're a musician and you want to sample someone else's work, you should do further research and proceed with caution.

✔ **The effect of the use upon the potential market for or value of the copyrighted work:** This factor concerns the extent that your copying has harmed the author's right to exploit the market for the material. Obviously, because of the ease of copying material on the Internet, a single isolated copy may be picked up and copied again and again, thereby ruining the market for the original.

Without specific facts, it is impossible for me to give further guidance on what may or may not be fair use. For more information on fair use, or any aspect of copyright law you should hire an attorney for guidance. For answers to general questions, www.copyright.gov contains excellent resources.

Downloading a movie or television show in its entirely so that you can watch it on your own computer is not considered fair use, even if you could have watched the same movie or television show on your TV at home.

Introducing the public domain

Works in the public domain, are those that no longer have copyright protection. They can be used freely without the permission of the former copyright owner.

For example, the works of William Shakespeare are in the public domain. Similarly, many content creators make their works available for free, or so long as you give them credit. Read the small print!

Typically, works enter the public domain after the copyright exclusivity period has expired. Determining whether the copyright protection has expired is made more difficult because of the numerous term extensions that have occurred over time. For more information on figuring out whether a copyright has expired, the U.S. Copyright Office has published Circular 15a, available online at www.copyright.gov.

If everyone jumped off a bridge . . .

Just because a work is available online doesn't make it automatically part of the public domain. Copyright protection is automatic, and the burden is on the user not to infringe. Even you.

You may feel as though you're safer if *everyone else* in the universe has a copy of the new Britney Spears song. ("They can't possibly prosecute *everyone!*") No, a copyright holder probably can't catch everyone, but that doesn't make your crime valid. Even if a work is floating around the Internet in a million public locations, as ubiquitous as Starbucks, you're not more entitled to break the law.

Put simply, a copyright holder isn't required to sue or prosecute everyone who violates his or her copyright. But that copyright holder sure as heck can come after you if he or she desires. When the temptation to follow the trend comes over you, remember, it's not your job to worry about what everyone else is getting away with. The law is the law.

Handling content you create

You can always use works you create in any way, without worry. If you're an employer, you own the works created by your employees under the *work-made-for-hire* rule. That rule specifies that unless otherwise specified in writing, the employer owns the copyright of a work made for hire that is created within the employee's course and scope of his or her job.

Likewise, original creations of your own belong to you. They can be distributed as torrents, but you should probably set up a license that governs what copyright rights you're willing to share with others. I get into all that in Chapter 14.

Blaming technology for infringement?

You may be tempted to say that technology is to blame for copyright infringement. After all, without BitTorrent or one of the other peer-to-peer technologies, finding that copy of *Revenge of the Sith* wouldn't be very easy, right? But technology is not to blame. File sharing, in and of itself, is not an act of copyright infringement. If you own the data being shared, or if you have a license to copy or distribute it, the technology you use is relatively unimportant from the standpoint of copyright law. In fact, the ethical issues raised by the new technologies are quite interesting if you're into this sort of thing.

BitTorrent technology is not designed to facilitate infringement. Can it be used to download copyrighted material? Absolutely, but that isn't its sole purpose or even a substantial reason for its creation. Courts look to see whether there are substantial, noninfringing uses of the technology to determine its purposes. If the court finds substantial, noninfringing uses, then the inquiry focuses on how the technology is used to determine whether infringement has occurred. Case law continues to be developed as P2P technologies are created and advanced, so it's hard to predict what will come.

(continued)

(continued)

In 1984, the U.S. Supreme Court heard the Sony Betamax case (*Sony Corporation of America v. Universal City Studios*), which became a watershed case for the fair use defense to copyright infringement. The case allowed the use of VCRs so that users could record and "time-shift" their favorite television programs. However, among its other arguments, Universal claimed that merely supplying the *means* of infringement was sufficient for vicarious liability under the Copyright Act.

The Supreme Court rejected Universal's argument, but by analogy to patent law, suggested that if Sony had sold the Betamax with constructive knowledge that customers used the equipment to make unauthorized copies of television programs, it could be held contributorily liable for the infringement by those users.

In the lower court, Sony introduced evidence of the many noninfringing uses of the Betamax, including the fact that some programs like "Mr. Roger's Neighborhood" were happy to have their programs copied for later use.

Comparing the infringing with the noninfringing aspects of the Betamax, the Court noted that "the sale of copying equipment, like the sale of other articles of commerce, does not constitute contributory infringement if the product is widely used for legitimate, unobjectionable purposes. Indeed, it need merely be capable of substantial noninfringing uses." Subsequently, the debate has centered on what is meant by a "substantial noninfringing use" of the technology. This has been true for several other cases you might find interesting reading:

- *A&M Records v. Napster,* in which the Court of Appeals refused to impute liability on Napster's owners merely because peer-to-peer file-sharing technology can be used to infringe music copyrights but because Napster had *facilitated* that infringement by providing users with technical support. Read more at www.ce9.uscourts.gov/Web/ OCELibra.nsf/0/cc61d7c45e059bd 4882569f100620da0?OpenDocument.

- In *MGM v. Grokster,* the U.S. Supreme Court focused on the actions Grokster took in advertising its system to users who formerly pirated music from Napster, therefore inducing users to infringe copyright, the court determined. You can read more here: www. eff.org/IP/P2P/MGM_v_Grokster.

Part III

Creating BitTorrent Content

The 5th Wave   By Rich Tennant

THE NEW HOLLYWOOD

CUT! PASTE! TORRENT!

In this part . . .

*G*ot ambitions to be a newscaster or a filmmaker? BitTorrent is a terrific technology to use for distributing your latest creation without running up huge bandwidth costs or buying time on your local cable channel. But it all starts with actually creating your content. Use Chapter 7 if you're a budding radio broadcaster and you need to get up to speed on microphones, recording techniques, and audio-editing software. Chapters 8 and 9 are directed to the new videographer. In Chapter 8, get specific recommendations about equipment and great tips on filming techniques. Chapter 9 takes you from film to filmmaker by showing you some common editing techniques that give your creation professional polish.

Chapter 7

Creating Audio Files

. . . .

. . . .

*T*he power that comes from sharing files with BitTorrent isn't just a result of being technologically sophisticated; BitTorrent enables digital content creators to transform themselves into distribution mega centers.

Whether you aspire to be a rock star, a radio talk show host, or the world's next big composer — you can get your audio content to the ears of your listeners without the headache or expense of setting up a traditional broadcasting channel.

Not so long ago, the idea of starting a radio station or becoming the host of a variety style radio show featuring your closest friends was next to impossible. But, now, using your home personal computer and BitTorrent as your means of distribution, you can avoid costly bandwidth bills and limitations traditionally associated with offering content for open download on the Internet.

In this chapter, I talk about how to get started recording audio on your computer, editing content for playback, and exporting the audio into a usable file format. You can find several free or inexpensive tools out there, so don't worry about expense. Using this guide, you can create audio files for distribution via BitTorrent easily and simply.

You also get a quick overview of how to create high-quality audio files, from acquiring recording equipment, setting up the recording environment, and then getting your audio onto your computer. This chapter can't give you everything you could possibly need to know, but it gets you started.

Getting Equipped

If you're already addicted to creating BitTorrent audio content, you're not alone. Many people on the Internet are creating their own audio programming, and using BitTorrent as their distribution medium to the world.

Good gear, the proper setup, and a quiet place to record make all the difference between a great audio experience and one that makes you grit your teeth.

Creating your own radio content can be quite a thrilling experience, but creating usable audio takes some time and care. If you don't pay any attention to the quality of the broadcast, no one else will pay attention to the broadcast either!

Having said that, it really doesn't cost very much to get started. You only need a few things in place before you can get up and recording your own content quickly. The following sections tell you about a few of the things you need to begin.

Before you record your first track of audio, you need to consider a few of the technical aspects of recording. You should decide what kinds of audio you plan to record and allow that decision to help you to determine what tools you should use.

Here are a few of the questions you should ask before you make any decisions about which audio software to purchase and what kind of environment you should be recording in:

- ✔ Are you recording talk radio?
- ✔ Are you recording a few people?
- ✔ Are you recording a single artist playing a musical instrument, or are you recording a choir?
- ✔ Are you recording a huge event with a hundred-piece orchestra?

The answers to these questions help you decide how much, and what kind of equipment you need, especially when it comes to microphones. Clearly, if you are only recording a single subject, your microphone needs are vastly different than if you are recording an orchestra.

In any situation where you are dealing with multiple microphones you need to add a mixing board to your equipment so that you can input all your microphones onto your recording device. I talk more about microphones and other equipment later in this chapter.

After you determine what kind of audio you need to record, you can choose appropriate software to make your recordings. Most BitTorrent users creating their own audio — of themselves or of a small group — don't need to invest in high-end audio-editing software and equipment. Even if you're not ready to make a purchase just yet, just knowing what's available can do you a world of good, in case you have big expansion plans for *after* you strike it rich!

Your level of expertise today, and the level of knowledge you want to attain, play a big part in determining the appropriate software solution. More expensive packages tend to have several options, and can be quite overwhelming to the average or casual user.

You can find hundreds of different audio packages out there. They range from expensive packages with all of the bells and whistles to lower-end, open-source applications that are released to users for free. These are the main considerations to think about when looking for audio software:

- ✔ **Price:** The first thing you must determine is what your budget can support. Can you afford to purchase a professional package? They tend to be of a better quality but are pretty expensive for the hobbyist.

  The free packages may suit your budget, but usually require attention and a little patience (depending on the support provided by the maker). Also, packages are often free because they are in development; additional features (perhaps the cool ones you need) may be developed more slowly.

  The pros and cons to expensive and free software play directly into what you want to accomplish with the program. That's why price shouldn't be your only consideration. Consider the rest of the items in this list.

- ✔ **Ease of use:** Do you need to read a manual for three days before you can make your first mix? Is the tool easy to figure out? A good audio program can get you up and recording — though not proficient — within 30 minutes. If tools are so hidden that you spend minutes poking through menus to find the most basic (and essential) functions, move on to another software application.

  Each package works a little differently, and you should be able to find one that suits your individual style better. Most recording software companies provide demo versions of their software, so you can try the software before purchasing. Go to your local music store (one that sells instruments) and ask some questions. Most instrument retail stores have knowledgeable staff to help you in regards to the software. Reading reviews and drawing up a list of your must-have features can also help you make a decision.

- ✔ **Mixing skills:** Your current level of experience with mixing is also important. Mixing is what happens when you take multiple audio tracks and put them together. For instance, a common radio news technique is to mix a reporter's voiceover with short comments by an interview subject, and sometimes to also add in background sounds from the interview location (street noise, for example). Mixing is a talent that is often learned through trial and error or by doing some reading on audio production. Depending on what you want to accomplish, you may need to do a lot of mixing, or hardly any at all. If mixing is important, look for a software package with easy-to-master mixing tools.

✔ **Sound quality:** Does the software make audio files that sound good? Some sound editing programs are focused on creating particular kinds of audio. For instance, some are better for spoken-word pieces, some are targeted to musicians. The final determining factor should be whether you're getting a good result for the audio you are working with.

The cost of an audio software program doesn't necessarily correspond with its usefulness! Expensive, high-end products can still have bad software design and may not be very intuitive to use. They may even be more difficult to use than a more basic program, even for standard functions. For beginners, starting small isn't a bad way to go.

Whether high-end or low, the audio software you choose should definitely have the ability to turn out high-quality audio files suitable for release on BitTorrent.

Choosing a Software Option

If you are just starting to create audio for the wonderful world of BitTorrent, try out the open-source audio software packages first. After you're comfortable with those, research the higher-end, more powerful tools for editing your sound. Be sure to take advantage of any software package that you can download and try without paying first, even if the program is limited during the trial. Until you actually use some of this software you won't know what works for you and what doesn't. Plus, using open-source options is in the spirit of the BitTorrent way.

Some audio-editing software packages are free; others require you to purchase them. If you are serious about recording on a regular basis, the investment may be worth it. The following sections give you an overview of several good packages you can try out.

Audacity

The program of choice for many home audio recorders is a free, open-source program called Audacity, shown in Figure 7-1. Audacity is a multitrack recording program that allows anyone with a microphone (properly set up, of course) to record audio and mix it all together. It is a small download and is simple to install and use.

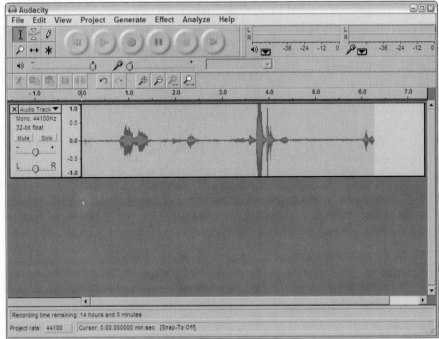

Figure 7-1:
Audacity's
built-in tools
permit easy
recording,
displayed in
an easily
editable
waveform.

Audacity is one of the best open-source recording packages out there. Audacity is available for Windows, Mac OS 9 or X, and Linux/Unix. You can download it at `audacity.sourceforge.net`.

It has many powerful features, including audio filters and free mixing of multiple sound tracks. You can export files in a variety of audio formats: MP3, Windows media audio, WAV files, or RAW audio. With a little experimentation and close attention to the instructions, you should be able to record your first radio program in less than a day.

Recording and importing with Audacity

Audacity can record live audio through a microphone or mixer, or digitize recordings from cassette tapes, vinyl records, or minidisks. With some sound cards, it can also capture streaming audio. Some of the other great features are:

- ✔ Recording from microphone, line input, or other sources
- ✔ Dubbing over existing tracks to create multitrack recordings
- ✔ Recording up to 16 channels at once (requires multichannel hardware)
- ✔ Monitoring volume levels before, during, and after recording

Editing sound files with Audacity

Audacity features some powerful tools to make changes to your recorded audio. All of the editing tools are easily accessible. You can quickly edit with cut, copy, paste, and delete functions. You'll especially love the unlimited undo that makes editing easy ("Now with fewer headaches!").

Audacity puts no limit on the number of tracks that you can record and edit — a wonderful trait in a free package.

Saving and exporting with Audacity

Audacity can export Windows Media audio, MP3s, WAV, AIFF, and RAW audio files. Each export is easy to do, and offers options for changing the sound quality in order to end up with a reasonable file size.

Acoustica MP3 Audio Mixer

Don't let the name fool you. The MP3 Audio Mixer from Acoustica doesn't just make MP3 files (although that is its most common use). It can also produce and mix Windows Media files, among several others.

Of the packages discussed in this chapter, the Acoustica mixer may be the easiest one to use right out of the box.

Acoustica MP3 Audio Mixer is directed at non-professional hobbyists, and it is definitely a good package for beginners to start with. The time elapsed from installation to your first generated MP3 can be as little as a few minutes. Acoustica MP3 Audio Mixer is shown in Figure 7-2.

Acoustica has a series of complementary software packages that work with MP3 Audio Mixer and are worth evaluating if you wish to stick with this line of software. This package is currently available only for Windows, and costs about $25. There is a seven-day evaluation version available for download from its Web site: www.acoustica.com/mp3-audio-mixer.

Recording and importing files with Acoustica MP3 Audio Mixer

You can import WAV files, MP3s, or Windows Media files, and then edit them easily using drag-and-drop functionality. Mixing the tracks, fading volumes, and track characteristics are all accessible with a single mouse click. Recording is as simple as clicking a track to record and clicking the Record button. Sound is recorded and saved instantly into the selected tracks.

Multiple tracks   Record button

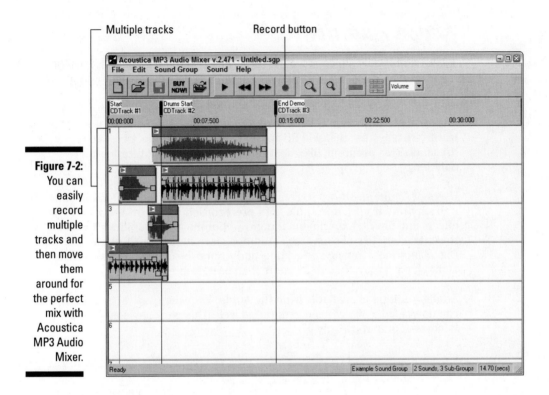

Figure 7-2:
You can
easily
record
multiple
tracks and
then move
them
around for
the perfect
mix with
Acoustica
MP3 Audio
Mixer.

Editing files with Acoustica MP3 Audio Mixer

By simply dragging tracks and audio selections, you can make changes to
each of the audio tracks. This process can be fun — and even addictive!

You can *fade* sounds in and out, and mix audio with Acoustica's easy-to-use
interface. A fade is the transition from silence to sound, or vice versa; it's a
fairly common audio-editing technique you should definitely look for in your
software. You can also control playback for each track individually.

Saving and exporting files with Acoustica MP3 Audio Mixer

Acoustica is made for the MP3 market but can export MP3, WAV, and WMA
files. It also has an optional Real Media plug-in that can be used to create Real
Media files. Each file type can be exported by this software and can be saved
in a variety of qualities, from CD quality to radio quality.

Adobe Audition

Adobe Audition is a professional audio-editing suite developed by Adobe, the makers of the popular creative programs Adobe Photoshop and Adobe Illustrator. This package has everything you could ever want.

Well, you probably don't really want the price tag. But for $299, you get a feature-rich system that will do anything the home audio mixer could ever dream of. This program, like most Adobe offerings, is not for the mere dabbler.

Users of Audition, shown in Figure 7-3, can mix their recorded audio sources into separate tracks, mix audio with prerecorded video, or use over 50 digital effects and filters. Experiment and grow your mastering abilities by changing the characteristics of each track. Audition also offers MIDI (Musical Instrument Digital Interface) mixing and editing, and a full suite of other tools to make any audiophiles happy, though it's more than most hobbyists need.

Adobe Audition is available from the Adobe Web site (www.adobe.com). You can download a 30-day trial version, as well. This package is available for Windows computers only.

Figure 7-3:
Adobe
Audition
looks
intimidating
but is
correspond-
ingly
powerful.

Recording and importing files with Adobe Audition

Like any recording package, recording audio with Audition is as simple as selecting a track and clicking the Record button. Sound is recorded and saved instantly into the selected tracks. You can import any media into a track, from MIDI sound files to video files.

Editing files with Adobe Audition

Adobe Audition uses common commands like cut, copy, and paste. This familiarity makes the editing process quick and also enables you to apply your effects quickly.

The nice thing about most packages is the editing is usually controlled by clicking and dragging. Figuring out how to mix elements may take some practice, but Adobe Audition has some tools to help you along. It also has a built-in help system that contains a wealth of information to help you create great-sounding files.

Saving and exporting files with Adobe Audition

Audition can save and export in a number of different file types. Users can create audio exports for streaming media, MIDI, raw audio formats, and MP3 or Windows Media.

Choosing Your Hardware

By far, the simplest solution for acquiring audio is to record it directly onto your computer. Get started quickly by simply opening up the audio-editing software you're using, plugging in a microphone, and away you go. Using software and a mic is a great way for beginners to get started because you don't rack up additional hardware costs and because you can play up the familiarity you already have with your computer.

On the downside, hauling your computer around to the places you want to record isn't always practical, especially if you don't have a laptop. As well, computers are known to crash, and audio software can be buggy. You can easily lose an important recording because your instant messenger program starts up at the wrong moment.

The solution? Do your recording on a device specifically intended for that purpose, like a tape recorder, minidisk recorder, or even an MP3 recorder.

With increasing frequency, even mobile telephones have built-in recording devices that create audio feeds, which can be converted into MP3 files and ultimately released on BitTorrent. You may want something a bit more stable than a mobile phone for recording purposes, but the idea does open quite a few opportunities you may never have considered.

Dedicated recording devices, like portable MP3 players, also feature built-in microphones that can record audio anywhere. Many actually record directly into the MP3 format, saving you time you might have spent converting files later. The player/recorders available today are cheap, portable, and can store a lot of audio at a decent quality. Even the popular iPod from Apple can be converted into a portable recording device with the purchase of a special microphone.

Recording Hardware Information You Need to Know

As you look around for a recording device to take on the road, try to find one that lets you simply transfer files from the device to your computer — having to re-record your audio is no fun, especially if you capture it in digital format to begin with.

The following list gives you some of the common elements of a recording kit that you might take away from your desk and onto the street, or into a bar, restaurant, or office. You may not need everything on the list, so pick and choose items to fit your own needs:

- **Microphones:** On a tight budget? Inexpensive computer headsets (a microphone attached to earphones) can get you started quickly. When you are ready to upgrade, look for an *omnidirectional* or *semi-directional* microphone (they usually cost between $50 and $150). The better the microphone you use, the better your audio quality is!

  An omnidirectional microphone picks up sound from every direction. A semi-directional microphone enables you to determine the direction sounds are picked up from.

- **Mixing board:** When you need to record several people talking, a mixing board can be really useful. Mixing boards enable you to use several microphones and control the volume of each microphone separately. This flexibility is especially useful when you have one person who speaks very quietly and another who practically yells. Mixing boards can cost $100 or thousands of dollars, depending, of course, on how many bells and whistles you want.

✔ **Headphones:** Headphones are great — they block any noise that isn't being picked up by the microphone and they let you know quickly if something has gone wrong (a microphone suddenly stops working, for example). You can find microphones that cover your whole ear for $30 to $75.

✔ **Cables:** Connect all your equipment together with the appropriate audio equipment. Radio Shack is a great source for audio cables and adapters, assuming the right cables don't come with the hardware you buy.

✔ **Extra batteries, power cords, and extension cords:** Don't forget all those power adapters for your hardware! There's nothing worse than having to call off your whole recording session because you forgot to bring an extra AA battery!

✔ **Tapes:** If you're recording onto tape, be sure to bring extra reels or cassettes.

Most good electronics stores carry a variety of microphones, headphones, and mixing boards. If you are shopping online, try B&H Photo, a top-notch source for all kinds of audio and video equipment (see Figure 7-4).

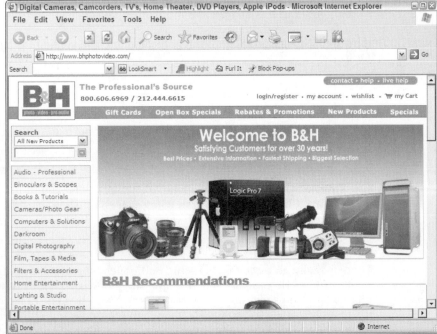

Figure 7-4:
B&H Photo carries a wide selection of all kinds of audio-recording equipment, from tapes to micro-phones.

Recording Audio and Speech

The recording process is simple. In fact, it really is the easy part compared to deciding between all the options in equipment and software available. Keep in mind that when you record your own audio content, you may need to get creative to get around extraneous noises and other distractions.

For example, perhaps you live in a noisy part of town; you may need to move your recording studio to a closet; or maybe you have to put your favorite barking pet outside for the afternoon. In either case, getting creative with the recording process often has more to do with problem solving than it does with managing what is being said, sung, or played by your performers.

If you are just recording yourself, all you need to do is plug your microphone into the audio input on your computer, click the Record button on the recording software of your choice, and start talking, playing, or singing.

If you want to get more advanced, you can purchase a mixing board from your local music store (prices may range from $100 and up into the thousands), the appropriate cables, headsets, and microphones, and record away using the same software. (See "Recording Hardware Information You Need to Know," earlier in this chapter, for more information.)

Here are the steps to follow when recording into the software program Audacity:

1. **Run Audacity.**

2. **Plug in your mixer or microphone to the computer's microphone port.**

   If you are using a mixer, plug in your microphones, CD players, electric guitars, tape players, or other devices.

3. **Click the Record button on the main Audacity Recording toolbar.**

4. **Talk, sing, play music, or otherwise generate the sound you want to record. Click the Stop button when you're finished, as shown in Figure 7-5.**

5. **Save your audio file.**

There is really no right way to record audio files on your home computer. That's right — there really isn't a proper way of doing it. Think of your home BitTorrent radio program as a starting point. If you become hooked and want to create better audio programs, you can purchase better equipment and get recording.

The sky is really the limit here in terms of what you want to create. BitTorrent has made many a home broadcasting addict. Come to think of it, home broadcasting has also made a lot of BitTorrent addicts, too.

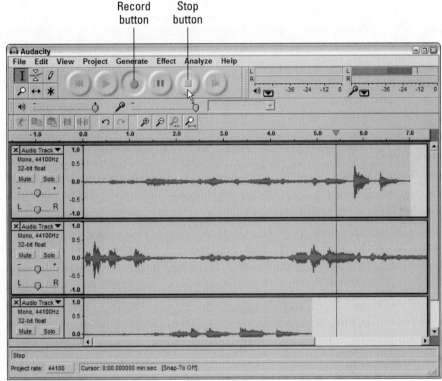

Record
button

Stop
button

Figure 7-5:
Recording is
a fairly
simple
process
with
Audacity.

Setting up your recording environment

Pretend you are about to record and edit the best audio program in the world. It might be a speech, or maybe a talk radio program where you inter-view some expert (or a panel of experts).

What do you need to do during the recording phase to make your editing process run smoother? Well, here is some advice to remember:

- ✔ Try and record all of your audio in as quiet a space as you can.

- ✔ Select a space without an echo. Hard surfaces, like bathrooms, aren't ideal. The listening audience will hear an annoying echo.

- ✔ Make the space comfortable and free of distractions. Nothing makes an editing headache worse than trying to edit out the squirming of an uncomfortable guest, or the sound of someone shuffling paper.

- ✔ Record room noise. What? Record the room? Yes. Making edits in an audio file is better if you have some spare room noise to overwrite coughs, stutters, and other undesirable noises.

Most often, all you need is a really good microphone and a quiet, echo-free bedroom. Yet, this may not be possible if you live in a home with three and a half kids, two dogs, and visitors in the basement. Pay attention to when it is quietest in your chosen recording environment. When is street noise minimized? When are the neighborhood kids out playing tag? What time does the construction crew arrive? You may have to work around other people's schedules to get the best possible results.

Making the recording special

If you really want to make your audio recording shine, effectively using multi-track mixers is a skill that will blow all of your listeners away.

Imagine you have a panel of amazing political experts, all with something brilliant to say. If all of them are wearing separate microphones and each microphone is plugged into a mixing board, some audio-editing software can record each microphone separately — onto its own track.

The result is an amazingly layered audio file that permits you to edit out the sneezing on one microphone without losing the scintillating commentary on another.

The point is to know what you want to accomplish and to have the equipment you need to properly accomplish the task. If you're just starting out, running low on cash, or only interviewing a single person, maybe you don't need a mixer. But if this audio thing is a life-long dream, you need a mixer, and the advice of a good resource on mixing.

Editing Audio Files

The editing process is a highly subjective process between people and different pieces of audio. The way you handle a recording made at a restaurant varies vastly from how you edit a recording made during a music concert.

Most Internet audiophiles make more voice recordings than music (the sound of their own voice is attractive, perhaps?). When editing for voice, there are a few common editing tasks you can use to clean up your recording:

✔ **Replace unpleasant sounds and mistakes.** For example, if your recording is interrupted by a ringing phone, or your interview subject grabbed a file folder and looked up some facts, you may want to take those noises out. If you record some background noise in the interview environment, use that *white noise* to overwrite the undesired sounds.

✔ **Take out unneeded words, like exclamations and pause words.** If your interview subject says "um" a lot, you can take those ums out — improving the quality of your recording without destroying the veracity of what was said. Most interview subjects appreciate editing that makes them sound better, especially when you clean up stuttering. *Pause* words (um, uh, ah, oh, and so on) are often strangely obtrusive in an audio file when you don't have visual cues to distract you from noticing them.

✔ **Got a fast talker on the line?** You can add white noise in between words and sentences to space out the interview and make it a little easier to understand.

✔ **Use *fades* and *cross fades*.** A fade is a form of audio blending. Typically, fades are used to move from scene to scene in your audio. For instance, adding a fade to background or transition music helps to eliminate the jarring effect of a full-volume transition.

When you're editing, listen and try to remove the following:

✔ Obtrusive noises in the distance (barking dogs, garbage trucks)

✔ Signs, yawns, and other audible breathing noises

✔ Local background noises (doors closing, glasses tinkling, phones ringing)

✔ Stuttering and other mistakes ("Let me phrase that another way.")

✔ Any sounds caused by the interview subject moving around in a chair or touching the microphone

✔ Burps, sneezes, and other less savory sounds

The basic editing process works like this:

1. **As you listen to your file being played back, the cursor moves along the waveform. When you hear something you don't want in your file, like a sneeze, stop the cursor.**

2. **Use the cursor to highlight the offending sound, as I do in Figure 7-6.**

3. **Cut, copy, paste or delete your selection.**

4. **Repeat as needed throughout the entire file.**

    Don't forget to save the new version of the file before you close it.

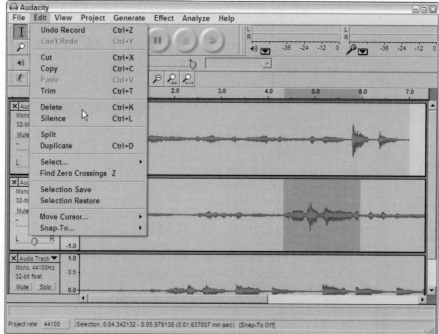

Figure 7-6:
To remove
an unwanted
noise,
highlight
it in the
waveform
and
delete it.

Exporting Audio

The most common file format found on the Internet these days is MP3. It has been all over the news, and portable MP3 devices created to play this file format are in wide use.

If you want to make sure that most people can easily listen to the audio content you produce, choose audio-editing and recording software that can export directly to the MP3 format. If the software you want to use doesn't allow you to export MP3s, look around for a plug-in you can add, or a file conversion utility you can use.

Audacity, for example, does not export to MP3 out of the box. Users must download an MP3 encoder in order to export MP3s.

Exporting an MP3 is done through the use of an *encoder*. Encoders are pieces of software that encode a sound source into an electronic form that can then be edited and saved. You want one that can export a very high bit rate, so that you end up with a high-quality file. The term *bit rate* refers to the amount of detailed data contained within the original source recording.

Some software applications come with an integrated encoder, or offer a plug-in that adds MP3 encoding functionality (sometimes there is a charge for these extra plug-ins, sometimes not).

The audio files you capture and save in any recording you make will have a RAW level of audio. RAW files are uncompressed — and huge. The longer the recording is, the larger the file is.

So, to make the file size a little more reasonable and deliver it via a network like BitTorrent, you need to compress the audio into another format, like MP3.

What happens when a file is compressed? The lower the bit rate, the lower quality the sound file has. When you save a file with a lower *sample rate* or *bit rate,* your audio software throws away some portion of the original analog record. The result is that the size of the file can be greatly reduced. As you decrease the bit rate, you decrease the quality, and you decrease the file size.

Because you're actually removing part of the original recording when you save a RAW file as an MP3, the result won't sound quite as good as the original. In fact, the lower the bit rate you choose, the lower the sound quality your file has.

In general, you want to record your audio at a high bit rate, and then save it into a format that uses a somewhat smaller bit rate in order to make the final file a reasonable size. Figuring out just how to use bit rates is a big topic, however, and you may want to refer to *MP3 For Dummies* by Andy Rathbone (Wiley) or *PC Recording Studios For Dummies* by Jeff Strong (Wiley). In Figure 7-7, I set the bit rate of the MP3 file before I export a recording using Audacity.

Depending on the software you use to record and mix your audio source, you may want to experiment with different settings until you find a reasonable balance between quality and file size. The recipe is different for each piece of audio. After all, there is no sense in smashing down a five-minute piece of audio the way you would one that is two hours long.

Finding a good balance between quality and file size when exporting audio is a bit of an acquired touch and is based on what you prefer, how you intend to deliver the file, and what the file needs to sound like to work well. BitTorrent makes the overall sizes of files less of a concern, so I often err on the side of higher quality (and bigger files) these days.

Of course, there are other file formats you can use to export and release your audio. But, currently, MP3 is an Internet standard, and it is nearly guaranteed that your listeners have a player on their computer that can handle MP3s, no matter what kind of computers they use.

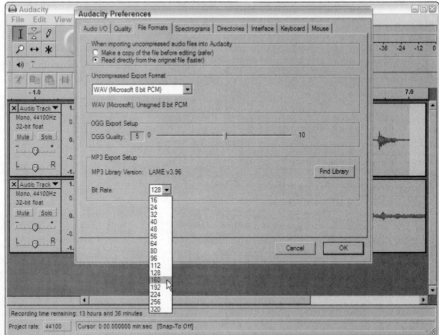

Figure 7-7:
Using
Audacity,
you can
set the
preferences
for the bit
rate at
which you
want to
export.

If you choose to export your audio as another format (like AAC, M4A, WAV, or RM), make sure you include instructions with your file for those who download it, explaining what kind of file it is, and how they might go about playing it.

Chapter 8

Shooting Digital Video

*O*ne of the exciting benefits of technologies like BitTorrent is that it enables more people to create and distribute large media files. Would-be broadcasters no longer need to work for television networks or pay to put their shows on cable. Families looking to share wedding videos or vacation footage can do so without paying a mint in Web hosting and video streaming fees.

By using BitTorrent, you can create your own videos and put them online. This chapter is all about getting started shooting video (whether in your garage or basement or somewhere a little more exotic).

In this chapter I share some recommendations on buying good consumer-level video equipment, and give you some basic tips for shooting video effectively. Because I don't know just what kind of video you want to create, think creatively about how to apply these tips to your situation.

Toward the end of the chapter, you discover how to move video from the camera — or from a DVD or VHS tape — into your computer so that you can edit it. In Chapter 9, you can find out more about editing video on your computer.

Keep in mind that Chapters 8 and 9 are meant to get you started with video shooting and editing. For more advanced instruction and techniques, I recommend you read *Digital Video For Dummies,* 3rd Edition, by Keith Underdahl (Wiley).

Getting Equipped

To get started with video, you need to invest in some hardware and software. The good news is that the cost of digital video cameras has come down in recent years, and you can find plenty of consumer-level solutions to choose from. Nonetheless, putting together a good video kit involves some expenditure, so plan your budget accordingly.

If you plan to do somewhat more professional shooting than the standard home movie, this is the minimum equipment you need to shoot video:

- A camera, preferably a digital video camera
- Headphones
- Tapes or other recording media, cables, power cords, and batteries
- A microphone or two
- A tripod

Of course, this list would be much longer if I included all the extras you can add to your video kit; these are the minimum requirements.

If you're going to use more than one microphone for your video shoot, you also need an audio mixing board that can accept multiple microphone inputs and produce a single audio output. Audio mixing boards are covered more fully in Chapter 7.

Choosing a camera

You can choose between several types of cameras, but the best choice is usually a digital video camera, often abbreviated as *DV camera*. DV cameras capture images electronically and store them magnetically on a tape. The data is stored digitally, and the resulting video is very high quality. Even mass-market DV cameras come close to creating broadcast (television) quality images and sound. I highly recommend that you purchase a DV camera, or upgrade to one when your budget permits it.

One reason people sometimes hesitate to buy a digital video is that they have a number of old tapes in VHS, 8mm, Hi8, or other formats. A digital video camera can't play back those old tapes, but keep in mind that you're limiting the quality of your future video if you base your camera choice on those old tapes. If you really need to access that older footage, consider having it digitized and put onto DVD (several companies can do this kind of work for you) or buying an inexpensive used camera or player that will play those tapes for you. Getting copies of this media made in other formats is a good idea anyway because VHS and 8mm tapes do have limited lifespans.

DV cameras are available at many price levels and have come down to quite affordable levels as more and more consumers — rather than professionals —

have purchased them. The bad news is that buying a camera involves more than just checking the price. You have several types of DV cameras to choose from, and the market continues to grow.

Of course, each camera has different strengths and weaknesses. Keep in mind that spending extra time on research is important; you shouldn't use shortcuts in the search for the right camera.

Differentiating between formats

Some decisions are quite easy. For instance, you can purchase cameras (and tape decks, DVD players, and so on) that use the NTSC, PAL or SECAM formats. If you're not familiar with these acronyms, fear not. Knowing which format is right for you is simply a matter of knowing where in the world you live:

- **NTSC (National Television Standards Committee):** Used in the United States, the Philippines, and Japan.

- **PAL (Phase Alternating Line):** Used in most of Europe, Australia, South America, and southern Asia.

- **SECAM (Sequential Couleur Avec Memoire):** Used in France, much of Eastern Europe, Russia, and central Asia.

These three formats don't speak to each other, and are designed to prevent copyright violation across these major regions. They all have different strengths, but that doesn't matter, because you need to purchase the accessories and components used where you live. In fact, you may have a hard time finding components for other formats!

Deciding on a recording media

As you consider which camera is best for your needs, you should determine what kind of media you want to use for taping. DV cameras come in several flavors, as detailed in Table 8-1.

Table 8-1	Major DV Camera Types	
Camera	*Type of Media*	*Computer Connection*
MiniDV	MiniDV tapes	IEEE-1394 FireWire
Digital8	Hi8	i.Link
DVD	DVD-RAM, DVD-R	DVD drive
CD-R/W	CD-R/Ws	CD drive

Making compromises

As you start to research MiniDV cameras, consider the following:

✔ **Comfort:** Does the size and shape of the camera suit your shooting style? Is it physically comfortable to use?

✔ **Ease of use:** How easy is the camera to use? Are record and zoom buttons easy to access? Can you load a tape without removing the camera from a tripod?

✔ **Quality:** How good is the picture quality?

✔ **Bells and whistles:** Which features are those you simply must have, and which are just attractive?

✔ **Price:** What can you afford to spend? If a MiniDV (or any camera, for that matter) looks and works great but is out of your budget, set it aside and save up for it later.

As with most electronics purchases, you must find a balance between all these issues, and reach a compromise. Think hard about which of these is the most important for your purposes as you read through camera technical specifications and feature lists. Whatever you do, don't make an impulse purchase!

Each camera type is useful for specific purposes, but if you've never owned a digital video camera, and aren't sure what to buy, MiniDV is the best choice. MiniDVs are popular and come in a variety of makes and models, so you should be able to find one that suits both your needs and your budget. In addition, these cameras are often both smaller and lighter than most other camera types. MiniDV tapes are available in several lengths, but 60- and 90-minute tapes are the easiest to find.

Most MiniDV cameras use the IEEE-1394 FireWire interface to connect to a computer, which ensures quick transfer of data. It's increasingly common for today's computers to come with FireWire ports as a default feature, and it can be added relatively inexpensively to older machines.

Selecting features

MiniDV cameras range in price from $250 to $2,000. The difference in price has a great deal to do with picture quality and other features. Here are a few features you should weigh when making your choice.

✔ **Zoom:** Camera spec sheets list both optical and digital zoom. *Optical zoom* is the zoom factor that the camera's lens can achieve. *Digital zoom* is a bit of a fake. Digital zoom enlarges the image without actually adding more data, so the result can be fuzzy. If you need a lot of zoom, look for a camera with a good optical zoom range, or one for which you can buy separate lenses. Don't be lured in by digital zoom specs.

✔ **Resolution:** A digital image is composed of lines and pixels. The more of these the better, in terms of image quality.

✔ **Size:** Some DV cameras are so small they can actually be hard to use. Although smaller cameras are lighter to carry around, make sure you can actually push buttons and rotate knobs before you buy.

✔ **Connections:** How many microphone jacks does the camera have? (Most only accept one.) Is there a headset jack? Many MiniDV cameras can also input and output video in S-Video format, which can be very useful for acquiring video from old tapes, or playing back your video on a television. Also check for a USB port, which can be quite useful.

✔ **Special effects:** The camera you're considering may promise all kinds of in-camera effects, but with some practice you can recreate many of these effects using digital video-editing software, and with better precision. In other words, you shouldn't necessarily base your final decision on whether the camera provides these effects.

✔ **Battery life:** If you have to interrupt your video shoot every 25 minutes to replace the batteries, you are not going to be a happy camper. Look for a camera that uses longer-life lithium-ion batteries, and don't forget to check out how much extra batteries cost.

Using research resources

Eventually, you have to go into a store and actually hold cameras. That experience will be less overwhelming if you already have some idea of the kinds of cameras you want to try. Online research can help you narrow down your choices. These Web sites and publications publish reviews and comments:

✔ **CNET** (www.cnet.com): CNET is a great resource of news, tips, and reviews for all kinds of computer hardware and electronics. The site's camcorder section, shown in Figure 8-1, is attractive, easy-to-use, and even includes feedback and ratings from people who purchased the camera.

✔ **Videomaker magazine** (www.videomaker.com): You can read the consumer video production magazine Videomaker online or in print. In both editions you find advice from experts in the field, reviews, and lots of do-it-yourself articles written for beginners and professionals.

✔ **Consumer Reports** (www.consumerreports.com): This magazine has a very useful product selector that walks you through the options available. It's a great resource for narrowing down your choices based on price and features. You can subscribe monthly or annually.

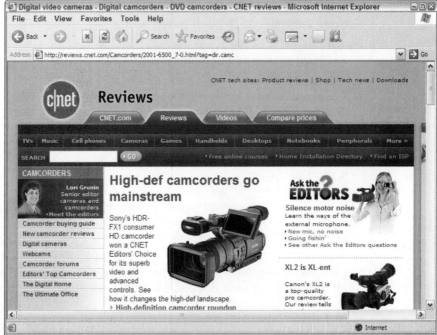

Figure 8-1:
CNET
Reviews is
an excellent
source of
reviews
from writers
and camera
owners.

Buying a tripod

One of the easiest ways to destroy your footage is to not use a tripod. Most consumer-level video cameras are very small and light, and it's tempting to simply hold the camera in your hand when you shoot. Unless you have a very steady hand and walk very smoothly, however, the resulting video looks very jerky and unprofessional. Whenever possible, set your camera up on a tripod, and use the tripod's zoom, pan, and tilt features to adjust your shots. When you need to move the camera, pick up the whole tripod and carry it with you.

While shopping for a tripod, consider the following issues:

✔ **Weight:** You have to carry the tripod with you, so you need one that is light enough for you to carry comfortably (along with your other equipment). Most tripods collapse down, but they can still be quite heavy.

On the other hand, don't get a super-lightweight tripod, either. Superlightweight tripods can border on being flimsy, which is not a trait you want in the hardware that's holding your brand-new video camera. You need to find a happy balance between a tripod that's light enough to carry but sturdy enough to support the camera during use.

✔ **Height:** You should be able to use your tripod comfortably standing or sitting. You may forget that you may need to sit during long video shoots, so before you make your tripod purchase, try setting up the tripod and using it while in a chair. Some tripods aren't configured for optimum comfort. The camera should sit at your eye-level (whether you're sitting or standing) so that you can look through the viewfinder or use an external preview screen.

✔ **Type of tripod:** You can purchase folding tripods, table-top tripods, mini tripods, car window tripods, c-clamp tripods, or monopods/unipods (these have only one leg and are great for steadier shooting when you can't use a normal tripod). Use the kind of shooting you're doing as your guide when you purchase a tripod. You may even need to purchase more than one tripod for maximum flexibility.

✔ **Tripod head:** Some tripods are sold with a *head* — the connecting piece between the tripod and the camera — and some are not. Be aware that you can purchase heads that allow pans and tilts, panoramic shots, and rotation, and that are configured for specialized shooting angles. Many tripod heads include a *level,* as well, which can come in handy when you must place the tripod on uneven ground. Your needs here will be determined by the type of shooting you plan to do, and sometimes also by the kind of camera you use. If you aren't sure which kind of head to get, start with a tripod that gives you a good range of *pan movement* as well as *tilt.*

Most good camera stores carry a wide selection of tripods and heads. Bring your camera to the store and don't be afraid to ask the salespeople for advice and recommendations. Don't be shy about setting up the tripod with your camera in the configuration you expect to shoot in. Buying a tripod should be a very hands-on experience! Among the best tripod and tripod head manufacturers are Benbo, Bogen/Manfrotto, Bushnell, Kodak, Nikon, and Zeiss. You can find a wide selection to look at online on the B&H Photo Web site (`bhphoto video.com`). Figure 8-2 shows some Bogen/Manfrotto tripod systems.

Pan, tilt, zoom

If you're brand new to the world (and lingo) of digital video, here's a quick rundown of a few basic terms:

✔ **Pan:** When you pan, you shift the camera from left to right (or right to left) across the viewing area.

✔ **Tilt:** Tilting is the opposite of panning; this action has you moving the camera top to bottom or bottom to top across the viewing area.

✔ **Zoom:** When you zoom in or out, you're enlarging or reducing the image.

Figure 8-2:
B&H Photo
is a good
resource for
research-
ing or
purchasing
tripods
and other
camera
and video
hardware.

Selecting a microphone

When shooting video, never disregard the importance of high-quality sound.
The audio portion of a video is at least as important (and maybe more important) as the picture.

If you don't believe me, try watching a television program with the sound off.
Chances are that the plot of the program is pretty hard to follow. Now listen
to the sound without watching the picture. Can you understand what is going
on in the program? Listening almost always provides you better understanding of what is happening than just watching the picture.

Whether you're taping a wedding, a family vacation, an interview, or a rock
concert, sound is crucial to getting the job done effectively. Using the right
microphone in the right situation can help you create a usable piece of video
that has good sound quality.

If you would like to find out more about microphones, the Audio-Technica
Web site has a good and very technical guide to understanding and using
microphones at www.audio-technica.com/cms/site/9904525cd25e0d8d/
index.html. It is shown in Figure 8-3.

Figure 8-3:
The Audio-
Technica
Web site
provides a
good tutorial
on how
micro-
phones
work.

The Shure Web site has a good guide to selecting a wireless microphone system online at `www.shure.com/booklets/intro/intro_to_wireless.asp` and a guide to setting up and operating a wireless system at `www.shure.com/booklets/wireless/wireless_page1.html`.

Because the proximity of a microphone to the mouth may produce pops and hisses, consider adding a windscreen to your kit. (Windscreens also come in handy if you're filming outside.) Although you can purchase a commercial windscreen, a quick solution is to stretch a nylon stocking over an embroidery hoop, wire, or wooden ring; simply place the screen between the microphone and the mouth and you've got yourself a windscreen. Keep in mind that the screen will be visible when you shoot video!

The following sections offer details about several kinds of microphones.

Introducing shotgun microphones

Shotgun microphones are a kind of *unidirectional* microphone. (I talk more about microphone direction in the sidebar "Directional properties of microphones" in this chapter.) Shotgun mics listen to the sounds in front of them and don't pick up much sound from behind or to the side.

Directional properties of microphones

Omnidirectional microphones pick up sound from all directions at the same time, and at the same level. There is one exception to this rule: The body of the microphone blocks sound, so the shape of an omnidirectional microphone matters. Omnidirectional microphones provide close to 360 degrees of sound pickup around the microphone, as shown in the following figure.

Unidirectional microphones pick up sound best from the front — the direction in which the microphone is pointed. Sound from the side and rear of the microphone is audible, but not as loud as that in front. Unidirectional microphones come in four flavors; the difference has to do with the *pattern,* or shape, in which the microphone picks up sound. The four types are:

✔ **Sub-cardiod:** Sub-cardiod microphones give you about 170 degrees of audio pickup around the front of the microphone.

✔ **Cardiod:** These are the most common directional microphones, and are designed to give about 120 degrees of pickup. You can see the cardiod pattern in the figure.

✔ **Hyper-cardiod:** A hyper-cardiod microphone has 100 degrees of audio pickup.

✔ **Line:** This microphone creates a 90-degree shape in audio pickup. A shotgun microphone (which I discuss elsewhere in this chapter) is a line microphone.

Omnidirectional
microphone pattern

Directional
microphone pattern

If you can only afford to buy one microphone, a shotgun mic is your best choice. In addition, you usually need only one shotgun microphone, even when taping multiple people.

You can mount a shotgun microphone on the camera itself, or on a *boom* — a long rod that's extended over the shooting area. If you mount your shotgun microphone on a boom, add another person to your camera crew to hold and move the microphone. *Boom-mounting* shotgun mics provide better sound than camera-mounting because the mic is much closer to the sound source. Shotgun microphones are also extremely useful when you don't want the microphone visible in the video. Position a boom-mounted shotgun mic slightly above, below, or to the side of the audio source, but wherever you put it, make sure it's pointed at the audio source.

Getting ahold of a handheld microphone

Handheld microphones are excellent for high-quality vocals, as when you tape singers and speakers. Most handheld microphones are unidirectional, so they pick up a speaker or singer very well, and noise from behind and to the side of the microphone less well. (See the sidebar, "Directional properties of microphones," elsewhere in this chapter, for an explanation of the difference between omnidirectional and unidirectional mics.)

Hold or place handheld mics at a 45-degree angle to the speaker's mouth, not perpendicularly, and between 6 and 16 inches away from the speaker's mouth. A handheld microphone can be held or placed in a microphone stand (floor, podium, or tabletop).

When two speakers are sharing a handheld microphone, you may notice some variation in their audio levels, or volume. Placing the microphone closer to the quiet person can alleviate this problem, or the two speakers can reposition themselves as each speaks.

Though powerful, handheld microphones can be a real problem for those who aren't used to using them. I can't tell you how many times I have watched speakers start off well, holding the microphone at the right angle and distance, only to see them begin to gesture with it to make a point or absent-mindedly lower it until it is somewhere around their waists. For novices, consider putting your handheld microphone in a stand and placing the stand on a podium.

Pinning your hopes on lavalier microphones

Lavalier microphones are unidirectional microphones, and are sometimes called *lapel* or *personal microphones.* They are only useful for picking up audio from a single person. Clipped to clothing, lavalier microphones are usually quite small, unobtrusive to the eye, and pick up very little background noise. They're particularly effective if your speaker wants the freedom to move around a bit and needs to keep his or her hands free.

When you have multiple speakers using lavalier microphones the resulting audio can be very good, especially because the mics can't be inadvertently repositioned during a talk, or left behind at a podium. However, some speakers create noise by fiddling with them, especially during periods when they aren't the focus of the shoot. These mics can also rub up against clothing and jewelry. I have also seen situations where speakers on a panel forget they are wearing microphones and whisper to each other while another panelist is speaking — the result is less than secretive!

Lavalier microphones should be clipped to the outermost layer of clothing, about 6 to 14 inches from the mouth, and generally pointing toward the mouth. As much as possible, position the microphone directly under the mouth, rather than to the side. Most microphones of this kind come with small clips, but you can also use tape to attach them to clothing and even skin. Be careful that the person wearing the lavalier has enough slack in the cable to move without dislodging the microphone.

Purchasing headset microphones

Headset mics are unidirectional microphones designed to minimize pickup of all that background noise. Announcers and sportscasters often use headset microphones because they work well in noisy environments. The addition of headphones allows them to hear what they sound like — you might be surprised how useful this is to a speaker — despite deafening crowd noise.

Headset microphones are, pretty obviously, only useful for gathering audio from one speaker, but you can mic several speakers using headset microphones, and the result will be quite good. Because the speaker is physically wearing the microphone he or she can't leave it behind, and the mic can't easily be moved away from the correct position. For the purposes of a video shoot, however, remember that headset mics are extremely visible, and in fact actually obscure part of the speaker's face. They look downright dorky.

A good-quality headset microphone can be used effectively in situations with very loud background noise, but don't try to use the kinds of microphones used with office telephones or Internet telephony in their place. Telephone headsets, though they include a microphone, are simply not of high enough quality to serve for most filming purposes.

Jamming with instrument microphones

Instrument microphones are designed to sit in front of, or attach directly to, a musical instrument. They are occasionally even placed inside an instrument. These microphones are unidirectional and are usually used to isolate or amplify a particular instrument — from drums to electric guitars.

Installing instrument microphones is a specialized skill, and the subject of much debate even between audio professionals. If you must arrange this kind of setup, expect to spend a great deal of time listening to the instrument being played alone and in combination with all the other shoot elements.

Getting techno-cool with wireless microphones

Handheld, lavalier, headset, and instrument microphones can also be purchased as wireless microphones systems. A wireless microphone transmits the audio it picks up back to the receiving box wirelessly. The box is then plugged in to the camera audio pickup jack.

The benefits of using a wireless microphone are pretty obvious — fewer visible cables mean better pictures, and fewer chances that cords can be tripped over or pulled loose. In situations where you have multiple microphones, cables can be confusing and unattractive. Wireless microphones are also invaluable in situations when you need to position the camera some distance from the microphone. Wireless systems can transmit from 100 to 1,000 feet.

Wireless transmission is hindered by metal objects, furniture, electronics (such as computers and televisions), and some lights. Power cords that are positioned too close to the microphone or the receiver can cause interference. Some video cameras even interfere with good transmission! If you hear hums and crackles when using a wireless microphone system, try repositioning the receiver and the microphone until the noise is diminished.

Audio pros often set up reserve wired microphones when using wireless systems so that they don't lose the audio completely if interference occurs in the middle of a shoot.

(Not) Using internal camera microphones

Most cameras come with a built-in microphone. Don't use them. They are omnidirectional, and pick up almost all the noise in your filming situation indiscriminately. Thus, the important sounds — voices and music — may be lost underneath meaningless background sounds, like traffic. The microphone should be close to the audio you want to record, not close to the camera.

Using headphones

Whenever possible you should shoot video while listening to it through headphones at the same time. This technique has several benefits:

- ✔ You can easily tell when environmental noise is interfering with the voices or music you want to pick up, and make adjustments or pause taping to deal with them.

- ✔ Using headphones cuts down the amount of noise you're hearing yourself. Because most video shoots involve microphones, there is quite a bit of environmental or situational noise you can hear standing behind the camera that may not be picked up by the microphone. Wearing headphones ensures that you're hearing what the *camera* is hearing — or not hearing.

- ✔ You know when the microphone stops working, or the sound gets bad. If you're listening to what the camera hears, you will know whether a microphone quits working, runs out of batteries, or becomes poorly positioned. If you're not using headphones, you won't know this until you watch the recording and it's too late.

✔ People won't talk to you. I'm always surprised how often passersby stop to talk to a camera person, especially one who is positioned behind a tripod. Their comments and questions are invariably picked up by the microphone, and become part of the recording. Wearing headphones tends to reduce the number of times this happens.

When buying headphones you don't have to break the bank, but you should avoid really cheap headphones. Look for headphones that completely cover the ears, offer fairly good audio quality. You should be able to find a suitable set in the $50 to $150 range.

Audio-Technica, Behringer, Bose, Denon, Sennheiser, and Sony all have headphones that work well for video shooting purposes.

Remembering the essentials

After you select your primary video shooting components, you need to add a few more items to your kit:

✔ **Tapes/media:** Always include a few extra tapes in your video shooting kit. Buying extra tapes may add to the expense of your shoot, especially when you're using digital video, but paying for extra tapes is undoubtedly less expensive than having to re-shoot an entire segment because you ran out of tape the first time. Bring extras even if you can't imagine needing them. You can use them next time.

✔ **Cables:** Some audio components are sold with connecting cables; many are not. You probably need to add audio, video, power and other cables to your kit. Don't skimp on these cables. The quality of the cables and adapters you use contributes significantly to the picture and sound quality of the final product, so this isn't the place to pinch pennies.

✔ **Batteries:** Many video and audio hardware pieces use batteries (especially microphones), and you should have backups and extras on hand. Think in terms of having more than you could ever possibly need, and consider bringing a battery charger just in case.

✔ **Power cords and adapters:** Any component that requires power probably requires an adapter and a cord. Including a couple of extensions cords is also a good idea.

✔ **Gaffer's tape:** During shoots when you have to string cable a long way or across walkways, you should secure your cables to the ground using cloth gaffer's tape. Gaffer's tape looks a bit like duct tape, but doesn't leave behind the same sticky residue.

Shooting Video

As you get started shooting video, remember that many people do this work professionally — and that most of them work as part of a larger team. Producing a good piece of video can be a massive undertaking, if your goal is to produce the nightly news, for example. Of course, plenty of videographers work alone and with basic equipment with great results. The following sections give you a broad overview of tips and ideas. Use what applies best to your situation.

Planning a shoot

So you've got a great idea for a video shoot and you can't wait to get started? Great! But before you run out the door with your camera, you need to take care of some arrangements and issues. Sure, you can shoot video without planning your shoot, but a little preparation results in a better experience — and usually in better video.

The scope of your shoot naturally determines just how much planning is necessary before you get into the field, but assuming that you don't have to build a life-size replica of the Titanic, this list should take care of most situations:

 ✔ **Scout the location.** Before you show up with a camera, visit the location you plan to shoot. Spend some time there at the same time of day you plan to shoot. Watch what happens to the light, and where shadows fall. Walk around the area and figure out just where you will put the camera, where your power will come from, whether you need additional lighting, and where the action of your video will take place. If you are driving to this location, is there nearby parking available? If the shoot will take a while, are there bathrooms you can access? These details aren't glamorous, but they are important!

 ✔ **Get permission.** If you are shooting video in your living room, you don't really need to get permission to be there (although if you have roommates it might be a good idea!), but almost anywhere else you choose to shoot video you need to make sure you are allowed to be there. I don't mean to imply that you can't go to the park and shoot video of your child without getting a permit, but I have found that as soon as you set up a tripod or run a power cord, people tend to get a little touchy. Do yourself a favor and find out in advance whether you need to talk to someone in order to clear your shoot, especially if you plan to have lots of people and equipment in place.

Be prepared to get turned down; many people don't like the disturbance of a video shoot. In some cases, you may be required to get a permit, although this is true mostly in cities where filming happens on a large scale, like New York and Los Angeles.

If you get permission to shoot in a location and need to use a power outlet, be sure to ask first.

✔ **Post announcements.** If you're filming in a public location that people may walk through without realizing they are being filmed, you should put up a notice warning them that they may end up on tape.

Videomaker magazine has a good, quick reference guide, shown in Figure 8-4, to the legal issues you face when you film. You should be aware of copyright and privacy issues before you yell, "Action!" You can read this guide online at www.videomaker.com/scripts/lobby.cfm?id=10.

✔ **Double-check your kit.** Many video professionals create checklists of equipment that they can go over before they go to a shoot. Create a general checklist of materials that you need for every shoot, and then one that is specific for the current shoot. Put *everything* you need on the list, no matter how trivial it seems. Having a checklist and using it makes a huge difference in how smoothly your shoot goes, even if you're just going over to the neighbor's backyard.

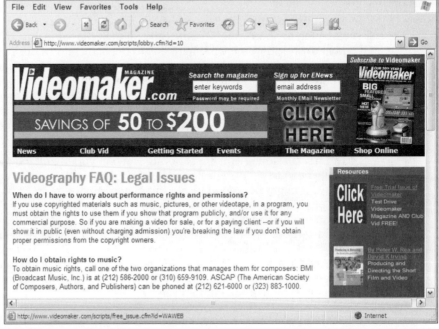

Figure 8-4:
Brush up on the legal issues involved in filming on the Videomaker magazine Web site.

The other important part of double-checking your kit is checking your equipment. Is it all in good working order? Are microphones actually in their cases? Did you put your camera away upside down last time? Is the extension cord a tangled mess? Making sure everything works, has fresh batteries, and is in the right place makes setting up your shoot go much more quickly.

✔ **Find a crew.** Using the term *crew* might be overkill. After all, you probably aren't out filming a television show. Still, even during an informal shoot, take along a friend or two to help you schlep equipment around, post signs, guard the camera when you have to go to the bathroom, and keep people from walking in front of the camera. If you opt for a boom-mounted shotgun mic, you definitely need someone to position it throughout the shoot.

✔ **Arrange transportation.** If you're traveling any distance at all (even to the neighbor's backyard!), you probably want to make sure you have transportation that will hold all your equipment, and any extra people you are taking along. If your video shoot involves getting talent to the location of the shoot, make sure they have a reliable way to get there. Don't forget to arrange a way to get everything and everyone home again!

Video equipment tends to be bulky and awkward, even if you don't have much of it. A good luggage cart can be very useful if you have to move things far from where they are unloaded.

Setting up your camera

Okay, so you're on the scene and ready to start shooting. Before you press the record button, run through this list:

✔ Are cables taped down and power cords plugged in?

✔ Are your extra tapes unwrapped and accessible? (You won't be happy to hear yourself unwrap cellophane from a tape when you watch your video later!)

✔ If you have helpers involved, do they know where they should be and how to operate any equipment they are supposed to use? They can't come ask questions after you press the record button, or those questions will end up on the tape!

✔ Have you taken some test footage and viewed it?

✔ Are your lights positioned correctly so that the picture is usable?

✔ Have you got all microphones plugged in and turned on? Have you listened to some recorded footage to make sure your sound levels are clear and loud enough?

✔ Have you tested your tripod to make sure it can tilt and pan smoothly without interfering with headset, microphone, and power cords?

✔ Are you seated or standing comfortably so that you can reach the camera, tripod, and other components?

Only when you've run through this list can you begin shooting.

Shooting footage

You pressed the record button, didn't you? Great, now you are officially putting sound and audio onto your tape. Here are a few do's and don'ts that can help you create good shots:

✔ ***Don't* be afraid to stop and start again if things go wrong.** Thanks to the magic of video editing you can remove miscues and mistakes when you edit your video.

✔ ***Do* use the pan and tilt features of your tripod, but *don't* get carried away.** Overusing pans and tilts can make viewers queasy, literally. Try to pan only once per shot, and do it slowly. Tilting is a little trickier to do. The important thing when you pan and tilt at the same time is to try and keep the horizon line level, if at all possible.

✔ ***Don't* zoom so much.** I know that earlier in this chapter I talked about buying a camera with a good optical zoom, but you should actually avoid zooming during taping as much as you can. Using the zoom feature a lot also makes your viewers queasy. When you do zoom in or out, do it slowly. Or, move the camera.

✔ ***Do* move the camera around.** If you can do it, move the camera to a new location to get different shots and angles. Pans, tilts, and zooms can only give video footage so much visual interest.

The MediaCollege Web site, shown in Figure 8-5, is a free educational Web site about electronic media. It has a great set of illustrations for setting up camera shots of people and situations. Ever wondered how to frame a close up? Visit www.mediacollege.com/video/shots to find out how.

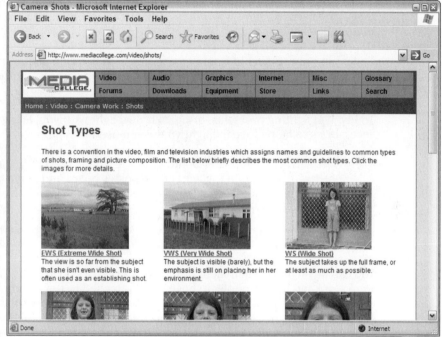

Figure 8-5:
The Media-
College
Web site
illustrates
common
shots and
guidelines
for using
them.

Handling Lighting Issues

Lighting is a big issue when shooting video — you need enough, but not too much. If you're shooting outdoors, light conditions change as the day goes by, and weather conditions shift. Indoors, you may be dealing with flickering fluorescent bulbs or windows. Getting set up properly can be a daunting proposition. Unfortunately, getting too specific about lighting would take me too far away from the topic of this book; after all, there are entire books devoted to this subject! However, I do have a few words of advice on the subject. A little practice and some research can improve your knowledge in this area, if only to know that you should always arrange to shoot video in naturally well-lit locations.

Some cameras come with a built-in light that points toward whatever the camera is aimed at. Although this light is sometimes helpful, it won't suit every situation. When indoors, fluorescent lights actually produce reasonably good lighting conditions, when positioned well.

Positioning can correct many lighting deficiencies. Set up your subject so that light falls upon it from a window or lamp. Position the camera so that it doesn't block the light.

Never put your subject in front of a window. This is called backlighting, and the result is that the subject appears as a shadow in contrast to the brightness of the light behind them.

To head off lighting problems, bring your own light with you, along with a few accessories to help move the light where you need it to be:

✔ White surfaces like poster board or fabric can be used to bounce light to another location. Aim the light at the poster board and move the poster board around until it is angled to project light onto your subject, or wherever you need it.

✔ Semi-opaque fabric screens can be used between the light and your subject to soften and diffuse the light.

You can buy lighting equipment in camera stores, or you can go to a hardware store and buy a couple of those lights attached to power cords used in attics and on construction sites, or any other suitable looking solution you can find. These work lights are sometimes sold with stands and hooks so that you can position them when shooting. Because they're meant to be moved around, they're usually collapsible.

If you're shooting for more than one day and your lighting situation is particularly problematic, you may be able to rent lights.

If you would like to add a lighting solution to your video shooting kit, a good all-purpose solution is a three-light system. A set of three lights enables you to light your subject from the front and both sides if needed, and offers a more even distribution of light. Your system should also allow you to add light screens to soften the light, and bounce screens to move it around. You can find some very nice three-light systems sold as packages. These frequently include carrying cases and collapsible stands.

Check out the lighting tutorials at the MediaCollege Web site, including the one for using a three-point lighting system (see Figure 8-6), at `www.media college.com/lighting/`.

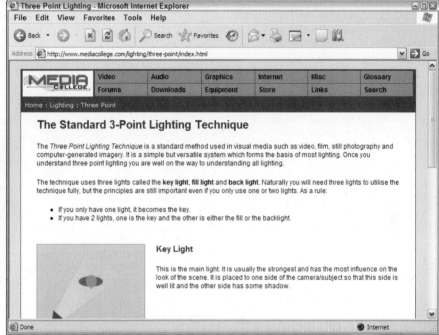

Figure 8-6:
The Media-
College
Web site
includes a
lighting
tutorial for
three-point
lighting
systems.

Cleaning Up

After you turn off the camera you have a few tasks remaining before you get back to your computer and edit your video.

The most important thing you should do while and after you shoot is label your tapes. Trust me. Sitting down in front of four tapes without labels when it comes time to edit can be frustrating and confusing!

As soon as you take a tape out of the camera, engage the tape protection feature that prevents you from taping over the footage. Most MiniDV tapes come with a little slider that prevents a camera from recording on the tape if you happen to accidentally put it back in the camera.

Before you leave the site of your shoot, make sure you have all your equipment and cables. Leaving a power cord plugged in to the wall socket after you pull the other end out of the component is a common mistake.

I am sure I don't have to say this, but I will anyway: You should pick up and dispose of any trash you leave behind, and don't forget to remove any tape you used to secure cables and signs you posted either.

Chapter 9

Capturing and Editing Digital Video

. . . .

In This Chapter

▶ Choosing the right hardware and software

▶ Getting video off the camera and into the computer

▶ Adding transitions, effects, and audio

▶ Turning your edited video into a digital file

. . . .

*V*ideo editing was once solely the domain of film professionals and Hollywood creative types. Today, lower computer prices and a more technically savvy consumer population have led to a surge in available video-editing software. This new popularity means that video editing is easier and faster than it has ever been — but that doesn't actually mean it's easy!

Even a short video is full of effects, transitions, and titles. By the time you watch a piece of video, someone has thought about every frame it contains. Thanks to your computer and some video-editing software, that someone is now you.

When I make it sound like so much fun, you might be asking yourself why you should edit your video at all. Editing is a process that enriches video. You can remove mistakes and unnecessary footage, choose the best of several shots, tell a more coherent story, and add sound effects, visual effects, voiceovers, and music. The result is a dynamic, exciting presentation. Visual imagery accompanied by sound is one of the most compelling human experiences around.

In this chapter you discover the available hardware and software that make or break a good video-editing experience. Then, begin the editing process by capturing video on to your computer.

Later in this chapter, I show you how to rearrange the order of shots, delete clips, add audio to video, and make transitions between scenes in your video. You find out a few tips and tricks along the way, and top it all off by exporting your file in a format you can use to share using BitTorrent.

Selecting Hardware and Software

The advent of digital video gives you the ability to create very high-quality video, and powerful but low-cost computers mean you can edit that video in the comfort of your own home. You can head down to any good computer store to get the equipment you need to edit digital video, and although you need to spend some money, your budget needn't been in the thousands of dollars, as it would have been not so long ago.

Software comes in all kinds of price ranges, and of course the more you spend, the more features you get. Nonetheless, I can tell you about some very good lower-cost solutions that meet nearly all your digital editing needs.

Choosing hardware

Selecting the hardware you use to edit your video is a bit of a task, but as with purchasing a digital video camera, the main work comes in doing your research before you buy. The issues involved include:

- Whether you should buy a Macintosh or PC to edit video on
- Whether you can just upgrade the machine sitting on your desk
- What your budgetary limitations are

Both Macintosh and PC computers are defended by die-hard fans who will argue until they are blue in the face about why their particular computer is the kind *you* should purchase. These are not the best people to take advice from, however. They are usually much more interested in promoting a particular computer platform than in making sure what you end up with suits you.

What you really need is a computer you will find easy to use and powerful enough for the kinds of video you will be editing. If you are more comfortable using PCs, then buy a PC. Vice-versa if you prefer Macs. You can find good video-editing software packages for both platforms, and both kinds of computers can be configured as video-editing machines.

Read on for info on the minimum requirements for a digital video-editing computer.

The computer you want to edit digital video on needs to have a fast — and quite large — hard drive, plenty of RAM, and a FireWire port or video capture card. Here's what you need your machine to have:

- **1 GHz processor:** Faster processors mean that the computer can think faster — any task that requires the computer to calculate will happen more quickly with a higher-speed processor. Editing video is a job that involves a lot of processor time, so look for at least a 1-GHz processor, and never go less than 500 MHz.

- ✔ **512MB to 1GB RAM:** The more RAM you can afford, the better. RAM is memory, and the more your computer has, the faster your machine can handle video editing, and the smoother playback of video will be. Keep in mind that in most computers RAM can usually be quickly upgraded, so if you only have the budget for 512MB now, you can save up and add more later.

- ✔ **50GB hard drive (or more!):** You will be shocked — shocked! — at how much space video takes up on your hard drive. These files are extremely large, probably much larger than any other kind of data you have dealt with before. Five minutes of uncompressed high-quality video can consume 1GB of hard drive space, so if you plan to edit long presentations, you may need even more than 50GB of hard drive space.

- ✔ **FireWire:** You need one FireWire port on your computer. It's helpful if that port is on the front of your machine so that you don't have to crawl around under your desk every time you want to plug your camera or tape player into it.

- ✔ **A video capture card if you need to digitize VHS or other analog video formats:** Video capture cards can usually accept both S-Video and composite video connections.

You don't need a video capture card at all if all your video is digital and can be inputted via FireWire.

Upgrading your current computer

When thinking about whether you can use your current computer, the question is a simple one — does your computer meet the requirements I list in the previous section, "Choosing hardware"? If not, can it be upgraded to meet them?

Upgrading is a tempting option because most people have a computer at home already. Remember that memory — RAM — is easy to upgrade. Processors, however, are not. If your computer doesn't already have FireWire, you can add a FireWire card, but these can be pricy items.

Your hard drive is another issue entirely. It is usually pretty easy to switch out an older hard drive for a new, larger one, assuming you can find one that will physically fit into the same slot. You can also add an external hard drive — or two! — to your system. There are many relatively inexpensive external hard drives on the market today. Look for one that can be connected via FireWire or USB 2.0, and that has at least a speed of 7200 rpm. However, realize that an external drive is always a little slower than an internal one.

If you buy an external hard drive on which to store digital video, and you also use FireWire to connect your camera to the computer, make sure your computer has two FireWire jacks!

If you can possibly do it, consider dedicating your video-editing machine to only being used for editing video — no e-mail, no game playing, no Web surfing, no Quicken. Video editing consumes a lot of space and requires a lot of RAM to run. If you can protect your video-editing machine from the new screensaver your son wants to download, and all those MP3s your daughter ripped, your machine will be a lot happier. Most of us can't afford to buy a dedicated computer, but if you are getting into video production in a serious way, it's something to aim for.

Basic components

Your video-editing setup, illustrated in Figure 9-1, has a few more components besides the computer:

- ✔ **A source playback device:** You can use your digital video camera itself, or buy a dedicated digital video player, to play the video you capture onto your computer.

- ✔ **Monitor:** If you can swing it, buy a nice, big monitor. Because there is so much happening on the screen while you edit video, those extra inches are really helpful. Better yet, get two monitors!

- ✔ **Speakers:** Your video has an audio track, right? Then you need speakers in order to hear it.

- ✔ **FireWire cable:** If you don't have one already, you need a FireWire cable to connect your camera to your computer.

If you plan to create voiceovers for your video, you may want to add a microphone to your setup, or you can simply record your voice using your video camera and handle it as you do video.

Choosing software

Your choice of software application is no doubt determined in large part by your budget, but don't focus so much on dollar signs that you lose sight of what you need to accomplish. If you're a hobbyist or beginner, you may want to start with an inexpensive (or even free) application to get a feel for how video editing works before you plunk down the money for a higher-end program. The following lists include editing programs for both Macintosh and PC computers, but it by no means includes every software program available. Feel free to use the program that came with your camera, or that you bought last year in a fit of optimism.

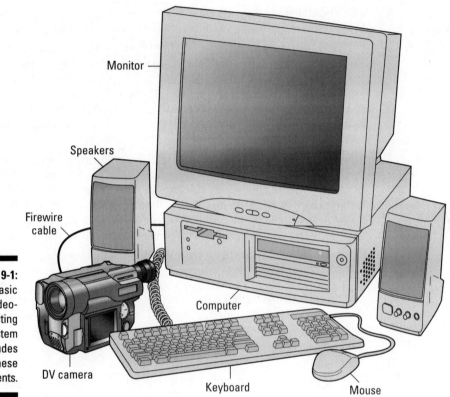

Monitor

Speakers

Firewire
cable

Computer

Figure 9-1:
A basic
video-
editing
system
includes
these
components.

DV camera

Keyboard

Mouse

PC software options

The following is a less-than-comprehensive list, arranged by price, of the most commonly used video-editing applications for PCs. I do my best to give you the most up-to-date information, although some info may change, and prices may fluctuate. Here are some products to check out:

✔ **Adobe Premiere Pro ($699):** This high-end, full-featured program enables you to edit multiple video tracks, add, edit, and mix audio, implement any of the many included clip transitions, and, of course, capture video. Some of the higher-end editing tools include color correction, titling, and graphics creation. If you are a user of Adobe Photoshop, you can import that program's files directly into Premiere, along with a wide variety of other image files. Download a 30-day trial version or purchase online at `www.adobe.com/products/premiere/`.

✔ **Avid Xpress DV ($495):** Touted as a professional video-editing solution, Avid Xpress DV is indeed a full-featured and powerful program. Edit, delete, and move video clips, integrate some of the more than 100 included effects, and implement automatic color correction. Round out your presentations with titles, credits, and text; add music, voice-overs, and other sound effects. Avid is the company that creates the video-editing systems used by many film professionals to edit Hollywood blockbusters (and stinkers). Find out how to purchase this product online at `www.avid.com/products/xpressdv/`.

✔ **Adobe Premiere Elements ($99):** Designed specifically for the home user, Adobe Premiere Elements offers many of the features found in Adobe Premiere Pro in a simplified interface. You can delete, move, and clip video, add titles and credits, and use some of the included slow-motion, warping, and transition effects. Download a 30-day free trial or purchase online at `www.adobe.com/products/premiereel/`.

✔ **Pinnacle Studio ($80):** Pinnacle Studio is a reasonably priced program that enables you to edit your video, add titles, and add music. It includes a number of cool special effects. Export your creations to tape, DVD, and Web-ready formats. This program includes some interesting automated features like color correction and audio noise reduction. Download a 30-day free trial or purchase online at `www.pinnaclesys.com/studio`.

✔ **Windows Movie Maker (free with Windows XP):** Use this program to edit and share home movies by using its drag-and-drop interface to move clips around and add transitions. This program is directly targeted to beginners. It is pre-installed on machines with Windows XP, but you can also download it from `www.microsoft.com/windowsxp/downloads/updates/moviemaker2.mspx`. Windows Movie Maker is shown in Figure 9-2.

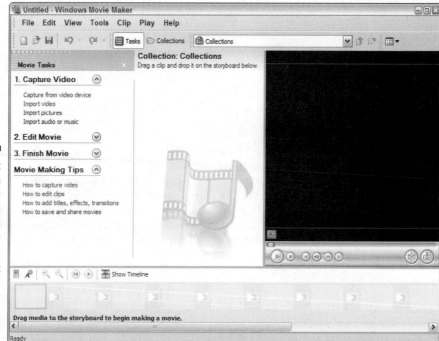

Figure 9-2:
Windows Movie Maker is a good place for beginners on a budget to start with video-editing software.

Macintosh software options

The following is a less-than-comprehensive list, arranged by price, of the most commonly used video-editing applications for Macs. I do my best to give you the most up-to-date information, although some info may change and prices may fluctuate. Here are some products to check out:

- **Apple Final Cut Pro ($999):** Final Cut Pro is a relative newcomer to the field of video editing, and brings a formidable set of tools to the table — at a formidable price. All the usual features are here: capture many video types, edit, cut, move, and delete clips, and more. Final Cut Pro has powerful audio editing, transitions, effects, credits, titles, and so on. The application is especially focused on delivering you a fast editing environment suited to the power of your machine. One of the features that sets this program apart is its ability to coordinate workflow between multiple editors. Purchase online at www.apple.com/finalcutstudio/final cutpro/.

- **Adobe Premiere Pro ($699):** This program enables you to edit multiple video tracks, add, edit, and mix audio, implement any of the many included clip transitions, and, of course, capture video. Some of the higher-end editing tools include color correction, titling, and graphics creation. Download a 30-day trial version or purchase online at www. adobe.com/products/premiere/. See the description in "PC software options," earlier in this chapter.

- **Avid Xpress DV ($495):** This professional video-editing solution, is indeed a full-featured and powerful program. Edit, delete, and move video clips, integrate some of the more than 100 included effects, and implement automatic color correction. Round out your presentations with titles, credits, and text; add music, voiceovers, and other sound effects. Find out how to purchase online at www.avid.com/products/ xpressdv/. See the description in "PC software options," earlier in this chapter.

- **Final Cut Express HD ($299):** Use the less-costly Final Cut Express HD to accomplish many of the things you can do in Final Cut Pro: titles, effects, transitions, and more. This application uses drag-and-drop functionality to make assembling your video easier. Import Adobe Photoshop graphics to spice up your presentation, and use the 99-track audio editor to add voiceovers, sound effects, and music. Purchase online at www. apple.com/finalcutexpress.

- **iMovie ($79):** Capture video quickly using Apple's iMovie, shown in Figure 9-3. This is a video-editing program targeted to home and hobbyist video editors. Apple has included a function called Magic iMovie, which imports video from your camera and breaks it into separate clips at each scene change, adds transitions and titles, and includes a soundtrack — automatically. You can definitely produce video quickly using iMovie. Purchase online at www.apple.com/ilife/imovie/, unless you have purchased a Macintosh recently, in which case it was included with your computer.

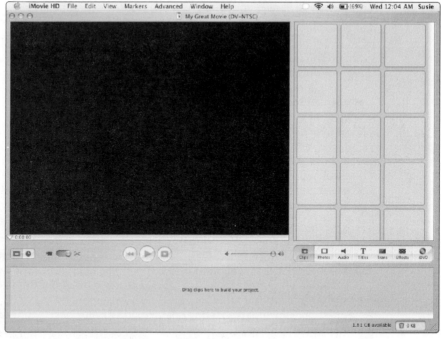

Figure 9-3:
iMovie
comes
pre-installed
on new
Macintosh
computers.

Capturing Video

After you have your hardware and software set up, and some videotape filled with golden moments, you're ready to get that footage onto the computer and start creating cross fades and sappy background music.

Get yourself started by setting up your computer to run the software cleanly and by getting your camera and tape out and ready.

Step 1: Configuring your computer

You need a healthy computer to run video-editing programs (especially those higher-end applications). In fact, video editing is just about the most intensive operation you can do on your computer. Ripping a CD, playing a DVD, and typing e-mails (all at the same time) don't come close to using the resources that are taken up by editing a five-minute video.

So, when you sit down to edit make sure your computer:

✔ Has a lot of free hard drive space.

✔ Is running current and solid versions of your operating system.

✔ Isn't running applications besides your video-editing software. Don't try to enter all your old receipts in your budget software while you edit video. You want every ounce of operating power running the video program.

✔ Isn't running a lot of background applications that use processor power. For instance, you should leave your virus protection running, but turn off optional tools and toys, like instant messaging programs.

A good place to check for some of those background applications is in your System Tray, that area of your Start menu on the far right next to the clock. Icons in that area often indicate applications that are running in the background.

✔ Has been recently defragmented and checked for errors. See the sidebar, "If you haven't defragged in a while," for a reminder on how to do this important system maintenance.

Step 2: Hooking up your camera

When your system is in good shape, you need to hook up your camera (or media player) to your computer. This is a pretty simple operation. Find your FireWire cable and plug it in to the FireWire output port on your camera, and in to the FireWire jack on your computer.

If you haven't defragged in a while

If you have blown off spring cleaning, you may need to defragment your hard drive before you can get up and running with your video editing. Here are the basic steps:

1. **Click the Windows Start button.**

2. **Choose All Programs⇨Accessories⇨System Tools⇨Disk Defragmenter.**

   A Disk Defragmenter dialog box appears.

3. **Select the hard drive you want to defragment (usually C:).**

4. **If you're not sure whether you really need to defrag, click the Analyze button.**

   Windows takes several minutes to analyze your hard drive and gives you its assessment. If you're advised not to bother with a defrag, then skip it for a week. If you're advised to defrag, skip to Step 5.

5. **Click the Defragment button to begin this exciting process.**

6. **Make yourself a cup of coffee. This process can take a while.**

Happily, you don't have to shut down your computer to hook up your camera. You can plug FireWire cables in to your computer all day long without causing an electrical short that will eat your computer.

After you hook up the cable, turn on your camera. If the device is connected successfully, your computer may make a happy chime and give you a `New hardware found` message as the system recognizes the camera.

Step 3: Getting video onto the computer

After you have your camera hooked up and turned on, launch the video-editing software you're using. For these instructions, I have used Adobe Premiere Elements, so if you're also using this program, you can follow along exactly. If you're using a different program, you may be able to find similar features, functions, and tools as you experiment with your first video.

Before you begin your video capture session, make sure the tape in the camera is cued up to the place where you want to start capturing video. Use your camera's VCR or Play setting, and use the Fast Forward and Rewind buttons to move around.

1. **Run Adobe Premiere Elements.**

2. **Click New Project.**

   Premiere Elements opens a New Project dialog box.

3. **Fill in the name of your project, choose a location to save it, and click OK.**

   Premiere Elements launches the project working windows: Media, Monitor, and Timeline, as shown in Figure 9-4.

4. **Turn your video camera on, and set it to run in VCR/Play mode.**

5. **In Premiere Elements, click the Capture button at the top of the application window.**

   Premiere Elements opens the Capture dialog box.

6. **Click Capture.**

   Premiere Elements tells the camera to begin playing the tape. As the video plays, Premiere Elements captures it onto the computer.

7. **Click Stop Capture to end the capture, or wait until all the video has been captured.**

   Voilà! The video is now on your hard drive! You can close the Capture dialog box to return to Editing mode.

Figure 9-4:
Don't be daunted by all the windows when you start a new project in Adobe Premiere Elements.

Editing Video

After you have some video on your computer, you make edits. What you choose to do with your video will vary each time you begin a new project, and in fact, many video editors make several edits before they end up with one they are happy with.

As a result, I can't give you exact instructions on how to edit your video; but I can tell you how to use some common video-editing techniques.

The first step in any video project is to get your video laid down on the *time-line* — a linear representation of all the footage in your project. The timeline shows you how long our project is, and the order in which the clips play. By moving pieces of video — or clips — around, you can change the sequence of the presentation.

If you use Adobe Premiere Elements to capture video, the application automatically saves it all to your computer and also places it inside your current project. While capturing, it breaks the video into pieces. You can see those inside the Media window in Figure 9-5.

Figure 9-5:
After
capturing
video,
Premiere
Elements
creates a
file for each
scene in the
Media
window,
and places
them in the
Timeline
as well.

Playback head

Many programs, including Premiere Elements, place video into a Timeline, breaking each scene into a separate clip.

You can manipulate the Timeline by:

✔ Using the scroll bar at the bottom of the window to move the entire Timeline right or left, earlier and later in the presentation.

✔ Zooming in and out using the magnifying glasses at the top of the window. Zooming in makes the Timeline longer, because you're using smaller units of time in the Timeline.

✔ Moving the playback head, by clicking the mouse anywhere along the numbers marking out the Timeline. (Look for the playback head on the right-hand side of the Timeline window in Figure 9-5.) As you move the playback head, the Monitor — essentially a preview window — displays the frame on which the playback head is sitting.

Working with clips

Sometimes Premiere Elements does a great job of breaking your video into clips; sometimes you still need to make additional cuts, perhaps to remove pieces you don't want, or to move a piece from one spot to another.

Here are a few common tasks you can perform with Adobe Premiere Elements (your program has similar functions, but they may not work precisely the same way Premiere Elements does):

- ✔ You can delete a clip from the Timeline by selecting it and pressing the Delete or Backspace keys.

- ✔ You can move a clip by clicking-and-dragging it to a new location.

- ✔ You can shorten a clip by putting the mouse over the line separating two clips. The cursor turns into Trim In or Trim Out icon, depending on whether you are shortening the beginning or end of a clip. Click-and-drag to the point to which you want to trim.

- ✔ You can cut a clip by selecting the Razor tool (the icon looks like a tiny razor blade) and clicking in the Timeline with it. The video splits at the exact spot where you click.

When you delete a clip from the Timeline, it remains in the Media window so that you can put it back in the Timeline later if you change your mind. Just select the clip and drag it into the Timeline. Because clips remain in the Media window, you can also reuse one again and again in your Timeline, by dragging it in as often as you need it.

Adding transitions

When you play your video right now, each scene simply jumps to the next (this is called a *jump cut*). With the help of Premiere Elements, however, you can make all those transitions from clip to clip a little more attractive.

There are all kinds of transitions available to choose from. Popular transitions include

- ✔ **Cross Dissolve:** One scene melts into the next.

- ✔ **Page Peel:** One scene pulls away from the other, usually beginning with a corner.

✔ **Wipe:** One scene is covered over by the next, or *wiped* out.

✔ **Zoom:** As one scene ends, the camera zooms in. As the next begins, the camera zooms out.

You can easily get carried away by all the available transitions. They are so much fun to add to your presentation that you may forget to ask yourself whether or not they're appropriate. When adding a transition, always think about what you want the end result to be. You want newsy, documentary style video? Limit yourself to jump cuts and the occasional dissolve. Are you creating a video of your son's fourth birthday party? Go to town with the Zoom transition, or experiment with other transitions included in Elements.

Whatever approach you decide on, all transitions can be applied in the same way. Follow these steps to apply a Cross Dissolve and then use them with another transition:

1. **Click the Effects button at the top of the application.**

   Premiere Elements opens the Effects palette.

2. **Type** dissolve **in to the Contains box in the Effects palette.**

   Premiere Elements jumps to the spot in the window containing Dissolve transitions.

3. **Click-and-drag the Cross Dissolve effect onto the point where two clips in the Timeline meet.**

   Premiere Elements adds the dissolve.

4. **Position the playback head just before the dissolve and click Play in the Monitor window.**

   Premiere Elements plays the video on the Timeline that comes after the playback head, so you can see the dissolve.

If you want to remove a transition you laid down earlier, use the Timeline magnifying glass to zoom in until you can see the transition overlaying the video, as shown in Figure 9-6. Right-click it and choose Clear from the menu that appears.

You can also make your transitions longer. Again, zoom in on the Timeline at the point where the transition is. Put your mouse at the edge of the beginning or end of the transition, and when you see the Trim In/Out tool appear, click-and-drag to make the transition longer.

Sometimes you may lay down a transition and Premiere Elements comes back at you with an error message: `Insufficient frames available`. The default setting for the transition — its length — is longer than the available number of frames in the clips. Because the two clips must overlap for a certain amount of time, they must be long enough to do so without losing important visual imagery. This is why you should try to film a few extra seconds between scenes.

Figure 9-6:
Delete
transitions
by right-
clicking on
them and
choosing
Clear from
the menu.

When you get the `Insufficient frames available` message, go ahead
and click OK and apply the transition anyway. Premiere Elements compensates by creating copies of frames to make the transition work. Be sure to
preview the end result to make sure it works.

Applying fades

At the beginning of your video you should add a nice transition from no
image to the first frame of the video. Typically transitions of this sort are
added by creating a fade, usually from black, into the image, or from the
image to black (if the fade is added at the end of the video). Premiere
Elements calls this type of effect a *dip*.

It's a subtle effect, but one that can give your video a little bit more polish
and professionalism — you can't argue that those are good things! Here's
how to dip to black at the end of your video:

1. **Click the Effects button at the top of the application.**

   Premiere Elements opens the Effects palette.

2. **Type** dip **in the Contains box in the Effects palette.**

   Premiere Elements jumps to the spot in the window containing a Dip to Black transition.

3. **Click-and-drag the Dip to Black effect onto the end of the video in your Timeline.**

   Premiere Elements adds the dip.

4. **Position the playback head just before the dip and click Play in the Monitor window.**

   Premiere Elements plays the video on the Timeline that comes after the playback head so you can see how the fade to black looks.

You can also Dip to Black between clips, instead of using a Dissolve or other transition.

Adding titles

No video is finished until you give it a title, right? Premiere Elements has just the tool to overlay that title on top of your video, or on top of a black screen before your video starts.

After you complete the important job of deciding just what the title should be, follow these steps to create a title screen:

1. **Position the playback head at the point you want to overlay your title.**

2. **Click the Titles button at the top of the application.**

   Premiere Elements opens the Adobe Title Designer window, and the titles Template window.

3. **In the Adobe Title Designer window, select the Text tool in the left-hand palette.**

4. **Click anywhere inside the video image window and type the name of your video.**

   Stay inside the innermost white line to ensure that your text is visible on television screens, which frequently crop and blur around the edges of an images.

5. **To apply a pre-defined style, select the text and click one of the Style boxes on the right side of the Adobe Title Designer, as shown in Figure 9-7.**

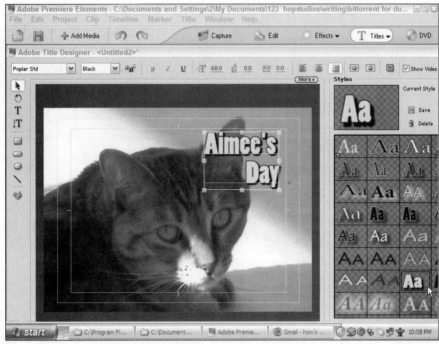

Figure 9-7:
You can
easily add a
pre-defined
style to
title text.

You can also select the text using the Arrow tool from the right-hand tool palette and make font face, style, alignment, and color changes using the appropriate menus.

6. **To add additional text, repeat Steps 2 through 5.**

7. **When finished, click Save Title.**

   Premiere Elements opens a Save Title window.

8. **Give your title a name and click Save.**

9. **Close the Adobe Title Designer.**

   The title is now visible in the Media window.

10. **Look for the track in the Timeline labeled Video 2. It is above Video 1, so you may have to scroll the window to find it.**

11. **Drag the title into the Video 2 track in the Timeline at the point you want it to begin, as shown in Figure 9-8.**

    Premiere Elements lays the title into the Video 2 track.

12. **Play the file from the Monitor window to make sure the title looks like you want it to.**

Figure 9-8:
Titles are
positioned
in the Video
2 track of
the Timeline.

Adding audio

I like to set my videos to music. Sometimes I shoot video with a particular song in mind, sometimes I find a happy solution later. Many videographers actually edit the pictures of their video to fit music, so that high points in the sound match dramatic visual moments. This is definitely an art form I haven't mastered, but the result can be beautiful productions.

You should choose songs you create yourself, songs you get permission to use, or songs from the public domain only. Copyrighted material is off limits unless you get permission! I tell you more about finding music you can use in Chapter 13.

Use these instructions to import and use an MP3 file as background music:

1. **Click File from the menus at the top of the application window, and select Add Media from the menu that opens.**

   Premiere Elements opens the Add Media window.

2. **Navigate to the location of the MP3 file you want to use, select it, and click Open.**

   Premiere Elements imports the media into the project and puts it into the Media window.

3. **Locate the Audio 2 track in the Timeline. It is below the Audio 1 track, so you may need to scroll down.**

   The Audio 1 track is reserved to sound attached to the video you lay down in the Timeline.

4. **Drag the MP3 file into the Audio 2 track of the Timeline at the point you want the music to begin playing.**

   Premiere Elements lays the audio file into the Audio 2 track, as shown in Figure 9-9.

Play your movie from the Monitor window to hear the music while you see the video play.

You can also add one of many audio transitions in the same way you have applied dissolves and fades earlier in this chapter. Some popular audio transitions are:

- ✔ **Reverb:** Do I really need to explain what this does?

- ✔ **Bass:** Everything's always better with bass, right? The bass transition automatically boosts all bass sound in the audio file.

Figure 9-9:
Add music files to your video by using the Audio 2 track.

Exporting Files

After you finish editing, you need to turn your file into something you can share with friends, family, your boss, or the general public via BitTorrent. Take a deep breath and prepare to show your creation to the world!

If you are reading this book, chances are you want to create a digital file that you can share via BitTorrent, but don't forget that you can also create CDs and DVDs of your files. You can even export out to tape, creating a new MiniDV tape (be sure not to write over your original footage!).

No matter what output you choose, you to get your video out of Premiere Elements and into a digital file, you need to export it. Premiere Elements is designed to let you export files in AVI, MPEG, QuickTime, or Windows Media format.

When you export, you may have the option to set the compression settings for the file. The more you compress a file, remember, the smaller it becomes — but the lower the quality it is, as well. Choosing a good compression setting is like walking a tightrope sometimes.

The good news is that if you're sharing files with BitTorrent, file size isn't as big a limitation for you as it would be if you were sharing files with other file-sharing services on the Internet. In most cases, you should opt for higher-quality video, even though the resulting file may be quite large.

After you start your export, be prepared to wait a while. Exporting, even on a very powerful computer, is a slow process. Start your export at night, and let your machine work through the data while you get some well-earned rest.

Follow these directions to walk through exporting a QuickTime movie file:

1. **Click File from the menus at the top of the application, and choose Export/QuickTime from the menu that opens.**

   Premiere Elements opens the Export QuickTime window.

2. **Select LAN (1024K) from the list of compression settings on right-hand side of the window.**

   If you want to customize the compression settings being used, click the Advanced tab and prepare to be daunted.

3. **Click OK.**

   Premiere Elements opens the Save File window.

4. **Navigate to the location you want to save your file, give it a name, and click Save.**

   Premiere Elements starts the Rendering process, as shown in Figure 9-10.

Figure 9-10:
Rendering
takes time,
but you can
follow the
progress
being made
in the
Rendering
window.

To ensure your computer uses all its processing power on the rendering process, close down all other applications (no Web surfing, please!) and screensavers while the process runs. Better yet, turn them off before you start the rendering process!

When your computer finishes rendering the file, be sure to open and play it. Watch at least a few minutes of the video to make sure that the compression settings you used haven't wreaked too much havoc with the quality of the file, and that it runs smoothly.

When you're happy with the file, you're ready to share it using BitTorrent. In Chapter 10 you see how to do just that.

Part IV
Delivering
BitTorrent Content

The 5th Wave   By Rich Tennant

"Would it ruin the online concert experience if I vacuumed the mosh pit between songs?"

In this part . . .

Movie in the can, audio broadcast fine-tuned to the last decibel, photo collection polished into perfection? Now you can take what you've created and put it onto the BitTorrent network. Chapter 10 walks you through using popular BitTorrent clients to create torrent files, including giving you some best practices that help you name things properly. You also get the nitty-gritty detail on announcing your torrent to a tracker, right down to how to install and run your own BitTorrent tracker (you *are* a glutton for punishment, aren't you?). In Chapter 11, you find some torrenting best practices and how to seed your files. Chapter 12 puts everything into perspective by showing you how to promote your creations online so that the world beats a path to your torrent.

Chapter 10

Making and Tracking Torrents

You want to make your own torrent file and share your newly created audio program or a home video. The video of your kids and the neighbor's dog in your backyard pool is hilarious. And that song you recorded with your brother-in-law during that party last weekend is a shining moment in your newly discovered music career. You already know that BitTorrent is the tool you want to use to share your creations with the world. Who knows? Maybe a Hollywood producer or a record company will see them!

But, how do you go about creating torrents? You already know how to download content using BitTorrent (if you don't, check out Chapter 2), but you may never have thought about how that information gets into the torrent file. In this chapter, you find out how to use popular torrent-making software to turn your creative adventures into files you can distribute using BitTorrent.

In this chapter, you also get information on how trackers are used to coordinate the flow of files on the BitTorrent network, and what your tracker options are as you get serious about sharing content.

After you finish reading this chapter, please also read Chapter 11 to find out about seeding your files to the BitTorrent network.

Creating a Torrent

Here is a simple walkthrough of how you get from a media file to a torrent file without too much trouble:

1. **Create media to share, whether it is text, audio, video, images, or a combination of some of these things.**

2. **Use a BitTorrent client of your choice to make a torrent by identifying the file you are sharing.**

3. **Choose a tracker, or use your BitTorrent client as a tracker.**

   The tracker is software in your client or on a Web server that connects the swarm of computers that are uploading and downloading the file, putting those with content in touch with those who need it.

4. **Seed the file or files.**

   Seeding is the process of making sure that at least one complete copy of your media is available to those trying to download it. Popular files may need to be seeded only once; as a file's popularity decreases it may need to be seeded again as those with the file stop sharing it. I talk more about seeding in Chapter 11.

The general process sounds simple enough, doesn't it? In fact, creating a torrent file really isn't difficult. If you are ready to try it, make sure you have the following items close to hand:

- ✔ **Files you want to distribute:** You must have the audio, video, images, text, or other files that you want to distribute ready to go — edited and put into a format you think most people will be able to open and use.

- ✔ **Torrent maker software:** To make a torrent, you need one of the BitTorrent clients that can make torrents. The Official BitTorrent client can make torrents, serve as a tracker, and seed your file.

- ✔ **Access to a tracker:** To create a torrent, you need access to tracker software installed on a Web server, or to use a BitTorrent client that acts as a tracker. Later in this chapter, you can find out more about installing your own tracker and getting access to public trackers.

- ✔ **Ability to seed:** After you have your torrent file and your media file ready to go, you must *seed* them into the BitTorrent network in order to make them available.

   Seeding a file is an essential step. You can seed the file using your BitTorrent client by keeping that client running. I talk about seeding in Chapter 11.

Making a torrent

Throughout this chapter, I use the Official BitTorrent client, available from www.bittorrent.com, to demonstrate the process of creating a torrent. When you use the Official BitTorrent client's Make Torrent utility, all options are contained in one simple window. You can navigate your media files quickly and easily, and you can select media to add to a torrent with a click of the mouse. As a beginner, don't hesitate to use the default values for your settings.

The simplicity of this software is a major strength. Faced with too many options, even a seasoned pro can be overwhelmed; this package is a great one to use to make your first torrent.

You must put your file into a format most Internet users can listen to; MP3 and WAV are both good options.

Here's how to create a torrent file of your audio or video that can distribute your media:

1. **If you haven't done so already, create a folder on your computer that contains only your file(s).**

   You can put the folder anywhere. You can put it on your desktop, in your My Documents folder, or wherever makes sense to you. Make sure this folder contains only the file(s) you want to share.

2. **Run the Official BitTorrent client.**

3. **Choose File⇨Make New Torrent.**

   The BitTorrent Metafile Creator window appears.

4. **Click Add.**

   The Select File window appears.

5. **Locate the file(s) on your computer and click OK.**

   You can choose a single file, or you can select an entire folder of content to share. Depending on what you are sharing, you may want to create a torrent for a single file, or one that shares a bunch of related files at the same time, like a photo collection.

6. **If you want to share an entire folder, locate the folder and click Select Folder, as shown in Figure 10-1.**

7. **Select your torrent piece size.**

   If you're not sure how small to make the piece, go ahead and select the default setting. The sidebar, "Blowing torrent files to pieces," later in this chapter, offers more information about how piece sizes work.

8. **To use the BitTorrent client as your tracker, select the DHT radio button.**

   If you want to use a tracker Web site as your tracker, click the Use Tracker radio button and enter the tracker URL in the text box. You can read more about using tracker services and setting up your own tracker later in this chapter.

9. **Click the Make button, as shown in Figure 10-2.**

   The Official BitTorrent client creates a torrent file in the same place as your media file(s). When the file is done, the Done window appears.

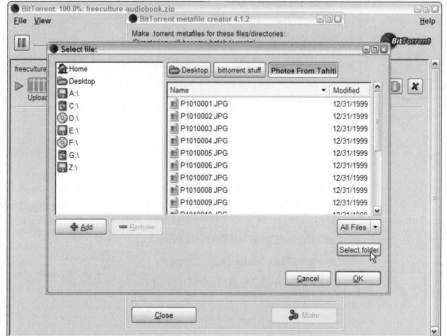

Figure 10-1:
You can use
the Official
BitTorrent
client to
create
torrent files
from a
single file
or from a
collection
of files.

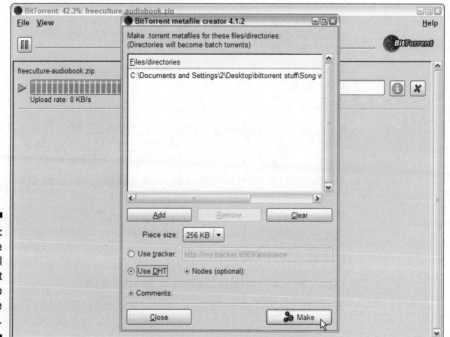

Figure 10-2:
You can use
the Official
BitTorrent
client to
create
torrent files.

10. **If you want to seed your file now, click Start Seeding. If you want to seed your file later, click OK.**

    For more on seeding, read Chapter 11.

When trying to share a large collection of files, many users find it helpful to compress them into a single ZIP file or RAR file (ZIP and RAR are the most common file compression file types). While this is an easy step from an organizational point of view, remember that creating an archive file adds an extra step for the person downloading the content. Because users still have to decompress the file(s) when downloading is complete, things are just a little bit harder. If your potential audience is likely to have problems figuring out how to decompress an archive file, you should simply create a torrent for the folder containing all your files instead of compressing all the files into a single archive. When users download your files, they end up with a handy folder of your content.

Making a torrent with Azureus

Azureus (`azureus.sourceforge.net`) is a very popular Java-based torrent software application that runs on almost every kind of computer platform there is. You can use this free program to download torrent files and also use it to make torrent files.

One of the nice benefits of this program is that it uses a list of trackers within the software that are updated automatically each time the program starts, so you may find newer and larger tracker systems when generating each of your torrent files. You can also use Azureus itself as the tracker.

Blowing torrent files to pieces

BitTorrent is powerful in part because it breaks files into *pieces,* creating smaller chunks of data to be passed around the network. When all these pieces are assembled you have a complete file.

When creating a torrent file, you get to choose how large its pieces are. Because the files are traded by numerous people, you want to make them as easy to transport as possible. Breaking the files into small, manageable bits prevents slow network connections. BitTorrent pieces enable users to download different parts of the file from different locations. Getting files from multiple locations means that the whole process uses less bandwidth.

When it comes to making your own torrents, you should feel free to experiment with piece size. Remember that larger pieces can cause higher bandwidth loads. Having too many tiny pieces to find and download can also cause problems during downloading. As a beginning user, you may want to stick with the default setting (usually 256KB).

Another benefit for this package is the fact that it is created in the multiplatform Java language. You need to install the Java Runtime Environment in order to use Azureus, but don't let this step scare you! The program walks you through the installation process. This additional functionality makes Azureus the most portable package around, with versions for nearly every type of operating system.

The only downside to using Azureus is that it's almost too complete. It contains numerous and confusing options, which are almost guaranteed to put new users off balance. Azureus is the program to use after you're comfortable making and sharing BitTorrent files.

Use these directions to create a torrent with Azureus:

1. **Run Azureus.**

2. **Choose File⇨New Torrent.**

   The Make a Torrent window opens.

3. **Decide whether you want to use the embedded Azureus tracker or whether you want to use an external tracker instead.**

   For more information on trackers, please read Chapter 11.

   If you want to use the embedded tracker, but can't select it, you may need to turn it on by Selecting Options from the Tools menu, and opening the Tracker preferences.

4. **Select whether you are creating a torrent for a single file or a directory (folder).**

5. **Click Next.**

6. **Use the Browse button to find the file on your computer that you want to create a torrent file for.**

7. **Click Next.**

8. **Use the Browse button to tell Azureus where to save the torrent file.**

9. **Select the piece size you want to use.**

   You can find out more about piece sizes in the sidebar, "Blowing torrent files to pieces."

10. **Click to add a check mark to the Open the Torrent for Seeding When Done box if you want to seed your file immediately.**

    Need to know more about seeding? Read Chapter 11.

11. **Click Finish, as shown in Figure 10-3.**

    You can seed the file when you're ready by selecting File⇨Open Torrent File (for seeding). . . .

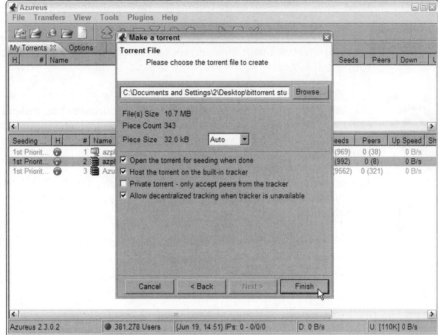

Figure 10-3:
Make a
torrent
quickly and
easily using
Azureus.

Tracking Your Torrents

Trackers keep, well, *track* of all the people who are downloading and seeding a torrent, putting those users with pieces of the file in touch with those who don't yet have those pieces. Clearly, the tracker is a pretty important part of the whole BitTorrent network!

A tracker is usually a piece of software installed on a Web-accessible computer (most often a Web server), and it's sometimes also associated with a Web page that lists torrents the tracker is tracking. You can find tracker Web sites to use or you can install and run a tracker on your own Web site, if you have one.

In the spring of 2005, many of the most popular BitTorrent clients were released with a way to bypass the need for external tracker software. Now these clients themselves act as trackers, greatly decreasing the level of technical skills needed by the average BitTorrent distributor. This new twist in the technology is sometimes referred to as *trackerless* serving, although of course it's a bit of a misnomer, because the tracker is still part of the process even though it is integrated into the client.

Most clients still offer both options — tracker and trackerless distribution. Generally speaking, you get a very simple process when you use the client as a tracker. However, if you use a server-based tracker, you get better statistical information about your files and those who are downloading and uploading them.

If you're new to BitTorrent, or only seeding a few files, I strongly recommend you use a BitTorrent client as the tracker for your files. The Official BitTorrent client can act as a tracker for you. However, if you're interested in finding out about using a public tracker site, or in figuring out how to run your own tracker, this section runs you through the basics.

The process of *serving* up your torrent file using a tracker is a fairly simple one, but it does contain a few points where confusion may get the better of even the most seasoned BitTorrent user.

In fact, for some readers this chapter is the most challenging and frustrating in this book. If you start to feel daunted, remember that you aren't alone in feeling this way.

In Chapter 11 you get help in properly preparing your files — ways to set up file organization, and correctly name files — that can help make the process of keeping tabs on your content easy.

Serving trackerlessly

Many of the popular BitTorrent clients now include torrent creation utilities, and many of these also offer trackerless torrent serving. The differences between the clients are small, and in this section I describe how to use the trackerless serving option. You can adapt the information in this section to the client you choose to use.

To serve a file trackerlessly, you need:

- ✔ A computer with extended periods of Internet access, preferably always-on broadband access like DSL or a cable modem.
- ✔ A way of getting people to your file, like a static IP address. (See the sidebar, "Psst, buddy. Want a static IP?" in this chapter for more information.)

Assuming you have both these requirements and have mastered the ability to create a torrent with your BitTorrent client, you only need to worry about seeding your files properly. There is information about seeding in Chapter 11.

TECHNICAL STUFF

Psst, buddy. Want a static IP?

Every computer connected to a computer network has an *IP address*. When you sign on to the Internet at home, your Internet service provider may assign an IP number to you at that point, in which case you have a dynamic IP address — one that is probably different every time you sign on. A static IP address is one that is yours whether your computer is online or not.

Static IP addresses for a home Internet connection are rare. Your computer's IP address may change weekly, monthly, or even daily, depending on how your ISP handles its servers and clients.

Trackers rely on static IP addresses. If you're running a tracker and a BitTorrent user makes a request of your tracker, the tracker needs to know exactly which computer has the data being requested, and the only way for it to reach your computer is if your IP address is the same as it was when the torrent was created. Before you pick up the phone to call your ISP about getting a static IP address, which will cost you a bit of money, consider using a *dynamic name service,* which is free.

There are a few dynamic name service (or DNS) providers out there that host name services for free. What's in a name? Since your dynamic IP address can change on a semi-regular basis, dynamic name services like DynDNS (www. dyndns.org) or EveryDNS (www.everydns. net) enable home users to assign a name to their particular IP address — when your home computer IP address changes, your DNS address changes, too!

Thus, if you have an IP address of 192.168. 1.100 and your dynamic name service assigns a name to it like jerrystracker.homeip. net, you won't have to worry about your tracker getting lost when your IP address eventually changes. If your Internet service provider changes your IP address to 192.168.1.200, your dynamic name service changes your IP address, and people can still find your tracker at jerrystracker.homeip.net — and you don't have to do anything to make it all happen.

The default setup of the DynDNS (or any other free service like it) is that you have to go to the DynDNS site to update your IP address manually. But, you can also get a software package that updates your address at regular intervals. Your DNS service provider has a list of them and instructions on how to install them. There are also alternatives with firewalls and routers.

More often, firewalls and routers offer built-in functionality for DynDNS and several other dynamic name services. Each time the IP address changes on your firewall, the firewall tells the dynamic name service that your address has changed.

Anyone who has a computer connected to the Internet has an IP address, and having a static address means you can more easily be found by hackers and viruses. Before you consider getting a static IP address, make sure you have a firewall to protect your computer. *Firewalls For Dummies,* 2nd Edition, by Brian Komar, Ronald Beekelaar, and Joern Wettern (Wiley) is a good source of information on choosing, installing, and setting up a firewall. If you want to find out more about IP addresses, read *TCP/IP For Dummies,* 5th Edition, by Candace Leiden, Marshall Wilensky, and Scott Bradner (Wiley).

Using a public tracker

Using a public tracker is a great solution for BitTorrent distributors who want a quick fix to the tracker problem. You can find many public tracker sites out there to choose from that track torrent files at no cost, requiring only registration for you to use them.

To serve a file using a public tracker you need:

✔ A computer with extended periods of Internet access, preferably always-on broadband access like DSL or a cable modem.

✔ Access to a public tracker.

✔ A way of getting people to your file, like a static IP address. (See the sidebar, "Psst, buddy. Want a static IP?" for more information.)

Remember that public trackers come and go because most of them are run by individuals. Check on your files often if you use a public tracker to make sure the site is still active and that your files are listed.

Because public trackers are in the business of matching files with those who seek them, they can be the subject of legal action when they host files that infringe copyright.

A few public trackers to begin with are:

✔ TorrentSpy.com (www.torrentspy.com)

✔ Torrent Reactor (www.torrentreactor.net)

✔ TorrentTyphoon (www.torrenttyphoon.com)

✔ The Pirate Bay (www.thepiratebay.org)

There are public tracker sites dedicated to particular subjects, or types of content. For example, the tracker site bt.etree.org shares live concert recordings by trade-friendly artists. Do a little research to find a tracker that suits you. You can find a list of trackers at www.bamber.org/wiki/ow.asp? LinksTorrents#h1.

Using a public tracker when you create a torrent with the Official BitTorrent client is pretty simple:

1. **Find a public tracker to use.**

2. **Check the tracker site's terms of use to make sure you don't need permission and that your content is appropriate.**

Visit the tracker Web site and check for a Terms of Use agreement. Some trackers, though public, put limits on the kinds of content they accept. Others require that you get permission before announcing your content with their tracker. You may need to register, as well.

3. **While making your torrent, select Use Tracker and type the tracker address.**

   The tracker site you choose provides documentation providing this address.

4. **Begin seeding using your BitTorrent client.**

   There is information on seeding in Chapter 11.

5. **Go to the tracker site and search for your file to make sure that it's listed.**

   Better yet, try to download your torrent yourself to make sure that everything is working properly.

Using a public tracker is a fairly straight-forward way to submit your tracking information. After you submit the file, it's searchable. People all over the Internet using the same tracker can connect and download your media file(s). If you want to be sure your torrent file is reaching as many people as possible, you can submit your file to multiple trackers.

Some torrent creation software packages make the process of announcing your files to trackers very simple. They actually list public trackers when you create the torrent, and you can simply select one. You can sometimes even choose to have the program submit automatically to a whole series of public trackers.

Submitting your torrent to a series of trackers automatically means you know just where your information is being submitted. Great! On other hand, not all public trackers are being used for legal purposes; many trackers cater to nothing but those looking to download illegally available copyrighted materials like TV shows and movies. These sites are open to legal attack, and often go offline — along with your tracking information. You probably prefer not to associate your content with pirated material, so do your homework before you pick a tracking site.

Running your own tracker

Using a trackerless BitTorrent client works — but only as long as you can keep your computer connected to the Internet. Public trackers are easy to use, but can go offline without warning. For a completely reliable tracking solution, the best option is to set up and run your own tracker. A tracker is a great idea conceptually, but when it comes to actually setting it up . . . well, here there be dragons.

Running your own tracker gives you ultimate control over where your torrent files live and how long they stay available, but a personal tracker is also something that requires attention and needs to be maintained.

To serve a file using your own tracker you need:

✔ A computer with extended periods of Internet access, preferably always-on broadband access like DSL or a cable modem.

✔ A Web site where you can install and run your tracker. If you need information on setting up a Web site where you can host your tracker, look at the section, "Taking advantage of Web hosting options," later in this chapter.

✔ Tracker software.

✔ A way of getting people to your files. If you are running your own Web site, you can place your files online, or run a BitTorrent client to seed them. If you seed them from your computer, a static IP address is pretty important. (There is more information about static IP addresses in the sidebar, "Psst, buddy. Want a static IP?")

The two main software packages to check out are Blog Torrent and Broadcast Machine. These great server-based software packages enable users to set up their own online torrent server systems with very few resources required.

Installing these packages requires an FTP client and a Web server. You can install this software on almost any Web server. Check with your Web host first before installing to make sure your server space meets the minimum requirements. If you do not have a Web site hosting account, this software may not be for you, and you must to stick to using your trackerless BitTorrent software or a public tracker to manage your torrent files.

Taking advantage of Web hosting options

You must have a Web hosting account in order to run a tracker yourself. To decide what kind of account you need, consider:

✔ Whether you plan to upload your media files and serve them from your Web site. If you do, you need a Web host with lots of disk space to store the files in.

✔ Whether you plan to use the Web site for running the tracker but want to seed your files from your BitTorrent client. If this is the case, you need very little disk space in which to store your files, because you won't be uploading your media files.

✔ Whether the Web host permits you to run a BitTorrent tracker. With all of the negative BitTorrent press running around the media these days (much of it filled with incorrect information about BitTorrent technology), many Web hosts don't want to allow torrent hosting. Some fear being named in copyright lawsuits, while others want to avoid dealing with the technical overhead and bandwidth issues that might be involved. (Serving BitTorrent files always involves some bandwidth overhead, even if it's less than what would be required to serve the same files in other ways.)

✔ Whether the Web hosting account is compatible with the tracker you want to install. Be sure to check the server requirements for the tracker. If in doubt, send the requirements to the Web host's technical support center and ask if the software will work on its system.

Of course, you can find many "free" Web hosting solutions out there. Places like Yahoo! GeoCities (geocities.yahoo.com) and Doteasy (www.doteasy.com) offer very minimal options for free Web hosting services. These solutions should work well for storing torrent files, because the files are quite small. A free Web host is not a good choice if you plan to serve your files from the Web server, since you will need more disk storage than is typically available with these kinds of accounts.

To use Doteasy's free hosting service you must purchase a .com, .net, or .org domain for $30. You get 100MB of space, which is plenty of room for a torrent listing. This solution works well for hosting torrents and Web pages, but the technical specifications of the server mean you probably can't install a tracker.

The more you know, the better your Web host decision will be. Shop around, see what is out there, and make sure the system you choose allows you to serve BitTorrent files. Not all Web hosts are willing to permit you to host a BitTorrent tracker.

Use a file transfer program (FTP) to install your tracker software and to put your torrent files online. You use an HTML file with links to those torrents so that people can easily get to your content.

Using Blog Torrent

Blog Torrent (www.blogtorrent.com) is, as the Web site claims, "awesome." The software is simple to use and is highly effective. Blog Torrent makes posting video, audio, images, and document torrents online easy, creating a network of true peer-to-peer content sharing using the BitTorrent technology.

The process works like this:

1. **Download and install Blog Torrent, following the instructions included with Blog Torrent.**

2. **Point your Web browser to the Blog Torrent directory on your server and set up a user account.**

3. **Create torrent files that use your new tracker.**

4. **Seed your files using your BitTorrent client.**

Finding cool hosting services

Here are a couple of Web sites to check out:

✔ **1&1 Internet, Inc.** (www.1and1.com) is a hosting service from Europe that has recently begun offering hosting services in North America. The company has several Web hosting packages that are affordable and are good places for BitTorrent files to live.

✔ **Nexcess.net** (www.nexcess.net) is a hosting service offering excellent customer service that is willing to host BitTorrent trackers and files at affordable rates.

That's it. After you set up your first account (and assuming you haven't received any obvious errors on your screen) you are ready to start setting up your first series of torrent files.

Installing and running a tracker requires a certain amount of familiarity with Web sites, especially uploading files. If you're new to creating Web pages, consider *Creating Web Pages For Dummies,* 7th Edition, by Bud E. Smith (Wiley).

After Blog Torrent is installed and running successfully, you can log in to the Blog Torrent system to begin using the tracker. You can upload torrent files to the Blog Torrent tracker by using the Upload a File link on the tracker's Web pages.

One innovation you may enjoy about Blog Torrent is that you don't have to create a torrent file. Simply upload the file you want to share, and Blog Torrent creates the torrent file and links to it automatically.

Use these quick directions to upload a torrent file using the Blog Torrent tracker:

1. **Go to the Blog Torrent Web page.**

2. **Click Upload a File.**

   Blog Torrent automatically opens the Upload window.

3. **Select the torrent file you wish to upload to the system, as shown in Figure 10-4.**

4. **Click Open.**

   The client uploads the torrent file.

Now, here is the real magic. After you upload your torrent, all you need to do is tell people where your Web site is; Blog Torrent takes care of the rest. All torrent offerings are listed on the front page of the site, which provides users with links to your torrent files. That is all there is to using the Blog Torrent software.

Using Broadcast Machine

Broadcast Machine (www.participatoryculture.org/bm) is a software solution (borne from the open-source code of Blog Torrent) that has numerous innovative features. Broadcast Machine has built some exciting functionality into its system, and, even more importantly, adds a superior interface.

Broadcast Machine is focused on publishing video, so if you're into publishing music, it might not be the right tracker for you. Even if you're focused on television and video, you may need to adapt a little bit to how things are done. Broadcast Machine's goal is to publish video into Internet television *channels.* You divide your video content into categorized sections. You can have multiple channels and organize them pretty much any way you want.

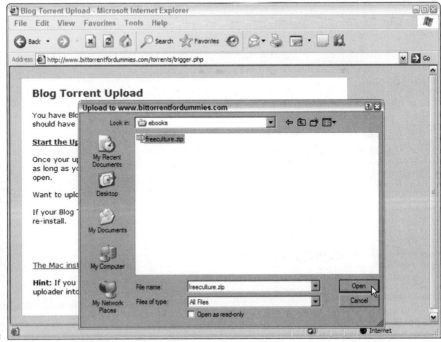

Figure 10-4: Blog Torrent uses a simple file selection box to facilitate uploads.

Installing Broadcast Machine is similar to installing Blog Torrent (as described in the previous section, "Using Blog Torrent."):

1. **Download and install the software package from Broadcast Machine's Web site.**

2. **Upload the program to your Web space.**

3. **Direct your browser window to the software and set up your first user.**

The quickest way to publish information to Broadcast Machine is to upload the files to the system itself, as shown in Figure 10-5. You can enter in as much information as you want to describe the files and make them more searchable.

Because using Broadcast Machine isn't for the novice, these steps give you just a bird's-eye view of how this tracker software works. For more information on Web publishing, check out *Creating Web Pages For Dummies,* 7th Edition, by Bud E. Smith (Wiley) and the Broadcast Machine documentation.

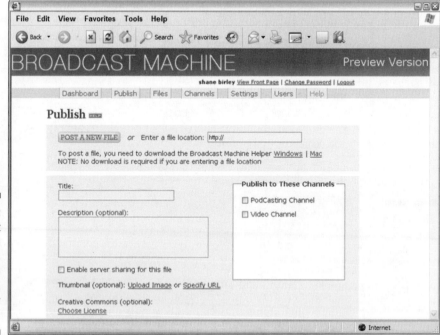

Figure 10-5:
Broadcast Machine has an easy-to-use publishing interface for new files.

Chapter 11

Seeding Your Torrents

. . . .

In This Chapter

▶ Making sure your file is available

▶ Covering seeding basics

▶ Organizing files like a pro

▶ Observing BitTorrent best practices

. . . .

Distributing your carefully created content through the BitTorrent net-work requires you to *seed* it. Seeding isn't terribly difficult, but it can be tricky to know when to seed and to choose the best way to do it. This chapter helps you get around the obstacles so that you can seed your own torrent files.

Although BitTorrent has been available for quite some time, it has only recently begun to hit the radar of mainstream computer users. That means its early years have been spent in the hands of experienced technical folks. The natural evolution of BitTorrent is taking it from a nerd tool to one of the most efficient and popular person-to-person protocols. Expect to see some exciting changes and efficiencies in coming months and years.

Until then, however, you and I are stuck with how things work today. In this chapter, I make you aware of some of the pitfalls of seeding your torrent files. I discuss the techniques and the technology, the processes and what you need to know in order to make your torrent available on the Internet.

Seeding Your Torrent

Seeding is the process of ensuring that there's a full version of the file you are sharing somewhere on the Internet. It's also the final step in BitTorrent distribution. You can't make your torrents available to others without seeding. This is a somewhat surprising statement, perhaps. After all, you've created torrents and gotten them noticed by a tracker. How is it that your torrents aren't already available?

If you are using a tracker, your file is announced by the tracker, and can be requested by others. But for the request to be met, the torrent must be seeded. You can seed the file yourself, and should, in order to make it possible for others to download the file and also become seeders.

After the file is seeded a few times, it's shared around the BitTorrent network. Now, every subsequent time you connect to the BitTorrent network, your file is presented for download, and you are a source for the complete file for other BitTorrent users. The same is true of anyone else who is sharing your file. But, you can't rely on other users to keep seeding your file. You may need to do it yourself. The more often you seed your file, the better distribution you get.

Some BitTorrent clients enable you to begin seeding the torrent file as soon as you create it. This is a good option, but you can (and should) always *reseed* the file when you think it is necessary. To see if you need to reseed, click the link to your torrent using a BitTorrent client — like BitTornado, shown in Figure 11-1 — that provides information about the file *swarm* (those sharing the file). If two or more seeders are online, you don't need to reseed at that time.

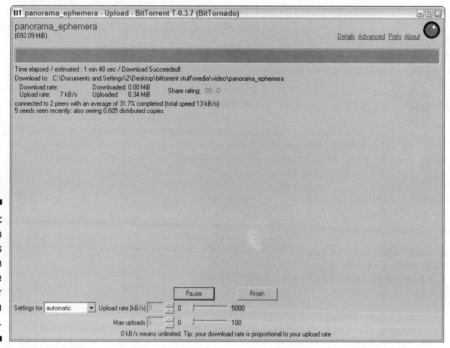

Figure 11-1:
BitTornado shows information about the swarm for the file you are seeding.

To seed your file, follow these steps:

1. **Click the torrent link for your file, whether it is on a Web page, your tracker, or a public tracker.**

   If you are using a public tracker, this link is on the tracker Web site. If you're hosting your own tracker, the link is on your own Web site.

   Your BitTorrent client launches.

2. **Tell the client where the file is by selecting the location on your computer.**

   The process of seeding, or transferring, begins at that point. When the file is uploaded and successfully shared to a few other people, it is fully seeded.

Continuously Seeding Your Files for Best Results

What makes the BitTorrent network function is the premise that file popularity grows steadily over time. As a file becomes more popular, it is more readily available from several locations around the world, with people continually sharing it for an extended period.

Files do sometimes disappear, especially those that are not as commonly downloaded. Often, these files are located on home computers which, from time to time, get shut off. But, with multiple seeds out on the Web, files are less and less likely to disappear.

To keep your files constantly seeded, keep your BitTorrent client running at all times, always seeding your files. If you can't keep your computer on and connected to the Internet all the time, be sure to seed whenever you're connected.

Another way to make your files more accessible is to place the actual media files (and not just the torrent files) on your own Web site. Because Web servers are usually online all the time, your files remain seeded. For more information on finding an appropriate Web hosting company, see Chapter 10.

Keeping Seeding Simple

The information in this chapter of the book can get a little confusing. The processes you need to follow tend to be straightforward, but because of the nature of the BitTorrent beast, some of the details are inherently hard to understand.

Looking into the BitTorrent crystal ball

A couple of exciting changes to the way BitTorrent works are on the horizon, so keep your eyes open.

The first trend on the horizon is a trackerless network. Trackers keep a listing of the files they have available and allow people to search their listings. You can think about a tracker like you do a computer desktop shortcut. Trackers, like desktop shortcuts, point to where the files are. But, just as you can easily delete shortcuts, trackers can be deleted — inadvertently or through technical error. You can't be a very good content publisher if your content isn't available. The video of your best friend's cat simply must be there when the night owl in Sweden tries to download it. If your tracker is down, or the public tracker you use loses your data, your Swedish friend may be out of luck. This inherent unreliability is one of the aspects of BitTorrent that long-time users consistently complain about. The ideal is to create a completely trackerless world.

In a trackerless world, every BitTorrent client on the Internet becomes a tracker. This way, there's no need for central tracker locations, making searching, uploading, and downloading torrent media more efficient and reliable.

A drawback for a trackerless world is that because users can't authenticate the quality of the tracker data, users may receive more broken or nonexistent links. But, overall, distributed tracker data is the future of the BitTorrent systems.

Another exciting development is a tool Microsoft is developing, currently called Avalanche. In the early summer of 2005, Microsoft released a press release indicating that it is working on its own "BitTorrent-like" person-to-person file-sharing protocol. (The name can be expected to change before the program is released, so don't be surprised if you hear program discussed by some other title.)

There is very little information on this tool at this time, but what is most exciting is that it proves that if big boys like Microsoft are paying attention, then BitTorrent is not just a nerd tool — it is a feasible file-sharing system. Because BitTorrent efficiently transfers information over the Internet, you can expect to see torrent-like tools to become more common in the coming years.

And, of course, you have several options to sort through. The choices you make depend upon your technical skill and how important it is to you that your files remain alive within the BitTorrent swarm.

Using these rules will give you a relatively stress-free experience using the BitTorrent network:

✔ Stay connected to the Internet so that you can seed and re-seed any files you have set up on a tracker.

✔ Use public trackers like TorrentSpy (www.torrentspy.com) and TorrentTyphoon (www.torrenttyphoon.com) to make sure that the tracking of your media files is as current as possible. This additional coverage can make a big difference in the lifespan of your torrents.

✔ Decide whether you want to seed your files using your BitTorrent client or whether you want to go to the trouble of setting up a Web site where you can place the files. If you do, your files remain seeded as long as they are on the Web site, but they can consume a lot of space in your Web hosting account.

✔ Use a single tool for your BitTorrent download, torrent creation, and seeding to keep the process as simple as possible. A good option for beginners is the Official BitTorrent client, available at www.bittorrent.com.

Whatever method you use to share your files, as long as you make a torrent file, send that information to a tracker or use your client to server tracker-lessly, make sure your computer is connected to the Internet, and keep your BitTorrent client open long enough to seed onto the network, you shouldn't have many problems.

Making Torrent Management Easier

You can make torrents by following the steps in Chapter 10. The process is relatively easy, and before you know it, you'll be seeding all kinds of cool files that you want to share with the world. But before you seed too many torrent files, you should know some details about how to make a proper torrent file.

You see, for the last two years, a rash of bad torrent files has infested the BitTorrent network. These files have been downloaded and then deleted from computer systems all over the world because those who created them didn't take the time to do things properly during the torrent file creation phase. Don't let that happen to you! Follow the advice in the following sections to make sure that when people click links to your torrents they can access your files.

Naming your files the smart way

All torrent makers everywhere need to know a few things when they name their files. (This is actually information you can apply to naming any files on any computer system for any purpose.) For some reason, naming rules are often ignored, even by savvy computer users. Computer users' attitudes are lax partly because many computer systems are so flexible about how files are named; your computer may let you to leave off file extensions and create 45-letter filenames, but other computers may not understand these filenames.

When you create files for Internet distribution, leave your personal choices at the door, and opt for straightforward names that make things easier for people and computers.

Here are some naming tips to remember:

✔ **Use lowercase letters.** Some people hate using only lowercase letters when naming their files. You may even prefer to name files with proper grammar: `PHOTO OF SUSIE'S LITTLE, YELLOW CAR.jpg`. One of the basic arguments for using lowercase letters is that some computers ignore filenames with all capital letters. If you use all capital letters, your filenames may not be usable on certain computers. Keep reading this list for punctuation rules in filenames.

✔ **Keep names short and simple.** The purpose of a good filename is to provide a brief, descriptive label of the file's contents. It shouldn't be a full-length sentence that offers a complete description. Make use of single words, dates, and descriptors to create effective filenames. For example, try a name like `050104photo_rover.jpg` for a picture of your dog (taken on a lovely, sunny day in May 2004) and avoid a name like `mydoglovesthesunandwatchhimeatbugsrightoutoftheair.jpg`.

Using long descriptions, or entire sentences, in your filenames is never good practice. Most computers truncate extremely long filenames, so much of your description may never even be seen. Save your descriptions for the Web page on which you create a link to the file.

Limit filenames to 8 to 20 characters. This way, the filename has a good chance of working on all computer systems.

✔ **Forget punctuation.** You should never use punctuation in filenames, with a couple of exceptions: underscores and dashes. Use only alpha (abc) or numeric (123) characters. Most operating systems prevent you from using punctuation in filenames, and many more simply choke on files that use unusual characters. You *cannot* use any of the following: `" \ / : * < > ? _`. Your computer may allow you to use a period (.) in more than one spot in the filename, but you should only use it once, just before the file extension.

✔ **Always use filename extensions.** Filename extensions enable computers (and people) to recognize what programs to use to open the files. If the file extensions are valid, computer operating systems know exactly what they are and instantly know what software can open the file.

These are common file extensions: `.doc`, `.xls`, `.pps`, `.jpg`, `.gif`, `.txt`, `.rtf`, `.tif`, `.mp3`, `.mov`, `.avi`, `.aif`, `.wav`, and `.ppt`. You probably see these every day on your own computer. If an extension is removed and forgotten, a computer doesn't know what the file is and won't open it. Never remove extensions when making torrent files.

Some computers hide file extensions even when they are part of the filename, and others tend not to include the file extension as a default when the file is saved. If your system performs this annoying favor for you, you can change your settings so that the extensions appear. In Windows XP, open Windows Explorer and Select Tools⇨Folder Options. In the Folder

Options window, click the View tab. Click the Hide Extensions for Known Filenames check box so that no check mark appears in the box.

✔ **Never use spaces.** Some computer systems love to hate spaces in computer filenames. They don't recognize them, and filenames come out looking very strange. Instead of leaving spaces, use an underscore (_). Underscores make filenames easier to read. For example, `photo_smart_dog.jpg` is easier to read on just about every computer system than `photosmartdog.jpg`.

Managing your files

Place your shared files into a single directory, or folder. Using the folder system is the easiest way to keep track of the files you want to share and ensure that files are where you think they are. If you spread out torrents and media files all over your computer, you will lose track of what you need to seed, what is old, and what you haven't even opened yet.

Managing your files is like taming a large closet filled with 30 years of memories and garbage. Get it under control, and get rid of stuff you don't need anymore.

Before you make a torrent file, you should organize a special directory that's dedicated strictly to files you are sharing and their related torrents. This way you ensure that all of your files are in one place, and you won't accidentally move them or delete them. *Note:* It's especially important that you *leave* files you're seeding alone. If you move them, your BitTorrent client won't be able to find them. Organizing the files is as simple as creating a simple directory structure. This structure may be divided up into the types of files. One directory could be dedicated to MP3 files, while another could house all of your shared video files. Making this distinction between the file types provides a sensible layout for later archiving to a blank CD or DVD. In Figure 11-2, you can see how I organize my files. Don't be afraid to group similar files in subfolders.

Make sure that you go to the trouble of organizing your media files before you start making torrents. I recommend the following file structure:

> Main folder: BitTorrent Media Files
>> Subfolder: Audio Files
>> Subfolder: Video Files
>> Subfolder: Photos
>> Subfolder: eBooks

In each subfolder you can create sub-subfolders for files you want to keep together.

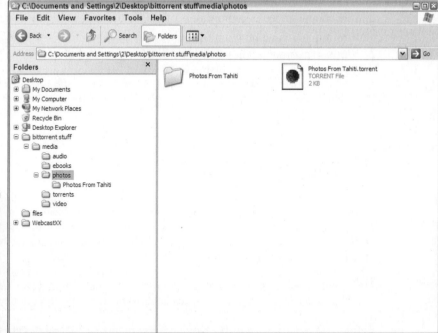

Figure 11-2:
Keeping
your files
organized
in folders
makes them
easy to find
and seed.

Using simple techniques for sensible filenames and keeping a record of the files you share in an organized directory structure go far in keeping files alive on the BitTorrent system. That'll make the people who receive your files happy. Likewise, you'll be happy if you can share your own songs, poetry, programming projects, and videos of you hamming it up at your sister's wedding without any hassle. In short, if you put in just the smallest effort, you can be a BitTorrent hero.

Maintaining netiquette

These are some simple rules that you can follow when you're making your own torrent files. If you follow these rules, you will be a star of the BitTorrent network and make other torrent sharers very happy.

Leeching is not nice

Torrent file sharing is something that, if done with respect to other users on BitTorrent networks, benefits everyone. The BitTorrent network runs on the principle of community sharing and respect.

TIP

Following torrent best practices

File-sharing technologies can easily be abused, or disabled, by not following some of the standard best practices. I've gathered a few do's and don'ts here that you should know about:

✔ **Do always select names that make sense to everyone (and not just you)!** A file called `day_at_the_beach.mov` makes a lot more sense than `xxr889thn.mov`. Straightforward naming helps everyone recognize the file for what it is, and no guessing is required.

✔ **Don't compress files into some kind of archive format that no one has heard of.** Most media files (like MP3 and AVI files) are

already compressed and won't shrink any further. When in doubt, compress the file using a standard format like ZIP or RAR and compare the file size of the archive with the original file.

✔ **Don't put extra files in your torrents.** Sometimes BitTorrent users place extra files into their torrent file that other users aren't expecting. This activity is (rightfully) considered suspicious!

✔ **Don't ever send viruses across BitTorrent networks.** Make sure to scan all the files you create and share with antivirus software before placing them into a torrent file.

To that end, if you're connected to the BitTorrent network long enough to complete a download of a file you really want, you should remain connected to the network long enough to share the wealth. Turning off the BitTorrent client and making those files inaccessible is called *leeching,* and users who make files inaccessible are known as *leeches* because they download as much as they want and then refuse to share anything.

REMEMBER

BitTorrent networks only operate at peak efficiency when users are connected to the Internet. Each file is shared around in tiny bits, making transfers quick and efficient. But, when you're not sharing with the rest of the users, this efficiency drops significantly.

There are no BitTorrent police who come to your door and request that you turn on your software client, but no one likes a leech, so help out the BitTorrent family and keep your client running and your computer connected to the Internet, even when you're not downloading content.

Staying cool with copyright

Do not, under any circumstances, torrent copyrighted materials. Only share torrent files for public domain and content that you create. If you're sending copyrighted materials across BitTorrent networks, you may hurt yourself, other users, your ISP, and ultimately, the entire BitTorrent network. Owners of that copyrighted material can, and often do, take legal action against those who illegally share their material.

You will find many out there who use the BitTorrent network to share files illegally — but you don't have to be so unoriginal. Isn't it fun to make and share your own stuff? Show off your guitar savvy, or set up a microphone and start your own radio program. Draw some awesome art and share it. Making a name for yourself as a content generator is much more exciting.

For more information about how downloading or sharing copyrighted material can affect you legally, read Chapter 6.

Chapter 12

Promoting Your Torrents

· ·

In This Chapter

▶ Remembering the basics

▶ Getting a Web site or blog

▶ Submitting a press release

▶ Taking advantage of basic Web site promotion tools

▶ Advertising on blogs and Web sites

· ·

*F*iguring out all the technology behind producing a film or audio broadcast, and then solving the technical puzzle of sharing that content using BitTorrent — those are tremendous accomplishments. But it's easy to forget that there is one more step in successfully sharing that content with others, and that is letting them know about it.

Marketing and promotion are the all-important follow-through tasks for any publisher, whether you're creating content alone in your garage or you're the BBC, a media organization that publishes content all over the world. If people don't know about your film, audio, book, photo collection . . . well, no one can benefit from what you have created.

This chapter is organized around helping you market and promote your digital content. Because you are creating files to be distributed with BitTorrent, I focus on Web and Internet marketing strategies, but don't overlook the offline world. You can advertise what you're doing outside of the Internet, as well. For example, you can use print advertising, attend networking events, or print and distribute stickers, to name just a few possibilities.

Online, however, your first task is to get yourself set up with a Web site, and then to use some tried-and-true optimization and marketing strategies to get yourself and your content known.

Remembering the Basics

A couple of important puzzle pieces have to be in place before even the most aggressive promotion plan in the world can work. First, you simply have to have created good content to begin with. And, of course, the technical aspects of getting it delivered to people need to be functioning correctly.

Creating good content

A good marketing plan can't save bad content. Always do the best job possible with what you create. *Some* people download a lot of BitTorrent content knowing that the files they end up with might not be perfect. For example, the version of *Star Wars Episodes III: Revenge of the Sith* that was going around the Internet at the time the film was released in theaters displayed a large counter at the top of the picture — evidence that the film had been pirated. You've heard the phrase "Beggars can't be choosers"? Well, thieves can't, either. Most of those who downloaded that torrent understood that the file hadn't been legally acquired and distributed, but were willing to put up with the counter in order to have a free copy of the film.

But for legally available content, the standard is different (especially if you charge money for it). Videos should have excellent picture quality; both videos and audio should sound excellent; photographs should be high-resolution, in focus, and color-corrected. Written materials should be spell-checked and use proper grammar. You get the idea.

Getting the technology right

It goes without saying that one important part of delivering BitTorrent online is to use the technology correctly. Don't forget these important technical steps to making and keeping your content available:

- ✓ **Seeding your content.** Seeding your content is the process of letting the tracker software you use know about your file, and where it can be found. As others download full copies of the file, they themselves become seeders, so it's important to seed your content yourself, and keep on doing so until at least two other seeds are online.

- ✓ **Checking to make sure seeds are still available.** Over time all the seeds of your content may stop being shared. In fact files have lifespans just like living organisms; as a file's popularity diminishes, as people clean off their hard drives or delete files they're done with, and so on, the files fade from existence. Be sure to get online to check periodically that at least a couple seeds of your content are still available.

The easiest way to do this is to start a torrent session and begin the download process. In Figure 12-1, you can see the swarm information (three seeds and one peer) for a file being downloaded using the BitTornado client.

✔ **Reseed when necessary.** If you don't have enough seeds of your content, you can reseed the content yourself.

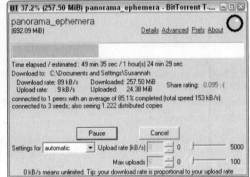

Figure 12-1:
BitTornado displays the current number of available seeds, and any peers that are currently acquiring the file.

If you need to review opening up your BitTorrent client and using it to point at and seed your file, or how to create your torrent, I suggest you turn to Chapter 11.

Getting a Web Site or Blog

Material that you want to promote online needs a place to live, and that, of course, is on a Web site. The type of site you choose to create may vary, depending on what you have produced and how serious you are about making a name for yourself as an artist, videographer, or musician, but at a minimum you should:

✔ **Buy your own domain name.** Domain names are inexpensive to purchase, and give you a unique Web identity. You can keep the name as long as you need it, and owning it means that no one else can use it.

Choose a name that it easy to remember, unique, and easy to spell. GoDaddy (shown in Figure 12-2), Network Solutions, and Dotster are all domain registrars you can use to look up availability of domain names, and then purchase them.

✔ **Get Web hosting.** A Web host is the Web server where your pages actually sit, and there are hundreds of options out there. Remember that if you plan to place your digital content online, you need to find Web hosting that can accommodate very large files. You can find free Web hosts, pay for hosting services, or, if you're super-serious (and *very* geeky), set up your own Web server. There is more information on setting up Web hosting in Chapter 11.

✔ **Publish an attractive, easy-to-use set of Web pages.** The type of Web site you create to promote your content will vary, depending on your content and how you want to use your Web site. For instance, a documentary film Web site might include small clips of the film that are watchable on the Web, a synopsis of the film, and a photo gallery, as well as the link to the torrent.

If you want to regularly publish audio torrents of a certain type — say, political commentary — you may choose to post each new torrent using a blog format. Each entry might describe the contents of the torrent, or include a text transcript, provide a link to the torrent, and of course give people a chance to leave feedback. (I talk more about using blogs to promote your torrents later in this chapter.)

Whatever you choose, concentrate on creating a Web site that is easy for people to use, puts important content high up on the page, has a clear navigation system, and works with the most common Web browsers, including Internet Explorer, Netscape, Mozilla, and, of course Opera.

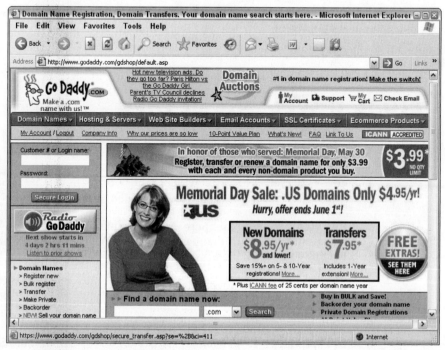

Figure 12-2:
The domain registrar GoDaddy allows you to check availability and purchase domain names.

Optimizing your content for search engines

One of the ways that people use to find content is by looking it up in search engines, or looking up keywords that you use on your Web site. The higher your site shows up in the list of search engine results, the more likely it is that people will find and visit your Web site. You can see a listing of Google search engine results in Figure 12-3.

The process of setting up your Web site to show up well in search engines is called *search engine optimization,* and although it may not feel much like marketing, it's a very important part of any Internet marketing plan. Here are the basic search engine optimization strategies:

- ✔ **Choose your words carefully.** Search engines use automated indexing tools to look at your Web pages. This means that machines — not humans — are reading your content, so you need to make it easy for the machine to understand what you're talking about (the happy side effect is that you also improve human understanding of your Web site, too!). Use simple, direct language when writing the titles of your pages and the text of each page.

  In addition, give some thought to the terms you think people might use if they were looking for content like yours. Be sure to use those terms, or keywords, on your Web site. You may have different keywords for each page or your Web site, so coming up with good keywords is an ongoing task.

- ✔ **Place your words carefully.** Most search engines give greater importance to words that are in titles, and that are higher on the page, so try to structure your Web pages so that important keywords are in those spots.

  Most search engines count the content on your home page as more important than the content on interior pages. Use words that describe your site on the home page. Avoid creating a home page that only displays an image or an animation, because search engines don't know how to read and understand this material.

- ✔ **Use important words frequently.** The more often you use a keyword, the more strongly a search engine matches your site with that term.

  Be careful! You can't simply use the same word 50 times in a row and call it done (this technique has been tried) because most search engines watch for that kind of abuse and penalize Web sites that use it.

- ✔ **Use keywords that are currently popular.** If you can think of legitimate ways to incorporate current popular search terms, do so. The use of keywords that are in the news, or that people are curious about, brings more people to your site, even if they weren't looking for your page or your content to begin with. Keeping on top of the trends is a good way to capture people who are simply surfing the Web instead of doing more targeted research.

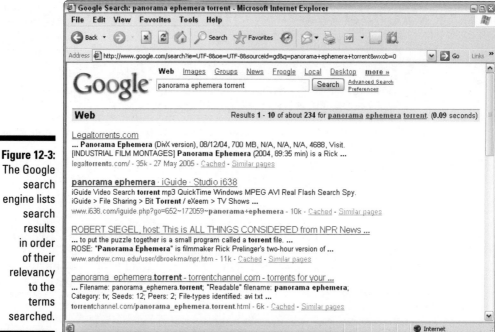

Figure 12-3:
The Google
search
engine lists
search
results
in order
of their
relevancy
to the
terms
searched.

✔ **Encourage others to link to your site.** The more links other Web pages make to your Web site, the more credit a search engine gives you. Basically, the search engine assumes that Web sites with useful information get more links, so they get ranked higher in search engine listings.

Search engine optimization is a big topic that I can only cover briefly here. If this is an important topic for you, I suggest you check out *Search Engine Optimization For Dummies* by Peter Kent (Wiley), and *Google For Dummies* by Brad Hill (Wiley).

Using a blog

The blog format is a great publishing tool for presenting recurring content, so if you plan to create a series of torrents, a blog is a great way to let people know about each new torrent as you make it available. Some of the big benefits to using a blog include:

✔ Your chances for improving search engines rankings increase, because each new post or entry is its own Web page. Having more Web pages means more opportunities for a page to show up in search engine results.

✔ Most blog software includes the ability to create an RSS feed. RSS, or *Really Simple Syndication,* publishes summaries of your posts to the major blog search engine and indexing Web sites like Technorati, increasing the chances of your content being found. As well, many blog readers use RSS feeds in newsreaders, so you can reach a large population quickly.

✔ The blogging community, or *blogosphere,* is all about sharing links and content, so publishing in a blog format, linking to other blogs, and commenting on other blogs, increase the chances that your page will be linked to in return. Those return links mean more eyeballs on your content, and higher search engine rankings overall.

✔ Blog software uses highly developed mechanisms for publishing content, so there is virtually no need for you to learn HTML to create your Web site. The publishing interfaces are quick to use and easy to figure out, and many provide good tools for uploading files.

✔ Most blogging services offer a set of reasonably well-designed templates to choose from, so you can also take care of designing your Web site design by simply starting a blog.

If you're interested in starting a blog, you can get going for free using Blogger, a free blogging service that is shown in Figure 12-4.

Figure 12-4: Blogger is a free blogging service that gets you started quickly.

Want to find out more about blogs? Check out *Buzz Marketing with Blogs For Dummies* by yours truly, Susannah Gardner (Wiley).

Submitting a Press Release

Creating a press release is certainly an old-school way of getting attention, but it's still quite effective. You can even write your own press release. A good way to get started is to find press releases written for similar purposes and use them as models for your own press release.

In general, however, a good press release should:

- ✔ **Get the attention of the reader fast.** Explain what's significant about what you're doing in the first sentence, and don't expect people to read any more than that.

- ✔ **Answer the basic questions.** Include all the facts about what you're doing, why, where, and when. Don't forget to tell people what you want them to do after reading the press release — for instance, visit your Web site.

- ✔ **Include your contact information.** Whenever possible, include a URL, phone number, e-mail address, and other contact information in the press release so that you can be easily reached.

- ✔ **Be short.** Don't create a press release longer than a single 8.5" x 11" page.

- ✔ **Be grammatically correct.** Journalists are often hyper-aware of spelling and grammar mistakes, and they may make judgments about you when they find them.

The point of a press release is to let people and news organizations know about something that is newsworthy, significant, or unique. For instance, announcing your new Web site probably isn't going to attract attention. But if you're doing something innovative or exciting, or if you're covering a topic that is especially important or exciting with your BitTorrent file, a press release may do just the trick to highlight the achievement.

When your press release is finished, a good way to get it into circulation is the use PRWeb, a free newswire service. PRWeb sends your press release to more than 100,000 media contacts and submits it to search engines. PRWeb is online at www.prweb.com, and shown in Figure 12-5.

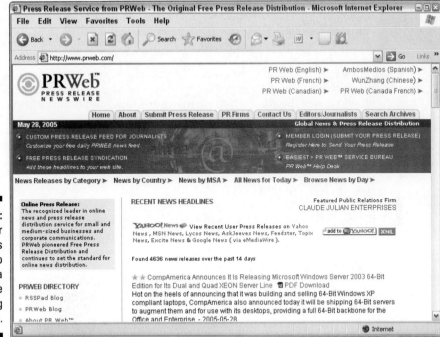

Figure 12-5:
Get your
press
release to
the media
for free
using
PRWeb.

PRWeb even offers a set of writing tips and guidelines for press releases, and a template you can use to get started. Take a look at the press release template in the sidebar, "Sample press release format" in this chapter. You can also send your press release to a mailing list, newspapers, radio stations, television stations, and contacts in your address book. Don't forget to put it on your Web site, too!

Sample Press Release Format

This model for a standard press release is reprinted courtesy of PRWeb (www.prweb.com) and can be found online in digital format. By the way, those pound signs at the end of the press release are journalistic lingo that indicate the end of the press release.

Headline Is in Title Case and Short, Ideally Not More Than 170 Characters; This Headline Is 138 Characters Long and Does Not Take a Period

While the headline uses title case, capitalizing every word except for prepositions and articles of three letters or less, the summary paragraph is a little longer synopsis in regular sentence form. It doesn't merely repeat the lead. It just tells the story in a different way.

City, State (PRWEB) Month 1, 2006 — The lead sentence contains the most important information in 25 words or less. Grab your reader's attention here. And don't assume that your reader has read your headline or summary paragraph; the lead should stand on its own.

A news release, like a news story, keeps sentences and paragraphs short, about three or four lines per paragraph. The first couple of paragraphs should cover the who, what, when, where, why, and how questions.

The rest of the news release expounds on the information provided in the lead paragraph. It includes quotes from key staff, customers, or subject matter experts. It contains more details about the news you have to tell, which can be about something unique or controversial or about a prominent person, place or thing.

"The final paragraph of a traditional news release contains the least newsworthy material," said Mario Bonilla, customer service representative for PR Web. "But for an online release, it's typical to restate and summarize the key points with a paragraph like the next one."

For additional information on the news that is the subject of this release (or for a sample, copy, or demo), contact Mary Smith, or visit `www.bogus.smith.com`. You can also include details on product availability, trademark acknowledgment, and so on here.

About XYZ Company:

Include a short corporate backgrounder about the company or the person who is newsworthy before you list the contact person's name and phone number. Do not include an e-mail address in the body of the release. Your e-mail address goes only in the "Contact e-mail" box when you first upload your press release.

Contact:

Mary Smith, Director of Public Relations

XYZ Company

555-555-5555

http://www.YourWebAddress.com

Include Safe Harbor statement (if applicable).

###

Taking Advantage of Basic Web Promotion Tools

Don't forget the power of the Web as you think about promotion.

✔ **Use e-mail to the fullest extent possible.** Your own address book may be full of people who are interested in what you're doing, and these people are often more than willing to tell others about it. E-mail everyone, but do so politely so that you aren't spamming your own contacts. Be sure to add your Web site address and a short explanation to your regular e-mail signature line, as well.

✔ **Locate Web sites that are related to your subject area.** If it seems appropriate, you can ask the Web site creator to participate in a link exchange. You can even create a small, attractive graphic that people can use when they set up the link.

✔ **Join a Web ring related to our topic.** A *Web ring* is a group of related Web sites (say, tattoo artists or Irish wolfhound fans) that agree to link to other Web sites in the ring. There is a directory of Web rings online at `www.webring.com`.

✔ **Find mailing lists, news groups, blogs, and forums that discuss topics to which your content is related.** Becoming a member of one of these groups and contributing useful information is a great way to attract an audience of people who value your opinions and information.

Whatever you do, *don't* spam one of these groups by simply posting a message asking people to come visit, unless that is the purpose of the group. No one likes a direct advertising message inserted into the middle of a conversation.

Advertising on Blogs and Web Sites

There are dozens of online advertising programs, and many Web sites that take text, image, and animation ads. Advertising, as you might expect, costs a bit of money to do, and you should be careful about where you decide to spend that little bit of cash burning a hole in your pocket. Still, used effectively and in a targeted way, you can advertise your content directly to those who are interested in hearing about it.

One good way to find effective advertising slots is to spend some time researching the sites that have an audience you think would like to use your content. (Watch for the ads of your competitors; the places they choose to advertise may also be suitable for you.)

TIP

When you find a Web site that attracts an audience that matches the one you would like to build, look around for advertising space on it. Also, look for a link to advertising opportunities in the navigation or in the advertising space. For instance, the blog Engadget (www.engadget.com) includes information about how to advertise and what it costs in the area it displays ads, as you can see in Figure 12-6.

Examining ad slots

Here are the basic online advertising formats:

- ✔ **Text ads:** Text ads are usually quite short, and always include a head-line, description, and link.

- ✔ **Pop-up ads:** Pretty much everyone hates this form of advertising, but it definitely gets attention. A pop-up ad is a secondary, usually smaller, browser window that launches automatically when a Web site page loads.

- ✔ **Banners and leaderboards:** Banner and leaderboard ads are usually displayed at the top and/or bottom of a Web page, and are optimized for good horizontal display space. A leaderboard is shown at the top of the Daily Pilot Web site (www.dailypilot.com), in Figure 12-7.

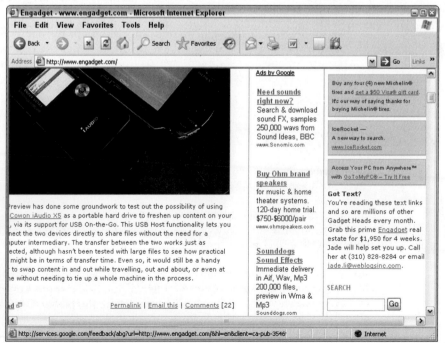

Figure 12-6:
Want to advertise on Engadget? The info on how to do so is displayed prominently on the right side of the home page.

Leaderboard

Figure 12-7:
The Daily
Pilot
newspaper
offers
advertisers
leaderboard
and
skyscraper
options.

Skyscraper

✔ **Boxes/rectangles:** These ads are often seen on the interior of pages, often with text wrapped around them.

✔ **Skyscrapers:** Skyscraper ads look like banners turned on end. They are quite tall vertically, and usually run alongside content in a right-hand column. You can see part of a skyscraper ad on the right side of Figure 12-7.

✔ **Buttons:** Buttons are small ads that individual Web site creators scatter across their pages, as suits their Web site's design.

Most of these formats have evolved to the point where there are standard sizes. You can get dimensions and see examples on the Internet Advertising Bureau's Web site at `iab.net/standards/adunits.asp`.

Finally, many Web sites and blogs offer sponsorship opportunities. These kinds of arrangements are more expensive. However, sponsors generally receive several ad slots, and sometimes other commercial messages are removed entirely.

Using ad programs

There are several Web site advertising programs that you can participate in to put your ads on Web sites that are related to your topic. Here's a rundown of your options:

 ✔ *Contextual* ad placement. Contextual ads actually have something to do with the Web page they are on. With a contextual advertising program, a cooking blog might end up with ads for kitchen supplies. The idea is that readers attracted by the content may also be attracted to advertising related to the content.

 ✔ *Niche ads* are designed to let you target the audiences of niche publications like blogs, hitting a target audience that has a high interest in a certain subject — and hopefully a lot of interest in what you are advertising, as well!

Google AdSense and AdWords

The Google AdSense program is by far the most popular of these advertising programs, and Web site owners can sign up to participate for free, earning money as Web site visitors click ads. The ads themselves change as the page content changes, and even between page viewings.

The Web site owner determines just where to put the Google AdSense advertising, and can choose between small text ads and larger graphic ads.

To place your ads on Web sites using the Google AdSense program, sign up for Google AdWords. Your ads are also placed next to relevant search engine results, on sites in the Google Network, in newsletters and e-mail messages, and even in the Google Gmail application. Google AdWords is online at www.google.com/adwords and is shown in Figure 12-8.

Blogads

The Blogads program was created by Henry Copeland to specifically target the blog-reading market. Advertisers can select the blogs they want their ads to appear on, and the bloggers get to choose whether to accept the ads. You can visit Blogads at www.blogads.com.

Blogads acts as the middleman, facilitating the placement of the ads and the financial transaction. Participating blogs include some of the most popular and successful blogs on the Web today, from politics to technology to photography.

A Blogad usually includes a text description, headline, link, and a good-sized graphic. You can see an example of a Blogad on Hugh Hewitt's blog (www.hughhewitt.com) in Figure 12-9.

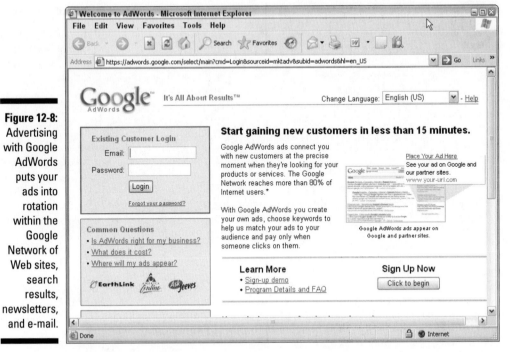

Figure 12-8:
Advertising with Google AdWords puts your ads into rotation within the Google Network of Web sites, search results, newsletters, and e-mail.

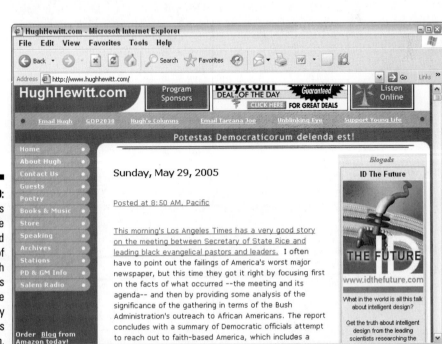

Figure 12-9:
The ads in the right-hand column of Hugh Hewitt's blog are placed by the Blogads program.

Pheedo (www.pheedo.com) and AdBrite (www.adbrite.com) are other blog advertising programs to consider.

Part V
Getting More out of BitTorrent

The 5th Wave   By Rich Tennant

In this part . . .

For the finishing touches, read through Chapter 13. Here you find a great guide to the various stock photography, fonts, illustrations, and video materials to flesh out your own work. If you need beach shots of Tahiti and (unfortunately) can't get there yourself to take pictures, this is the chapter for you. In Chapter 14, you find out how to protect your content while you distribute it. *You* can define just how you want to limit distribution and use of what you create. Then, in Chapter 15, take inspiration from what some forward-thinking businesses are doing with BitTorrent by taking advantage of its unique capabilities to distribute content quickly and inexpensively.

Chapter 13

Hunting for Additional Content

• •

In This Chapter

▶ Remixing from other creator's images, audio, and video sources

▶ Understanding public domain material

▶ Asking permission to use the work of others in your own

• •

Artists love to remix the culture they live in. Some artists build their entire careers on this concept. They borrow bits and pieces of other people's works and build upon them. They borrow an idea and morph it and modify it. This collaborative instinct has perhaps never been true than it is today, with technology so incredibly accessible to a much wider audience. Inexpensive tools that are easy to use, even by beginners, are everywhere.

The Internet and digital technology are responsible for much of your ability to see, hear, and read the creative works of people who you may never otherwise come across. The Internet enables you to see new ideas at work in new ways. The energy and creativity found online is inspiring, and it is causing all kinds of people to think about different ways of remaking creative media. Thankfully, a variety of artists already encourage others to sample and remix their work, and a wide range of places offer images, sounds, animations, and even video you can add to your own creative ventures without fear of violating copyright laws.

Being able to remix media is a creative process that requires dedication as well as talent. This chapter is devoted to helping you find resources for material you can use in your own work, and to help you figure out what to do when you want to get permission to use something in another person's work. The good news is that finding images, audio samples, and video segments is much easier in this day and age of the digital revolution.

Finding Images, Audio, and Video

If you want to use an image for your art but can't get it yourself (say you want to have a picture of a canyon, but you don't live near one) you can look in plenty of places to find a picture that might work. The same is true for audio files, video, and even animation!

I have not included many stock photography and footage houses in the following sections, but there are many excellent stock footage resources available. To find these resources online, type **stock photography** or **stock footage** into a search engine such as Google to find many good sources.

The following sections offer online resources to help you find pieces of media you can remix into your own creations. Not all of the content you'll find is free for the taking; in some cases, you may have to pay a fee, and in others you may need to request permission from the creator.

Because anyone can put content online, you may have to sift through some real dogs to find the gems. Don't get discouraged — keep looking!

Creative Commons Search

On the Creative Commons site (`search.creativecommons.org`), shown in Figure 13-1, you can use the Creative Commons Search Engine. The engine assists you in finding media that the original authors have already granted permission to use with certain restrictions. The restrictions vary from media to media, but each piece of media comes with a Creative Commons license that explains the use limitations set by the creator.

Figure 13-1:
Creative Commons provides a search interface to help you find media you can reuse in your own work.

LegalTorrents

LegalTorrents (www.legaltorrents.com) is a collection of Creative Commons-licensed works that cover the full range of media. You can find music, movies, and books here, and all of the media is available via BitTorrent. Many of the works listed on the LegalTorrents site are very unique and are definitely worth a look by any serious user of BitTorrent technology. Much of what is listed is of a high quality, but not everything can be reused with impunity, so be sure to check the license restrictions.

You can also find an RSS feed to keep up to date with new additions to the Web site.

DMusic

DMusic (www.dmusic.com) is one of the longest-running music portal sites on the Internet. The site has a long-established reputation for using Web technology to enable musicians to promote themselves by making some of their music available for download under a Creative Commons license. You can find a lot of content on this site, and some of it is really good. One of the key benefits to this site is you are able to communicate with the artists directly through the site.

CC Mixter

CC Mixter (www.ccmixter.org) is a community music-sharing site that was started by the folks at the Creative Commons. Visitors to the site can listen to, sample, mix, or interact with music in any way they choose. In November 2004, CC Mixter launched the site by promoting, along with *WIRED* magazine, 16 songs that were licensed under Creative Commons Sampling licenses.

If you want to resample and remix music, this site is for you. Borrow music, remix it, and then upload it back to CC Mixter to make the artists' work shine.

Opsound

Opsound (www.opsound.org) is a new record label that is looking for new ways to release music. The creators of Opsound want to create a way to harness the power of the Internet, with a special emphasis on enabling communication and sharing. You can find many music samples on the site worth checking out.

Nomads' Land

Nomads' Land (www.maion.com/photography) is an online stock photography Web site with some amazing shots from all around the world. The photos are covered under a Creative Commons license, and photos may also be purchased via the Web site, shown in Figure 13-2.

Common Content

Common Content (www.commoncontent.org) is an eclectic collection of works all licensed under Creative Commons licenses. The content on this site includes images, text, movies, and audio, and all the content is available for anyone to copy and remix. You can find quite a bit of fascinating content on this site.

Open Photo

Open Photo (www.openphoto.net) is a collection of photographs taken by photographers from around the world. These photos all have Creative Commons licenses and are of very high quality. Usage of most of these photos is allowed, but some require authorization by the photographer.

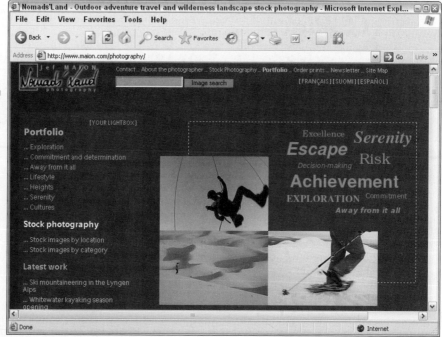

Figure 13-2:
Check out a wide selection of outdoor lifestyle photographs from remote locations by photographer Jef Maion on Nomads' Land.

Remix Reading

Remix Reading (www.remixreading.org) is an artistic project based in Reading, United Kingdom, with the aim of providing an environment that enables artists to get together to find inspiration in each other's works; the project encourages artists to remix other people's works and collaborate for a final product. You can find plenty of images, music remixes, and videos for artists of all sorts. All works are licensed with Creative Commons.

Internet Archive

The Internet Archive (www.archive.org) was founded in 1996 to become the largest and most comprehensive Internet library. Its purpose is to offer permanent access for researchers, historians, and scholars to historical collections that exist in a digital format. The Internet Archive provides visitors with access to a wide selection of text, audio, video, and software that can be used for free by anyone. Also, check out the Way Back Machine, which archives Web sites. The Internet Archive Web site is shown in Figure 13-3.

The word "archive" doesn't mean that this stuff is old! For example, I found a collection of amateur camcorder footage from the 2004 Phuket tsunami among other quite recent material.

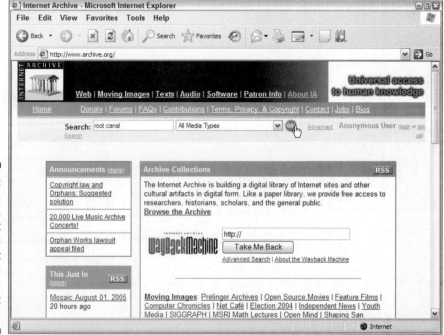

Figure 13-3: Search text, audio, video, and more at the world's biggest online library, the Internet Archive.

GarageBand

GarageBand (www.garageband.com) is a Web site dedicated to promotion and collaboration between up-and-coming artists. You can find a huge variety of music of all different qualities. It is interesting to view and listen to artists who are just honing their craft and making demonstration audio files to show their progress. You can leave instant feedback for an artist via the Web site.

Flickr Creative Commons Pool

Flickr (www.flickr.com/creativecommons) is a company that offers people a place to upload and archive their photos while also enabling others to view the pictures. Photos are from all over the world and all are submitted by active members of the Flickr community. Topics are wide ranging and vary in quality, but the collection is vast and multicultural.

The photos in the Creative Commons pool include images that can be reused with some restrictions by the photographer. The Flickr Creative Commons Pool is shown in Figure 13-4.

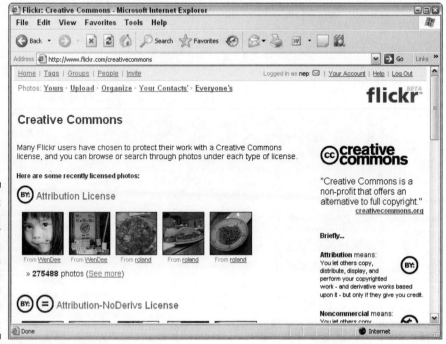

Figure 13-4:
Visit the Flickr Creative Commons Pool to find images from all over the world.

Open Clip Art Library

The Open Clip Art Library (www.openclipart.org) is a user-submitted collection of clip art from artists all over the world. The goal of this project is to create a large archive of clip art that may be used by anyone for any purpose. The quality of this clip art is amazing, and you can find images for all kinds of work. Creative Commons Public Domain licenses cover the entire collection.

Stock.XCHNG

Stock.XCHNG (www.sxc.hu) is a photo storage system originating in Hungary that promotes photographers and enables them to establish their own reuse terms. The collection varies in quality, but is quite broad; it numbers in the thousands. For a majority of the photos you must request permission from the authors in order to reuse them.

The Web Gallery of Art

The Web Gallery of Art (www.wga.hu) Web site, shown in Figure 13-5, is a virtual museum and database of European paintings and sculpture. Founded in 1996 in Hungary, the site has a large collection of images and is intent on making sure this art does not disappear. The Web Gallery of Art also intends to be an educational tool for art students worldwide. Images in these galleries are free for personal use and educational purposes, but require written authorization by the legal owner for other purposes. These works of art are definitely worth a look.

Magnatune

Magnatune (www.magnatune.com) is a new style of record label. The site wants visitors to know that the site's creators "are not evil." The artists listed on this label are treated fairly regarding their music and its distribution. And, the big plus is that you are free to listen to this music before you buy. Each track of an album is free for download and sharing, and is covered by a Creative Commons license.

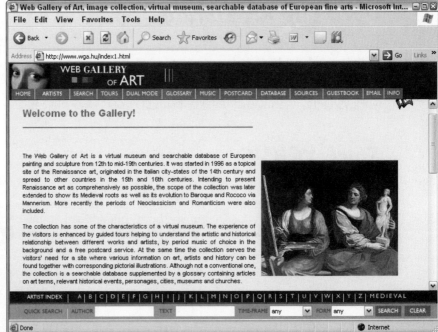

Identifying Public Domain Material

You can find a lot of content available in the *public domain* to work with. As with copyright, you can easily misunderstand just the scope of public domain materials. In a nutshell, creative materials that never had copyright, or whose terms of copyright protection have expired, are considered to be part of the public domain. Public domain works legally belong to everyone, and can be used by anyone.

Some creative materials are released immediately into the public domain and are available right when they are created. Torrent users and those who are creating their own torrent media may not realize the amount of content out there — and a vast amount is available in a digital format and is available for use.

One of the most interesting sources of public domain content is material created by U.S. government agencies. For instance, this means that movies created by NASA are in the public domain from the moment they are created — there is no waiting for copyright to expire.

Public domain media is free to use, even for profit, and does not have an *owner* or *copyright holder*. The media is available to anyone who happens to like the content. You can change it, edit it, extract portions of it for use, and generally turn what you find into something completely different. There are no restrictions on the media at all. Of course, the instant an artist uses these materials to create something new, that new work *is* copyrighted. You can always go back to the artists' source material (the public domain media) yourself if you like some of what you see or hear.

Public domain is not the same as *publicly available*. Just because you can very easily see, read, and make copies of media on the Internet does not mean that it is in the public domain. In fact, unless you find a notice that specifically identifies material on a Web site as public domain material, assume that it isn't.

Here's a list of sites that provide public domain media and art:

- **Free Public Domain Photo Database** (www.pdphoto.org): PD Photo is a large database of photographs that have been released into the public domain. The photos cover a wide range of topics and are all of a fairly high quality. All photos are free to use and are covered under Creative Commons Public Domain licenses.

- **Justinsomnia** (justinsomnia.org/gallery): This site is run by Justin Watt. He takes a series of photos and releases them into the public domain on his Web site. There are some incredibly brilliant images in this collection, and it's worth a peek.

- **U.S. Government Graphics and Photos** (www.firstgov.gov): This site (shown in Figure 13-6) is a collection of photos pertaining to the U.S. government. Most of these images and graphics are available for use in the public domain; they may be used and reproduced without permission or fee. However, some images may be protected by license. Thoroughly read the disclaimers on each site before use. For information about obtaining seals of federal agencies and the United States, please see the Government Printing Office Web site.

- **A listing of various U.S. Federal Government public domain images** (stellar-one.com/public/us_federal_government_public_domain_images.htm): This page contains a listing of common U.S. Federal public domain images. Images contained in this listing cover almost every possible subject, from machines to microbiology. Plan to spend a fair chunk of time exploring what's available here.

- **Classical recordings by MIT Choir and others** (hebb.mit.edu/Free Music): This site offers a collection of classical music recordings. Many of pieces available are recorded by the MIT Choir, but other groups are represented. There are some great quality recordings in this collection.

✔ **Washington State University Public Domain Resources** (`publishing.wsu.edu/publishing.wsu.edu_non_ssl/copyright/public_domain_resources`): Washington State University has a large amount of public domain resources listed, referencing all kinds of materials, including audio, images, photos, and movies.

✔ **Project Gutenberg** (`www.gutenberg.org`): Project Gutenberg, shown in Figure 13-7, is an ever-growing collection of novels and literature that have entered into the public domain. In the summer of 2005, the site listed 16,000 available texts.

✔ **Choral Public Domain** (`www.cpdl.org`): This is a Web site dedicated to providing access to musical scores and sheet music that have become part of the public domain. This is a fascinating site with a large collection of songs. If you are interested in rediscovering older music so that you can re-record it, the Choral Public Domain Web site is a good place to start.

✔ **Images Canada** (`www.imagescanada.ca`): Images Canada is a collection of images that reflect the events, people, places, and things that are part of Canada's cultural heritage. Non-commercial use is permitted for most images; commercial use requires the permission of the institution that created the image.

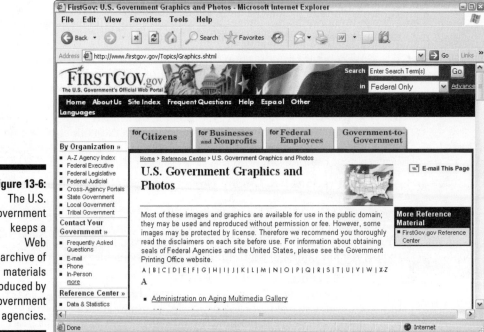

Figure 13-6:
The U.S. government keeps a Web archive of materials produced by government agencies.

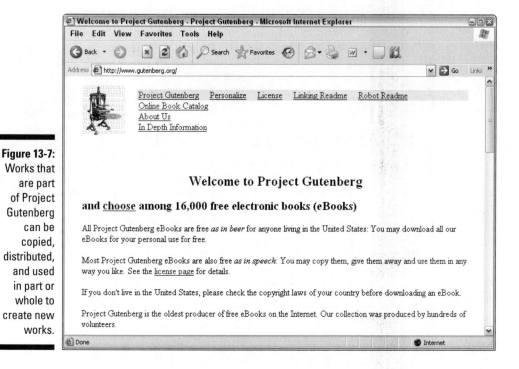

Welcome to Project Gutenberg - Project Gutenberg - Microsoft Internet Explorer
File   Edit   View   Favorites   Tools   Help

Back   ✕ ⬡ ⌂   Search   ⭐ Favorites   ⬡   ⬡ ▾ ⬡ ▾ ⬡ ⬡

Address http://www.gutenberg.org/   Go   Links »

Project Gutenberg   Personalize   License   Linking Readme   Robot Readme
Online Book Catalog
About Us
In Depth Information

                    Welcome to Project Gutenberg

and choose among 16,000 free electronic books (eBooks)

All Project Gutenberg eBooks are free *as in beer* for anyone living in the United States: You may download all our
eBooks for your personal use for free.

Most Project Gutenberg eBooks are also free *as in speech*: You may copy them, give them away and use them in any
way you like. See the license page for details.

If you don't live in the United States, please check the copyright laws of your country before downloading an eBook.

Project Gutenberg is the oldest producer of free eBooks on the Internet. Our collection was produced by hundreds of
volunteers.

Done   Internet

Figure 13-7:
Works that
are part
of Project
Gutenberg
can be
copied,
distributed,
and used
in part or
whole to
create new
works.

✔ **Eldritch Press** (www.eldritchpress.org): Eldritch Press is a collection
of books and literature in the public domain.

✔ **PD Info** (www.pdinfo.com): PD Info, shown in Figure 13-8, is a site with
links and information for music that has entered the public domain.
Check out the list of 3,500 songs in the public domain; there is even
sheet music for many of the songs.

TIP

Finding more information on the public domain

The list of public domain art and media provided
in this chapter is by no means comprehensive.
You can find many more resources than I could
possibly list here. To see more lists of possible
resources, please visit the following sites:

✔ **Wikipedia Public Domain Resource List:**
en.wikipedia.org/wiki/Wikipedi
a:Public_domain_resources

✔ **Wikipedia Public Domain Image Resources:**
en.wikipedia.org/wiki/Wikipedia
:Public_domain_image_resources

Figure 13-8:
The PD Info
Web site
has a good
guide to
identifying
works in the
public
domain.

Obtaining Permissions for Electronic Distribution

You may find a piece of media online that is covered by a Creative Commons license, but that requires permission to use under special circumstances. Or maybe the originator has said it's free to use, but you still want to contact the creator. Other times, you may come across work that is covered by full copyright, which means you need to get complete permission, and perhaps pay a fee.

If (or should I say when?) you find a photo, piece of video, some music, or some text that you simply must have as part of your creation and you aren't sure of the work's copyright status, you can request permission to use the work from the creator. You may be surprised at how willing creative people are to permit this kind of use as long as you include appropriate attribution and credit.

Expect to have a harder time with corporate publishers (like newspapers, magazines, television shows, books, and so on) or with individuals whose livelihood is tied up in the content they create. These organizations permit reprint and reuse, but usually require payment for their use.

If you do find something you want to use, send a formal request for permission that includes:

- ✔ Information about you and your project
- ✔ An explanation of why the work is important to your work
- ✔ A statement about how you plan to use the material, and whether the final product will be released to the public for free or whether it will be available commercially
- ✔ Your contact information

To make life a little easier, I've included a couple of sample letters you can use to get started.

Sample general permission letter

Dear Sir or Madam [or name, if known]:

I am currently creating a project called [name of project]. This project is intended for [describe the project].

I would like your permission to include the following material with this [project]: [Describe the content and where you found it on the Web].

The [content] will be used as follows: [Describe clearly how the project and content requested will be used — including whether you intend to alter or adapt the content in any way]. Once complete, the [project] will be accessible by [Describe type and scope of intended users].

My research indicates that you control the copyright for the material cited above. If not, I would appreciate any contact information that you can give me for the proper rights holder(s) — such as current address, telephone and e-mail address. Your permission will confirm that you have the right to grant the permission that I am requesting.

This permission to use the material requested includes non-exclusive world rights to use the material as I have described above. It will not limit any future use of the material by you or others authorized by you. If I require any additional uses of the material, I will contact you directly before I proceed.

Your prompt reply would be greatly appreciated. Should you require additional information, please do not hesitate to contact me at the following address: [Your contact information].

I am enclosing a second copy of this request for your records. If you agree to grant me permission to use the material as requested above, please sign the release form below and return one copy to me in the self-addressed return envelope.

Thank you,

[Your signature]

[Your name, typed]

RELEASE

Permission granted for the use of the material as described above:

Agreed to: _____

Name/Title: _____

Company/Affiliation: _____

Date: _____

Sample permission letter for use of content on a Web site

Dear [Sir or Madam] [or name, if known]:

I would like to use certain copyrighted material on a Web site to supplement existing content.

I would like your permission to include the following material with this Web site: [Describe the content and where you found it on the Web]. I would like this permission for the upcoming [number of years]. Any use beyond that time will be renegotiated.

The Web site can be described as follows: [Describe the Web site and include any features. Talk about the intended format for the content, such as sound or movie files — including whether you intend to alter or adapt the content in any way].

My research indicates that you control the copyright for the material cited above. If not, I would appreciate any contact information that you can give me for the proper rights holder(s) — such as current address, telephone and e-mail address. Your permission will confirm that you have the right to grant the permission that I am requesting.

Your prompt reply would be greatly appreciated. Should you require additional information, please do not hesitate to contact me at the following address: [Your contact information].

I am enclosing a second copy of this request for your records. If you agree to grant me permission to use the material as requested above, please sign the release form below and return one copy to me in the self-addressed return envelope.

Thank you,

[Your signature]

[You name, typed]

RELEASE

Permission granted for the use of the material as described above:

Agreed to: _____

Name/Title: _____

Company/Affiliation: _____

Date: _____

Chapter 14

Protecting Your Content

· ·

· ·

*I*f you distribute your audio, video, photo collection, text, or other content using BitTorrent, have you surrendered your copyright? This is a valid question, and one that this chapter answers.

In fact, you retain copyright of all your creative material, no matter how you choose to distribute it to the world. Using an Internet licensing organization called Creative Commons, you can even create custom licensing agreements to permit certain kinds of uses for your material. Getting that far means having a basic understanding of copyright itself, however, and what rights you have under the law.

Almost certainly you want to retain copyright of anything you create, but that doesn't mean you can't share it with others, or encourage them to redistribute it to their friends. In fact, if you use BitTorrent to distribute what you create, you ought to be sure you're okay with the content being redistributed, because the BitTorrent system is built for redistribution.

In this chapter, I walk you through the basics of copyright, and of making sure you let people know just what they can do with your files after they have them. I talk a bit about digital rights and explain what restrictions management is (and what that means to you).

Understanding Internet Distribution

Before I move on to copyright, there is one thing you need to understand: If you put a copy of your data on the Internet — in any format, anywhere — realize that you have just made that data public. At the least, it can be downloaded and viewed, read, or listened to. Depending on what kind of file you put online, anyone who downloads it may open it, edit it, or modify it for use in another creation. This action isn't legal, of course, but that doesn't mean it isn't done.

If you don't want people to have access to your files, don't put them on the Internet. It's that simple. After a file's out in the world, no matter what kinds of precautions you take — and I talk about some in this chapter — you no longer have much control over what happens to your content.

If you really, really need to protect what you create, BitTorrent isn't the distribution format for you. In fact, the Internet may not be the right place for you — using full-fledged copyright protection for your files virtually forces BitTorrent users to violate your copyright. You're sending a mixed message to other users if you put torrents online but don't want the files to be redistributed. You *must* get a Creative Commons license that permits redistribution if you intend to use BitTorrent for your files. See the following sections about getting official with your copyright.

Movie studios have certainly been struggling with this dilemma. Studios distribute to Academy members each year review copies of the films up for Academy Award consideration. Those members are supposed to watch the films and use them in making their decisions, but every year some of those versions show up in places they shouldn't be: pirated DVDs for sale off a side street, at video stores, and yes, for download on the Internet. How the films get in the hands of people they weren't intended for is a puzzle we don't have to solve. The point is, controlling content after you sell a copy or give a copy away is nearly impossible.

Not everyone is trying to profit from what you create. In fact, most people don't deliberately try to steal something they don't have rights to; but as digital technology has become ubiquitous and bandwidth becomes inexpensive, music, movies, television shows, and other traditionally copyrighted material is being shared in ways content creators never intended. You put your own content through the same risks that the big content originators do when you put it out into the world.

Mitigating the Feeding Frenzy

Of course, you can deal with the problem of exposing your files to willy-nilly file sharing. There are several strategies:

- ✔ **Clearly indicate that your work is copyrighted.** You may even consider registering your work with the U.S. Copyright Office. Even though your work is copyrighted the second you create it, reminding other people of the copyright can have a positive effect.

- ✔ **License your own work.** Your work is already copyrighted, but if you're using BitTorrent you probably don't mind people sharing it without your permission. Maybe you don't even mind others modifying your work, as long as you get some credit. Licensing your work clearly indicates what permissions you're willing to grant to people who have a copy of your file. You can license your work with Creative Commons or you could create your own license. Remember, unless you create a license for your work, all copyright rights reside with you. A license extends the rights you choose to others.

- ✔ **Take steps against any misuse of your content.** Ever heard the phrase "The best defense is a good offense"? That's certainly true in this case. You can never prevent all abuse, and you shouldn't try so hard that you actually prevent people from making appropriate use of your content. However, you can definitely take action against those who don't follow the terms of your license or observe your copyright. See the section, later in this chapter, called "Taking on Copyright Infringers," for more information.

Copyright is automatic and reserves all the rights to use and redistribute your content to you. A license is used to give other people some of those rights. You can have both a copyright and a license, but only copyright is automatic.

The important thing when thinking about limiting or expanding a license is to remember what you hope to accomplish by distributing your creations. Are you hoping to get your music heard by people who like it enough to use it in their own work? Are you hoping to publish your eBook with a mainstream press? Are you trying to get exposure for a documentary your sister created in order to get it accepted at a film festival? Let Table 14-1 help you make the decision.

Table 14-1		Deciding How to Release Your Content	
If You Want to . . .	*Then You Should . . .*	*But If You Want to . . .*	*Then You Should . . .*
Get your music heard	Distribute it freely	Encourage others to remix your music	Create a license that permits others to create derivative works
Let people read your book (and you don't care what people do with it)	Distribute it freely as a text file	Get a publisher to notice it and buy it	Distribute a single chapter as a PDF and license others to redistribute the book
Enable people to see your movie	Distribute it freely	Create buzz so that people will want to see it	Distribute a trailer that can't be modified and license it as free to distribute

Whatever your ultimate goal is, it should influence how strongly you try to protect what you put out into the world. Many amateur content creators are simply interested in having some impact on the lives of those who consume what they create. Others have a work that needs to stay intact but they hope to put in front of many people. Still others intentionally create something they hope inspires other creative people to take their material and create something of their own. Which case applies to you?

Understanding Copyright Basics

Copyright law governs what the U.S. Copyright Offices calls *original works of authorship* as soon as they exist in a tangible form. Think about it this way: If you can give the original or a copy of what you have created to a friend, you have a work in a tangible form. The delivery mechanism doesn't matter, either, so your friend can get the work digitally or you could physically hand it over.

Copyrightable works include:

- ✔ Architecture
- ✔ Choreography
- ✔ Dramas like plays, including any accompanying music
- ✔ Literature (including poetry, novels, short stories, memoirs, and other forms of both fiction and nonfiction)

- ✔ Movies
- ✔ Music, with or without words
- ✔ Sound recordings
- ✔ Visual pieces, from graphics to sculptures

You notice how logos aren't in there? Nor are ideas or inventions. You can't copyright an idea, invention, or logo (although you can patent inventions and trademark logos — but that's a whole other book).

Knowing your copyright rights

Copyright is born the moment the creative work takes tangible form, regardless of whether you publish the work or register it with the U.S. Copyright Office. As the creator of copyrighted material, you can:

- ✔ Make copies of it.
- ✔ Use it to make other works.
- ✔ Distribute it, sell it, rent it, or lend it.
- ✔ Perform it, assuming that's possible.
- ✔ Show it publicly, as when a painting is on a gallery wall.
- ✔ Broadcast it, if it's a sound recording.

You have the *right* to do these things, but rights aren't *guarantees*. For instance, you can use the Internet to broadcast your audio news story, but the local radio station doesn't have to air your story.

No one else has the right to display, copy, distribute, or broadcast your work unless you specifically give permission.

Making sure others know your copyright rights

Although copyright protection exists the moment your work is in a fixed form, it's a good idea to let others know that you are claiming copyright and that you plan to keep those rights (assuming you do). A copyright notice comes in handy.

There are three components to a copyright notice:

- ✔ The symbol © or the word Copyright. (You can also abbreviate this: Copr.)
- ✔ The year of first publication of the work. If there is no publication, use the year the work was fixed in tangible form.
- ✔ The name of the copyright owner (that's you!).

The copyright notice for this book is:

```
Copyright 2006 by Wiley Publishing, Inc.
```

Or:

```
(c) 2006 by Wiley Publishing, Inc.
```

Or:

```
Copr. 2006 by Wiley Publishing, Inc.
```

You actually don't have to use a copyright notice. Your copyright exists whether you attach one to your work or not. But using a copyright notice is useful for several reasons. The most important of these reasons is that it makes copyright ownership clear to everyone else. No one can claim ignorance if you have a clearly visible copyright notice.

A copyright notice is great, but remember that any material you distribute via BitTorrent is automatically redistributed because of the way BitTorrent works. Don't make people who download your file copyright infringers by putting a copyright notice on your work that isn't also accompanied by a license that permits redistribution, even if you plan to retain all other rights to your content.

Here are some easy-to-remember do's and don'ts for your copyright notices:

- ✔ **Do put your copyright notice somewhere prominent.** Place the notice on the cover of your eBook, in opening and closing credits of your film, and by all means next to any promotion link to the downloadable version of whatever your content is.

- ✔ **Don't go crazy.** You don't have to put it on every page of your eBook, or in every frame of your film. Littering your creative work with copyright notices doesn't look good and isn't necessary.

You often see copyright notices on every page of a Web site, but that's acceptable because a Web author can't predict what page visitors will see first, or whether visitors will see more than that one page. If you're a Web designer, you can err on the side of copyright overkill.

You should probably place a copyright notice — formatted correctly — on your work, even if you plan to let people use it freely in any way. After all, it can't hurt, and it can certainly help.

Getting Official with Your Copyright

You can register your copyright with the U.S. Copyright Office, and you can create a license for your work with an organization like Creative Commons. The following sections give you the lowdown on both options.

Registering with the U.S. Copyright Office

Just as you don't have to use a copyright notice even though it's a good idea, you also don't have to register your copyright with the U.S. Copyright Office. Doing so can be useful, however, and can save you time and trouble later. Here's a list of perks to registering your work:

- You get a public record of your claim.

- You can file a copyright infringement suit (in fact, you have to register your copyright before you can file a suit).

- If you register your work within five years of publication or creation, a court will accept as given evidence the validity of the copyright registration. In other words, if some other guy tries to say that your creation is actually *his* creation, your registration means you don't have to prove when and what is actually copyrighted.

- If you register the work within three months of publication or prior to an infringement, and you decide to sue someone else for infringement, your *statutory damages* (statutory damages are determined by law, not by your actual losses) and attorney's fees related to any court action will be paid by the defendant (assuming you win). If you don't register within three months, you can only get actual damages and profits.

- You're protected against the importation of infringing copies. For example, illegally made copies of your documentary can't be imported and sold.

Visit the U.S. Copyright Office Web site (shown in Figure 14-1) to find out how to register your copyright, if you think that's necessary, at `www.copyright.gov`.

If you register your work with the U.S. Copyright Office and plan to distribute it using BitTorrent, you also need to create a license that permits redistribution of your work. BitTorrent is designed to redistribute files as soon as they are downloaded, so you need to make sure you allow this use.

Figure 14-1:
The U.S.
Copyright
Office Web
site has
terrific
resources to
help you
register a
copyright.

Licensing your own content

Assuming that you want to license your work officially with the U.S. Copyright Office (see "Registering with the U.S. Copyright Office," earlier in this chapter), the next step you may want to take in protecting your content is to develop a license that specifies just what permissions you want to allow people who access your content.

For digital media, the best way to license your own work is by using the services of Creative Commons (`www.creativecommons.org`), a non-profit corporation started in 2001 specifically to help people handle their creative works in a digital environment. Creative Commons currently offers 11 types of licenses, all free, each outlining different terms of use for the media to which they are applied.

Avoiding mixed signals

If you distribute your content using BitTorrent, you must write a license that permits redistribution. Without this license, anyone who uses BitTorrent (or any other file-sharing product) is breaking the law if he or she uses the file-sharing technology for its intended purpose.

Only the copyright holder has the right to distribute works and make copies. If you put your work into the BitTorrent network without a license permitting redistribution, you're forcing anyone who seeds the file back into the community to violate your copyright!

All Creative Commons licenses are intended to be used by content creators who want to make their content publicly available (via BitTorrent or any other medium), and in some way control how that data gets used. You don't give up your copyright; you just extend some rights to anyone who gets the file.

Here are a few benefits of a Creative Commons license, based on the Creative Commons philosophy:

✔ Restricting access to a work with a full-fledged copyright notice doesn't help you gain the exposure and widespread distribution you may want. Setting up a license that permits others to distribute your work, or even to use parts of it in their work, gets you some of that exposure.

✔ You may enjoy the creative give and take that comes from contributing to and participating in an intellectual community, and the good feeling that comes with actively adding to the pool of content and knowledge available online.

✔ If you want to share your work, a Creative Commons license enables you to do so while still retaining some or even most of your copyright protection.

Creative Commons is probably the easiest way to create such a license. There are licenses available for:

✔ Audio
✔ Education materials
✔ Images
✔ Text
✔ Video
✔ Web sites

You can mix and match the rights you grant to your work in many ways. Here are a few:

- Other people can copy, distribute, display, and perform the work *only* if they give you credit.
- Other people can copy, distribute, display, and perform the work *only* for noncommercial purposes.
- Other people can copy, distribute, display, and perform *only* verbatim copies of the work, not derivative works based upon it.
- Other people can distribute derivative works only under a license identical to yours.
- Other people can do anything they like with your work.

After you make your selections, Creative Commons provides you with three forms of the license:

- A human-readable text version of the license (that is, one that makes sense to non-lawyers).
- A text version of the license to use in court (this one is for the lawyers).
- A code version of the license for use by search engines and other applications.

Creative Commons licenses *cannot* be used in conjunction with digital rights management tools. I talk more about digital rights management later in the chapter.

To create a Creative Commons license, visit www.creativecommons.org, and look for the category your content falls into. To create your customized license, Creative Commons walks you through a series of questions, as shown in Figure 14-2. Within minutes, you and your license are on your way.

Taking on Copyright Infringers

Copyright infringement occurs when someone uses your content in a way you haven't permitted, and in a manner the law reserves for you alone. It happens frequently, sometimes innocently, sometimes not. Most commonly the rights violated are those of reproduction (I made copies of audio tapes for my friends when I was a kid — didn't you?), performance, and the creation of unauthorized works based on your work.

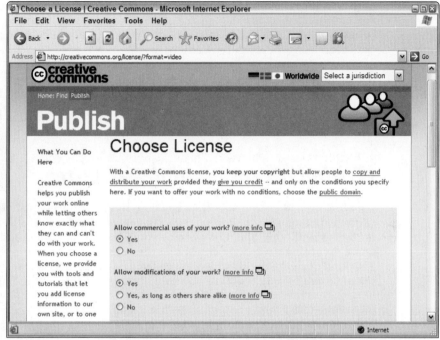

Figure 14-2:
Creative
Commons
enables you
to quickly
create a
license that
protects
your content
while giving
others
limited
rights to
use it.

There are only two possible exceptions to the typical rules of copyright:

- ✔ **Fair use:** Fair use enables you to quote a book in an academic paper, or show a screen shot of a movie in a review. It's a complicated area of the law, and judges rule differently when cases claiming fair use come to trial. Essentially, however, for the use to be considered fair it must serve some social or cultural purpose, for example, criticism, comment, scholarship, news reporting, and teaching. If you think what you want to do is covered by fair use, be sure to still give credit to the originator.

  A common fallacy is that the fair use doctrine permits you to sample 30 seconds of a song for use on your Web site or in your work. In fact, nothing in fair use specifies a number of words, or a time frame, that is permitted.

- ✔ **Parody or satire:** These two types of creation are specifically protected under fair use rules. If someone creates a humorous knockoff of your work, he or she may be able to claim that the takeoff was intended as a parody or a satire, and therefore acceptable, no matter how closely the work resembles yours.

In the world of file sharing, copyright infringement almost always involves someone making an illegal copy of copyright-protected content, and then distributing it. You can read more about how online piracy affects what you download using BitTorrent in Chapter 6.

If you find that your content has been distributed, used to create derivative works, or performed without your permission, you can take several steps to try to end the copyright violation. Almost all of these steps involve lawyers and the courts.

Writing a cease and desist letter

Your first step in ending an instance of copyright infringement should be to warn the person responsible for the infringement that he or she is, in fact, infringing your copyright; this warning should occur in writing, and it should contain a strongly worded request that the person stop the infringement. This kind of communication is often called a *cease and desist letter*. Cease and desist letters usually contain some kind of threat, spelled out or implied, that if the person does not stop the infringement, you will file a lawsuit. Builder.com, part of the CNET family of Web sites, has a sample version of a cease and desist letter online at `builder.com.com/5100-31-5082448.html`. It is also shown in Figure 14-3.

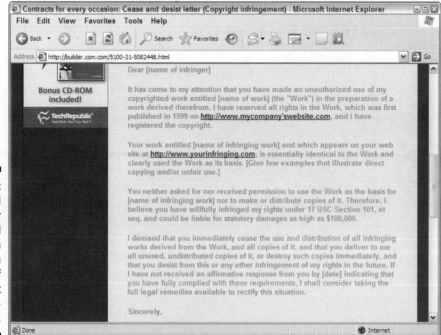

Figure 14-3:
A cease and desist letter is the usual first step in stopping an instance of copyright infringement.

These letters are, quite often, successful. (As it turns out, most people tend to want to avoid lawsuits.) In some cases, you may be dealing with an individual who doesn't realize that he or she is violating copyright, particularly if you didn't include a copyright notice or license with your work, or simply because the individual is ignorant of the law.

Lack of awareness is especially likely in the Internet age because files are readily accessible but are shared fairly anonymously across the Internet; when you don't know where files originate, you're less likely to think you're violating anyone's rights. Many people may realize that they're doing something wrong, but they think of trading copyrighted files as a victimless crime because they're so far removed from the originator of the file.

Sending a letter to the infringer's ISP

After you write a cease and desist letter, if the infringer continues to do bad things with your work of art, your next option is to send a letter to the infringer's Internet service provider. You can request that the ISP remove the problematic content, and quite often, ISPs will do so.

If things get so far that you have to contact the ISP, you should be aware that this action may not stop the infringer in the long run; however, it is a quick and effective solution to the immediate problem. If the infringer's ISP is not based in the United States, this course of action may not be quite as effective.

You can write these letters yourself, or hire a lawyer for maximum legalese impact.

When in doubt, contacting a lawyer

If you find that a cease and desist letter doesn't work, and contacting the infringer's ISP is also fruitless, or if you are experiencing widespread copyright infringement issues, it's time to consult a lawyer about whether you have a lawsuit. Assuming that you do think you have a case, you can start the paperwork required in filing the suit. If you haven't already done so, you should also register your work with the U.S. Copyright Office. You must register the work before you can proceed with a suit.

Defending Your Content with Technology

You have access to some technological tools that you can add to your arsenal of content protection. Most of these tools fall into one of two categories:

- ✔ Letting people know that your content is copyrighted, or that it is yours.
- ✔ Preventing people from editing or using part or all of your content.

Both of these strategies have to do with prevention of infringement of your content. Nothing is guaranteed to be wholly effective, but the techniques I outline in the following pages should make it harder for others to violate your copyright easily or unknowingly. Infringers simply have to go to a great deal of technical trouble to do bad stuff with your files, so the prevention option can be an effective deterrent.

Using information to your advantage

How you apply these strategies varies, depending on what kind of media you're dealing with. For example, a visual copyright symbol is next to useless if your content is an audio file. Here are some ideas for preventing users from abusing your copyrighted content:

- ✔ **Watermarks:** Watermarks can be visible or invisible. You are probably most familiar with them from television. The semi-transparent station identifiers that so many networks place in the corner of the screen are one version of a visible watermark. Usually, visible watermarks are small, persistent images or text. On video, they remain in place during the length of the presentation. In a set of images, the watermark appears on every individual image.

  Though watermarks are effective methods of branding or identifying visual content, they generally interfere with the image being shown. Because Web videos are often quite small to begin with, watermarks can create more problems than they solve online.

  Watermarks can consist of images or text. Possible textual messages include URLs, copyright notices, and names of authors. In Figure 14-4, you can see a watermark in use on an image from the stock photography Web site Photos.com (www.photos.com).

  An invisible watermark might change certain pixels of an image imperceptibly, or in visually subtle ways. Invisible watermarks are usually created so that you can track or detect the origin of a file, rather like some of the less visible security features in currency.

Figure 14-4:
The text on top of this image of a flower is a visual identifier known as a watermark.

✔ **Naming and metadata:** One important technique for letting people know that your content is copyrighted and belongs to you is to name it appropriately. Descriptive names are always important in order to understand what a file contains before users open it, and usually a good name includes the name of the work.

Adding your name to the filename can also help further reinforce your copyright. For example, the filename `gardner_parisphoto_louvre. jpg` gives users some quick information about the subject of the image, and it offers a subtle cue that the image belongs to someone (me!).

Many media creation programs, from Microsoft Word all the way up to Adobe Premiere Elements, enable (and encourage) you to add identifying information to your files, such as the title, subject, author, category, keywords, comments, description, copyright, and URL. All this stuff you include is called *metadata,* which is just a fancy way of saying that this information identifies the file in a way that's searchable by outsiders. You can see an example of the metadata information window from Microsoft Word in Figure 14-5.

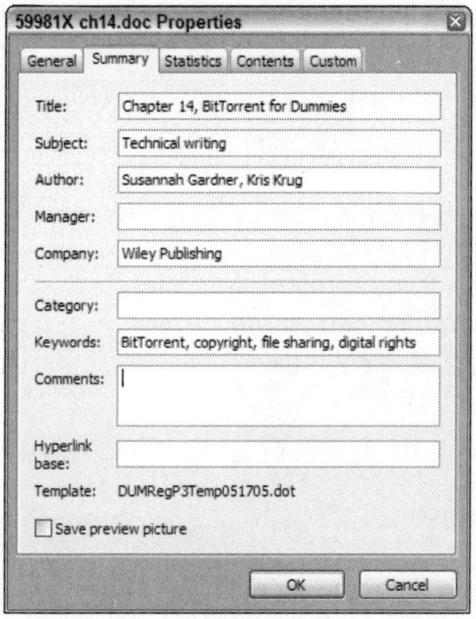

59981X ch14.doc Properties

General | **Summary** | Statistics | Contents | Custom

Title:	Chapter 14, BitTorrent for Dummies
Subject:	Technical writing
Author:	Susannah Gardner, Kris Krug
Manager:	
Company:	Wiley Publishing
Category:	
Keywords:	BitTorrent, copyright, file sharing, digital rights
Comments:	
Hyperlink base:	

Template: DUMRegP3Temp051705.dot

☐ Save preview picture

OK | Cancel

Figure 14-5:
Insert metadata into your file, as I have done here with Microsoft Word.

This metadata stays with the file as it travels, acting as an identifier that's separate from the content of the file. In the case of audio and video, this metadata is frequently displayed during playback in audio and video players, and it serves as a strong reminder to the watcher or listener about where the file came from.

If you use a blog or Web site to present your content you can also *tag* that content with keywords that describe it. Tagging is visible to humans, and also to search engines, and simply consists of creating a list of appropriate terms that describe you and your file's content.

✔ **Links:** Whenever possible, create a Web site or even just a Web page that describes your work and includes your copyright notice and any license you have set up to govern use of your content. Be sure to include contact information about yourself on the page.

With a Web page at your disposal, you can include the URL for the Web page in your file wherever possible. In the case of text, go ahead and put it on every page, if you like. For video, drop the URL into the credits. If the URL is short enough, you may even be able to use it as a watermark. In an audio file, read the URL out along with your copyright at the end of the broadcast.

The point here is to make sure that the viewer, listener, or reader sees a location to get more information about the file. Users may visit out of curiosity, or in order to get permission to use the file in some way. Take advantage of every opportunity to tell people who access your content just what they have, who originated it, and how they can legally use it.

✔ **Credits:** Movies and television shows have screen after screen of credits for a reason, and it isn't just about the actors' egos. Those credits are there in large part for the viewer. Curious about who directed? Watch the credits. Want to know who was responsible for costumes? The credits again.

People are very used to this format, and even if you don't have 570 people to list in your credits, the credits are one of the first places your viewers look to find out more about what they just watched. So don't skip adding credits to your video presentation, and make sure that you include yourself, your contact information, your copyright notice, any license you have for the content, and your URL.

✔ **Opening screens/pages:** An opening screen, or opening audio piece, is another way to ensure that nobody misses your copyright notice and other identifying information. In the case of a video, start your presentation with a black screen with large white text that states right up front who you are and what the viewer is entitled to do with the file he or she is viewing. Then move smoothly into your presentation. Spending ten seconds on something like this right at the beginning ensures that most people who open up your file are exposed to the copyright information they need.

For audio presentations, you can do the same thing, though of course you have to say the words out loud. Use this voiceover as an opportunity to introduce yourself, if you like, or even to promote other content you create. You can close with the same information as well, but audio typically doesn't have credits in the same way that video does, so an opening probably works a bit better.

In a text document, create a title page that contains all the important information. Again, because it is the first page, your information can't be missed.

Using technology to your advantage

Everything discussed in the previous section falls into the category of letting people know about you, and about what they can and can't do with your content. You're providing information to your audience, and that's a good thing. Of course, you can also be a little more assertive about preventing people from using your content, or pieces of it, in their own work, or passing it off as their own. This idea isn't rocket science, either; you've probably thought of it already. Simply deliver your file in a proprietary format that isn't editable. Here's a list of suggestions:

✓ **For text documents:** If you're distributing a text document like a book or article, you should use Adobe Portable Document Format, or PDF. A PDF is readable on any machine with the free Adobe Reader on it, but you can't copy and paste text out of it and into another document. PDFs also ensure that the document formatting is exactly as you intend, regardless of the operating system being used.

✓ **For audio and video:** Consider using Windows Media or Real Networks to encode your file. Both these formats can be played and saved onto a computer, but they can't be opened and edited. No one can snag your best sound byte for his or her own use, or grab the footage of your trip to Tahiti to put in a video presentation.

✓ **For animations and photo slideshows:** Macromedia Flash is a common Web animation program, frequently used to create interactive presentations and games. You can also use it to create a photo slideshow. Best of all, Flash produces a file format that can be easily distributed and viewed, but again, it can't be opened and cannibalized.

By using a proprietary, but common, piece of software to deliver your content, you don't prevent people from watching, listening, or reading. You do prevent them from pulling pieces out of what you have created.

If you are contemplating using this technique, do your best to make life easy on those who are downloading your files. Choose software most users are likely to have, and that is free to acquire. If you get too obscure, no one will actually be able to watch, listen to, or read your file, which certainly prevents them from violating your copyright!

Digital Rights Management

If you use iTunes, Rhapsody, or Napster, you're already familiar with *digital rights management (DRM)*. DRM technology adds encryption and content controls to digital files, with the intended purpose of protecting the rights of the copyright owner.

DRM content often:

✓ Is only playable on certain computers, or with certain programs

✓ Can only be copied onto a CD or DVD a certain number of times

✓ Can only be played or viewed a certain number of times

✓ Usually can't be edited

✓ Frequently can't be transferred to another computer, temporarily or permanently

For these reasons, digital rights management is often drolly called digital *restrictions* management. The drive behind the creators of these tools is to prevent copyright violation in every possible way, and by limiting what those who actually do have rights to the data can do with it.

Some DRM tools enable those selling digital content to price different levels of access at different price points, but really the point comes down to Internet distribution. DRM-controlled content won't work if shared with other users, over BitTorrent or any other technology. Consequently, you can't use DRM in conjunction with a Creative Commons license permitting redistribution.

Advocates of free speech object to DRM-controlled content on the basis that no existing DRM tool allows for legitimate, legal uses of data — those covered under fair use or parody.

Other critics object to the limitations placed on consumers, who if they purchased the same data from another source, might have much broader control over the same content.

Most DRM tools do permit the file creator to select just what kind of protection they want their data to have, and it is theoretically possible to create a DRM-controlled data file that can be distributed legitimately using peer-to-peer technology (like BitTorrent). So far, however, none of the major users of DRM tools permit peer-to-peer trading, and it doesn't seem likely to occur in the future.

As a creator of content, you can explore protecting your own content using digital rights management. However, most of the companies currently offering DRM tools market directly to music labels, studios, and other large media holdings. There is, as of this writing, no good solution for the home computer user with just a few files to protect.

I don't recommend using DRM for your BitTorrent files. The concept behind the BitTorrent technology is open, free, and reasonable access to files. Restrictions like those used in DRM cause real problems and conflict with the basic philosophy of this type of file sharing, and there is no DRM solution that actually permits free redistribution of the kind used with BitTorrent.

Chapter 15

Using BitTorrent in Organizations

In This Chapter

▶ Understanding why BitTorrent is useful for businesses and organizations

▶ Getting some ideas for using BitTorrent effectively

▶ Assessing what using BitTorrent means to your bottom line

▶ Looking at some real-world examples of BitTorrent successes

*I*n 2005, a *Washington Post* article said of BitTorrent, "It's too robust to stamp out with lawsuits, but too effective not to adopt for commercial use." And, in fact, the use of BitTorrent can significantly decrease distribution costs for companies that deliver digital products like software or training videos.

As yet, few companies are taking advantage of this opportunity. This reluctance to embrace BitTorrent has more to do with the newness of the technology than anything else — businesses, groups, and individuals are used to the idea that delivering large files online is both expensive and difficult. BitTorrent and other peer-to-peer file-sharing networks are changing this perception, but in such a way that it has stayed off the radar of industry, academia, and commerce. The college student with high-speed Internet access may have a better idea of BitTorrent's ability to handle large files easily and inexpensively than most IT experts in the corporate environment.

Though the Motion Picture Association of American and the Recording Industry Association of America have taken BitTorrent to task for facilitating copyright infringement, in fact this application may be the best technical solution out there for distributing video online, should those organizations ever decide to get with the program and follow the technological trends.

In this chapter, I look at some of the potential uses and savings available to groups who take advantage of BitTorrent, and give you some examples of people and groups that are doing just that.

Delivering the Goods via BitTorrent

BitTorrent is capable of delivering files hundreds of megabytes in size to hundreds of concurrent downloaders, all without the use of expensive video streaming servers, huge amounts of disk space, and tremendous bandwidth load on the content publisher. Upload the file just once, and then let everyone who wants a copy of the file do the work of distributing it for you.

Here's how this process works:

1. **A file is seeded into the BitTorrent network, perhaps uploaded to a Web server, perhaps served off a local machine.**

2. **As others start to request and download the file, the file's tracker (whether server- or client-based) synchs up those who have pieces of the file with those who don't.**

   The BitTorrent tracking potential is quite sophisticated. The tracker can determine what file pieces are at least available, which users have high-speed connections, what pieces are needed next, and what different pieces to send to different peers to ensure widespread availability.

3. **Those who begin downloading the file begin immediately to upload as well.**

   This unique aspect of BitTorrent creates a continuous exchange of pieces throughout the network, as shown in Figure 15-1. The result is that even if a file begins with a single seeder, it is soon being seeded by any peer with a small bit of the file, taking the load off the initial seeder. In addition, pieces do not need to be downloaded sequentially, so a peer can take advantage of any pieces that are available, not just the next one in line.

   The more requests are made to the tracker, the more peers that join the swarm of uploading and downloading. More requests and more peers mean faster distribution.

The final result of all this activity is a huge increase in the ability of a publisher to distribute a file quickly and without being limited by one Web site's Internet connection, one Web server's bandwidth capabilities, or one user's connection speed.

BitTorrent has the potential to be scaled to serve millions of file-sharers, none of whom are subjected to huge costs or bandwidth load.

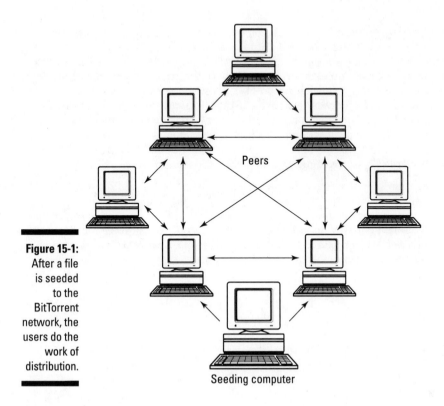

Peers

Seeding computer

Measuring Cost and Bandwidth Savings

Several elements are involved in serving very large files, no matter what they might be (audio, video, software, text, photos, and so on):

✔ **Web hosting:** For a Web site to be accessible on the Internet, it must be placed on a Web server. Web servers can hold text, HTML pages, images, video, or any other digital content. Web hosting can be acquired from a Web hosting company, or by setting up individual, dedicated Web servers. Web hosting packages are priced in part by the amount of Web space/media storage and bandwidth needed for the individual Web site. Costs vary widely, but begin around $10 a month and accelerate rapidly for Web sites with high Web space and bandwidth needs.

✔ **Web space/media storage:** Every digital file takes up a certain amount of space in the disk of a Web server. The larger the amount of space taken up, the higher the costs for a Web hosting account. Web sites that require storage space for very large files — like audio, video, and software — need a lot of Web space, which can be quite expensive.

✔ **Bandwidth:** Bandwidth is the amount of data that can be transferred on a Web site during a given time, usually one month. Small sites that don't get many visitors need very little bandwidth; large Web sites with lots of visitors need much more. Web sites that are providing access to extremely large files need a great deal of bandwidth. For example, a Web site providing access to a single 131MB file, with up to 50 users downloading it at the same time, needs about 6GB of bandwidth a month. Most Web hosting accounts include a certain amount of bandwidth, and charge more for use of extra bandwidth. Any content publisher putting up large files on a regular basis faces expensive bandwidth bills.

✔ **Streaming software, if needed:** Some media files — audio and video, usually — can be streamed to improve the user experience of those downloading the media. *Streaming media* enables users to hear or view it while it is being downloaded. Most streaming technology requires that the Web server have the streaming server software installed, for media files to be encoded in the streaming format, and for the user to have the player for the format installed on his or her system. The streaming server software, and licenses for the number of users who should be able to consume media at the same time, involve a significant outlay of money on the part of the publisher.

These ingredients for serving up files are necessary for every organization, from the largest multinational company to schools and single individuals. Clearly, individuals are less likely to be able to bear the costs associated with serving large files.

With BitTorrent, however, the scenario changes a bit:

✔ **Web hosting:** If a publisher wants to have a Web site, he or she must still purchase a Web hosting account. However, if the publisher only wants to share files using BitTorrent, having a Web site isn't mandatory, because the tracker Web site lists the file and gives others access to it. Or, the publisher could use a trackerless BitTorrent client.

✔ **Web space/media storage:** Publishers who share content via BitTorrent don't need to upload their files to the Web server. Even if they do so, the files can be taken down after they've been sufficiently seeded. This seeding technology greatly reduces the amount of storage space needed, which in turn greatly reduces the costs associated in the Web hosting account.

✔ **Bandwidth:** Those sharing BitTorrent files need only have sufficient bandwidth to seed their files once — other peers take over the process of distribution at that point. As a result, the need for bandwidth that permits a file to repeatedly download from a Web server is gone, and bandwidth needs are tied solely to the number of files being seeded by the publisher. Even if you need to reseed later, you still only need the bandwidth necessary to seed one copy of the file at any given time.

✔ **Streaming software:** Although publishers can still create Web content in a streaming format, the streaming server software doesn't have to be in place, nor are licenses that permit simultaneous playback necessary. The playback and encoding software for streaming files are typically free, so publishers can create files in the streaming format, distribute them via BitTorrent, and rest assured that users can play the files back easily — all without investing in the server software.

The traditional barrier to publishing large files on the Internet — cost — is vaulted when publishers use BitTorrent, no matter what industry you are part of, from academics to international finance. BitTorrent changes things for companies, groups, non-profits, research organizations, schools, and individuals who want to share large files with others at a low cost and without a lot of technical setup and maintenance.

The major hurdle to get over before beginning to use BitTorrent for distribution in your organization is one of education: Your users need to know how to acquire torrent files, and how to deal with them after the download is complete. They also need to know the ins and outs of file management so that they can maintain the files they upload (and upload them easily). Many Web publishers have chosen to deal with the learning curve by providing instruction and support for BitTorrent on their Web sites, and by being careful to create files that can easily be opened and played back on all kinds of computer platforms.

Getting Excited over BitTorrent Uses

Any organization or group with a lot of content to distribute can benefit from the financial savings of using BitTorrent instead of traditional FTP or HTTP transfers over the Web. Knowing this fact, though, doesn't mean you can't still miss the forest for the trees. If you plan to make media and other files available online and want others to be able to distribute them, do so using BitTorrent and be clear about whether you're permitting users to put the files into trackers and continue to share them. It's to your advantage if you do enable continued distribution, because users looking for the content won't have to come to you to download it.

Knowing the best uses for BitTorrent

BitTorrent distribution is best suited for

- **Big files:** Very large files, or sets of files that together are quite large. You can distribute small files with BitTorrent, but it's not the most efficient use of network resources.

- **Popular files:** Content that is going to be extremely popular during a short period. Bandwidth costs go up when you have lots of people trying to access the same file at the same time. If your content is going to be hot as soon as you announce it, BitTorrent can help you keep costs down and actually get people the files faster.

- **Non-super-secret files that aren't protected by copyright:** Content that can be freely distributed. I can't express strongly enough that the BitTorrent network isn't designed in any way for you to control access to torrent files. In fact, you can't predict where a file will end up when you release it to the BitTorrent network; nor can you predict how long it will remain available.

Introducing some cool distribution possibilities for BitTorrent

Here are just a few ideas for content suited for torrent distribution:

- **Distance learning:** Academic institutions and companies whose employees are geographically distanced from each other can distribute video lectures and presentations to outlying offices and branches.

- **Sharing of databases:** Companies and organizations that share large databases of contacts, records, files, and more can distribute the databases over a distance, *without* burning dozens of copies of a CD.

- **Libraries resources:** Libraries with collections of electronic research materials and archives can make these resources available to users, as some are already starting to do in other file formats.

- **Records:** Share records of employees, patients, and new members with remote locations that need access to the records. This potential offers a great opportunity to improve flexibility for international companies that frequently transfer employees from site to site.

- **Software:** Distribute software releases without incurring huge bandwidth loads every time you release a new bug fix.

- **Court documents:** Everyone knows being a lawyer means drowning in a sea of paper. How many trees could be saved if lawyers began sharing discovery documents as torrents instead of making 45 copies of the same content on paper?

✔ **Archives:** Any archive is rife for potential distribution via BitTorrent. Got a microfiche archive you just put in digital form? How about scans of all those old photographs? This content won't be changing anytime soon, so you can turn it into a torrent and call it done.

Looking at How BitTorrent Is Used Today

Companies and organizations — as well as individuals — are making use of BitTorrent in some creative and effective ways. These people all have one thing in common — a recognition that technology can make a huge difference in what they are trying to do.

Software

Distribution of Linux, an open-source operating system, is one of the best examples of effective BitTorrent use. As individual developers have created different flavors of the Linux operating system (and different versions of each flavor), developing a way to get the operating system out to those who wanted to use it has become a necessity.

These are very large files. You can use the word huge to describe them and not exaggerate. A distribution is often between 3GB and 5GB of data — that would be somewhere between 4 and 8 regular CD-ROMs of data.

Without distribution via BitTorrent, a Linux release could cripple a Web server. For that reason, Linux developers were among the very first to begin using BitTorrent for distribution, and it is now regarded as essential to the release of a new version.

Debian (whose Web site is shown in Figure 15-2), Red Hat, Mandriva, Fedora, and Connectiva are all Linux projects that distribute using BitTorrent.

Mattias Wadenstein of the Debian Project Group (www.debian.org) says that much of the impetus for distribution via BitTorrent came from users, and that as more users choose BitTorrent over other delivery methods, managing releases of new versions becomes easier. About 20 percent of those who download Debian now use BitTorrent, and the development group is hoping that figure grows.

Wadenstein's advice: "Try it, if you are already distributing via plain HTTP, provide BitTorrent as an alternative. And as BitTorrent becomes more available and integrated into browsers, it will be easier to use too. It is the future for large file distribution."

Makers of the Web browser Opera discovered what a problem downloads of their software could be in April 2005, when the sheer number of people trying to get a copy of the software got up to more than 100 per second. Opera Software's vice-president of engineering, Christen Krogh, called the incident a "technical knock-out to Opera's servers," and noted that "With BitTorrent, users would have had an alternative download mechanism."

So when Opera released the Opera 8.02 Preview 1 in July 2005, the company offered BitTorrent as one of the download options, as shown in Figure 15-3.

But Opera Software didn't stop there. The company included a new feature in this technical preview of Opera: BitTorrent is now built right into the browser. Want to download a torrent? Do everything directly through the Opera browser; no separate BitTorrent client is necessary.

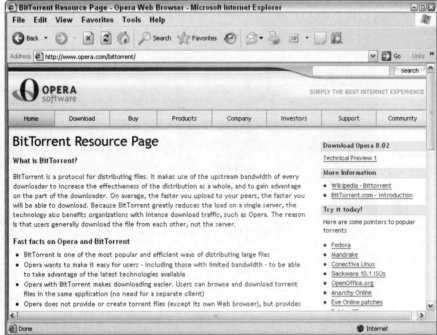

Figure 15-3:
Opera has
included a
full page
on its Web
site that
explains
BitTorrent.

You can find Opera browser versions for Windows, Linux, and Mac, all with
support for BitTorrent. According to Opera Software, BitTorrent support is
just the next logical step in supporting other file transfer protocols already in
use on the Web. For this company, the benefits of BitTorrent are so great they
have altered not just distribution of their product, but the product itself.

Games

Funcom's Anarchy Online is a science fiction-themed, massive, multiplayer,
online role-playing game that enables players to enter a world of monsters,
fantasy, and fantastic fighting. Players collect equipment, dispatch oppo-
nents, and advance through new levels, all while interacting with other players and the virtual environment.

In the eight months leading up to the game's four-year birthday, it attracted
more than 400,000 new signups, and a corresponding number of downloads
of the game client. At up to 1400MB a download, there was a lot of bandwidth
tied up in getting users set up to play the game (you can see the download
page in Figure 15-4).

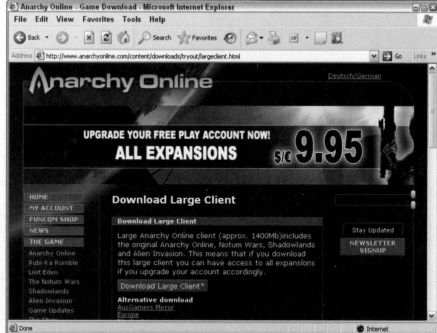

Figure 15-4:
To get
started
playing
Anarchy
Online, you
must first
download
the game
client using
BitTorrent.

A programmer at Funcom made the argument for using BitTorrent to distribute the game client, and as Jørgen Tharaldsen, product director for Funcom, says, "We haven't really looked back." In fact, says Tharaldsen, Funcom plans to do even more with BitTorrent when it releases new games in the future.

Funcom also uses BitTorrent to distribute large patches to the game, in the neighborhood of 100MB and under. Because players want the patches quickly, the surge of downloads when they become available actually improves the speed and quality of distribution.

The company deals with the rush by making the patch available on BitTorrent *before* the patch is on its regular FTP sites, thus steering a number of players into a method of downloading that is easier on Funcom's servers. "By using BitTorrent together with shifting downloads to alternate servers during these intense spikes in demand," says programmer Frank Stevenson, "we can significantly reduce our hosting costs."

Michael Mateas and Andrew Stern spent five years developing the artificial intelligence-based experiment in electronic narrative they call Façade. Their company, Procedural Arts, refers to Façade as both research and as art, but from the perspective of those who download it, it's an interactive game. Mateas, who runs the Experimental Games Laboratory at Georgia Tech, says the game is a "radical genre innovation that requires both design and technical innovation."

The game sets you up as the visitor of married couple Grace and Trip, shown in Figure 15-5. During your visit, their marriage starts to disintegrate before your eyes, and what you say to the two of them determines how the game plays out.

Façade was publicly released as a freeware download in July 2005. At 800MB it was too big to fit on a CD-ROM, and in any case, CDs require shipping and production costs. To save money, Procedural Arts opted to deliver Façade via a BitTorrent download, although you can also purchase a CD of the game from the company's Web site.

Music

At the South by Southwest *(SXSW)* Music and Media Conference held in Austin, Texas, in the spring of 2005, festival organizers worked with CitizenPod to produce a 2.6GB torrent of songs by the many performers at the festival.

More than 1,200 artists were part of the festival, and around 750 permitted SXSW to include their songs in the SXSW 2005 Showcasing Artist MP3 library in full, or in 30-second clips — all downloadable via BitTorrent.

Figure 15-5:
The interactive game Façade is available for download via BitTorrent.

Grace, are you angry at Trip?|

Text

Baen Books, a publisher of science fiction and fantasy books, has picked up on the power of word-of-mouth advertising and is fast capitalizing on it with the Baen Free Library.

Any author of a book published by Baen Books can participate in the Baen Free Library, which is essentially a collection of free titles that anyone can download. It may seem nonsensical to give away something that the publisher is also hoping to sell, but says First Librarian Eric Flint, "any kind of book distribution which provides free copies to people has always, throughout the history of publishing, eventually rebounded to the benefit of the author."

Baen Books is trading short-term profit (the potential sale of one book) for longer-term customer loyalty and an almost guaranteed increase in audience. After all, why wouldn't you recommend a good book to a friend if it was free?

An important component of the Baen Free Library, shown in Figure 15-6, is that the books can be freely redistributed via any method the reader sees fit. Baen Books has specifically established the library as a counter to some of the attitudes adopted by other publishers toward peer-to-peer distribution. And yes, you can find torrent files of these books. Visit the Baen Free Library at www.baen.com/library.

Figure 15-6:
The Baen Free Library is a source of free science fiction books that can be distributed into the BitTorrent network.

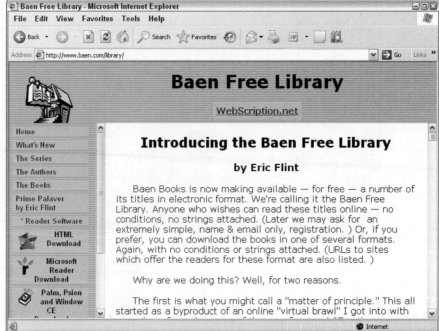

Video

Rocketboom is a three-minute daily video blog *(vlog)* put together by Andrew Baron and Amanda Congdon. Based out of New York, Rocketboom covers news stories in a non-conventional manner, ranging from celebrity lifestyles to science. A mixture of facts and analysis, the Rocketboom videos are a quirky mix of fun, sarcasm, and real information — it's news put together by actual people as opposed to dolls.

Rocketboom, shown in Figure 15-7, is available in several formats, from QuickTime video to torrents. You can get an RSS feed of Rocketboom as it is updated every day, as well. Here's what the Rocketboom Web site says about itself:

> *We differ from a regular TV program in many important ways. Instead of costing millions of dollars to produce, Rocketboom is created with a consumer-level video camera, a laptop, two lights and a map with no additional overhead or costs. Also, Rocketboom is distributed online, all around the world and on demand, and thus has a much larger potential audience than any TV broadcast. However, we spend $0 on promotion, relying entirely on word-of-mouth, and close to $0 on distribution because bandwidth costs and space are so inexpensive.*

Figure 15-7:
Get the Rocketboom video blog by torrent, QuickTime, or one of several other digital formats.

Part VI
The Part of Tens

"Honey — remember that pool party last summer where you showed everyone how to do the limbo in just a sombrero and a dish towel? It's being shared online as a torrent."

In this part . . .

I leave you with a set of three tens — 30 last tips, tricks, and suggestions to make your BitTorrent experience positive and enjoyable. In Chapter 16, I give you a comprehensive overview of the dizzying number of file types you can come across when you download content from BitTorrent. In Chapter 17, you get a chapter full of advice on how to protect yourself and your computer from viruses, worms, and spyware. It's sad but true — downloading files using BitTorrent means you're flirting with a few of these nasties. Last, but not least, is Chapter 18, a chapter dedicated to some of the best content I've found and downloaded using BitTorrent.

Chapter 16

Ten (Or So) Common File Formats for Sharing Your Content

*Y*ou encounter a dizzying number of different file formats when you share music, video, software, images, and other media using BitTorrent. This chapter touches on the range of these file formats.

These are brief overviews of the most common formats. You can find more information by searching about the particular file format in question at the Web site of the developer. I also include recommendations for formats you might choose when presenting your content.

Archived or Compressed Files

Many BitTorrent file creators choose to archive their files, sometimes for the sake of convenience, sometimes to bring down the overall file size of what they are sharing. The important thing to know is that when you download on of these files, you must *unpack* or *decompress* the archive before you can open the media files they contain.

Most of programs I list here open several kinds of compressed files, so you may only need one of these applications.

These are the most common archive file types:

- **ZIP:** ZIP files are produced by the WinZip program (available at www.winzip.com for $29). Files that are compressed with WinZip are referred to as *zipped.* You can use WinZip to both create and unpack ZIP files; you can also use WinZip to unpack most other standard archiving file formats. WinZip software often comes preinstalled on Windows PCs. You can download and use a 21-day evaluation version of the program, after which you are prompted with messages to purchase the software. WinZip is only available for Windows users, but you can open the ZIP format with almost any compression program, making it a good choice as an archive format.

- **RAR:** The .rar format is used to compress a series of files; it's a popular format among hardcore BitTorrent users because of its raw compression power. This format is native to WinRAR (available at www.rarlab.com for $29). WinRAR creates and decompresses .rar files and many other standard archive formats. You can download the 40-day free evaluation version of WinRAR, which is available for Windows, Macintosh, and Linux operating systems. Use the .rar format when you have several large files to compress into a single archive.

- **SIT:** StuffIt Expander is ideal for handling file archives with a .sit extension. SIT files are the compressed files created by the Macintosh OS by default, so StuffIt often comes pre-installed on Apple computers. You can use StuffIt Expander (www.stuffit.com, free) to open many standard archive file types, and the program has versions for the Macintosh, Windows, and Linux operating systems. The .sit format is native to Macintosh, and a good choice if Apple users are your target audience. *Note:* StuffIt Expander can only be used to open archive files, not to create them.

Video Files

Figuring out all the video formats available online can be one of the major technical headaches of using BitTorrent. This guide gives you the basics of the most common formats:

- **AVI:** Microsoft created its own video standard known as Audio Video Interleave. It is considered to be the Windows standard, and the most common Windows video file format in use. Because this file type was created by Microsoft, it plays with no problem in Windows Media Player (www.microsoft.com/windows/windowsmedia/default.aspx, free), which comes installed on all Windows machines. You can also play AVI files on Macintosh computers, and there is also a Macintosh version of Windows Media Player. AVI is a good choice for most video, but does create huge files.

✔ **QT (audio) and MOV (video):** QuickTime is an audio and video format developed by Apple. QuickTime is a versatile media system that enables users to play both video and audio files. QuickTime files play on both Macs and PCs. MOV files are quite common on the Web, especially because QuickTime playback is supported by all the major browsers. You can download the QuickTime Player (available at `www.quicktime.com` for free), although many media players can handle these formats. QuickTime provides excellent visual quality and good compatibility across platforms, making it a good choice for video you want to share with BitTorrent.

✔ **MPEG:** This file format is primarily used for video and is among the most common video file types shared on BitTorrent. Moving Picture Experts Group is a company that developed the standard for MPEG files. Most DVDs and video CDs use the MPEG format. These files can be large or small, depending on the type of MPEG, the compression technology used to encode the file, and the length of the video. MPEG files are compatible with most platforms and their related players so you don't have to download a specific player to play them. As a result, MPEG is a good choice for video you want to share with users on many different computer platforms.

✔ **RM:** Files with the `.rm` extension indicates that a file has been created in the native file format for RealNetworks. The `.rm` file extension usually indicates video that has been encoded to stream over the World Wide Web, and to play back in RealPlayer (available at `www.real.com` for free). Real media files tend to be good quality with low file sizes. (RA files are the audio version of this format.)

Streaming files aren't terribly commonly shared using BitTorrent, but they do have the advantage of being fairly commonly readable by different kinds of computers. Plus, the tools to create the files are free. Combine that with the free player, and RM, ASF, and WMV are a reasonable alteratives to use when you can't create files in QuickTime, MPEG, or AVI format.

✔ **ASF:** These files are created by the proprietary Microsoft standard for video streaming, Advanced Streaming Format. ASF files are usually streamed across the Internet but can also be played locally with Windows Media Player. These files have to be played in the Windows Media Player.

✔ **WMV:** Windows Media is a proprietary video format developed by Microsoft. The `.wmv` file extension indicates that the file is video, and is designed to be played by Windows Media Player. These files are encoded as streaming files, ideal for Web delivery. Windows Media files are often associated with `.asf`, or Advanced Streaming Format. You must use Windows Media Player to view WMV files. (WMA is the audio flavor of this format.)

Audio Files

The number of possible audio formats boggles the mind. Although some formats are proprietary, most can be played back on any media player on both PC and Macintosh computers.

- **AIFF:** The Audio Interchange File Format is an audio archive solution originally developed by Apple. Much like Microsoft WAV files, AIFF files aren't compressed and tend to be quite large. AIFF files are considered a standard in the storage of audio data on a computer. They tend to have a high quality of sound, but their size limits their usefulness for those wishing to use portable audio devices. The format isn't proprietary — you can play AIFF files in any media player. Because AIFF is pretty uncommon, some people may not know what to do with an AIFF, so they aren't the best choice for sharing audio with BitTorrent.

- **ASF:** See the entry for ASF in the section, "Video Files," earlier in this chapter.

- **CDA:** CDA stands for *compact disc audio*. Simply put, CDA audio tracks are the tracks found on audio compact discs. This audio format is used in compact disc players where the audio is then translated by your player and played through headphones or speakers. You can play these files in any media player that can play music CDs. When you see CDA files being shared, make extra sure that they are being made available legally, and aren't ripped from a commercial CD without permission.

- **MP3:** The MP3 format is the most popular audio format on the Internet. The MP3 format is so popular because it's a compressed format — which makes for small audio files. It's popular among Internet users who listen to music, archived audio broadcasts, or record their own audio at home. Most stores these days carry portable MP3 players and many home CD and DVD players play *burned* discs that use the MP3 format. Every media player on your computer plays MP3 files, making this format an excellent choice for sharing audio using BitTorrent.

- **RA:** See the RM entry in the section, "Video Files," earlier in this chapter.

- **WAV (or WAVE):** These files are created in the WAVE format developed and enhanced by Microsoft, which operates much like an AIFF, created by Apple. The files are large and are used mostly for archiving audio that must retain high levels of detail and quality. When making an audio CD from MP3 media, audio files are converted to WAV before generating the CD. This format can be played in any media player, and gives you good audio fidelity. It's a good choice for sharing audio using BitTorrent.

- **WMA:** See the WMV entry in the "Video Files" section earlier in this chapter.

Image Files

The good news about images you might download with BitTorrent is that there are very few operating system incompatibilities. Image formats have been around long enough that support for most formats is built in to all operating systems. A couple of formats are intended for high-end uses like printing; you can't open these formats without a proprietary graphics editing program. Aside from that, you should have an easy time opening most image formats you come across:

- ✔ **JPG and JPEG:** JPG (or JPEG) stands for Joint Photographic Expert Group, the originator of the file type. These files are partly compressed and commonly used on Web pages. They are ideal for images with lots of color, like photographs. You can open any of these files by simply double-clicking them. JPEG is a good format for sharing images with BitTorrent.

- ✔ **GIF:** GIF stands for Graphics Interchange Format. These files are another common Web standard. They are often used for graphic images such as drawings in one or two colors because the compression inherent to the format involves using a very small palette of colors. You can view GIFs by double-clicking, or by opening them using a Web browser, making them very accessible to those you share them with.

- ✔ **TIF or TIFF:** These files are short for Tagged Image File Format. This is a very high-quality format. These files are platform independent and can be viewed by most graphics programs.

- ✔ **PNG:** PNG stands for Portable Network Graphics. PNG was created to replace GIF images and TIFFs, but this transition hasn't really happened. Nonetheless, most computers have no trouble displaying these files.

- ✔ **BMP:** BMP stands for *bitmap*. These files are quite large, though not particularly wonderful in quality. BMP is a native Windows format, but the files open just fine on Macintosh computers. Still, BMP isn't the best choice for sharing content since the files are unnecessarily large.

- ✔ **EPS:** EPS stands for Encapsulated PostScript. These files are generally created for use by printers, so you don't find them often on the Web. They are very high-quality, and must be opened using a graphics editing program like Adobe Photoshop. EPS shouldn't be your first choice for sharing images using BitTorrent.

- ✔ **RAW:** These files are created by some digital cameras, and represent the data recorded by the camera before any file format or compression is applied. They are very large files, and very high-quality images. You must use a high-end graphics editing program like Adobe Photoshop to open RAW files. RAW usually isn't a good choice for sharing images using BitTorrent, because it is unfamiliar to most people.

Text Files

Text files are used to distribute books, manuals, or other lengthy written material. There are only a couple of possibilities for this format:

- ✔ **TXT:** These files are basic text files that can be viewed with any word processor, from simple applications like Notepad to Microsoft Word. These files offer no style formatting options (bold, italics, and so on).

- ✔ **RTF:** Rich Text Format was developed to permit reliable text document exchanges between different computer platforms. Unlike files with the .txt extension, Rich Text Format includes stylistic formatting like bold, italics, and so on. You can open files with the .rtf extension with any word processor application, from SimpleText to Microsoft Word.

If you do share text, but don't want it to be editable by others, or to let others copy and paste sections from your text, consider converting your text to the PDF format I describe in the following section.

PDFs

When publishers want to present material with a fixed, uneditable format, PDF, or Portable Document Format, is often their first choice. PDF was created by Adobe Systems (makers of Adobe Photoshop, among many other applications), to permit reliable delivery of brochures, artwork, text, and images over the Internet. The big goal of PDF was to make the display of the file the same, regardless of users' computers or operating systems. Fonts look as they were originally intended, even if you don't have those fonts on your computer. Layout elements stay where they belong, unlike Web pages, which can vary in appearance depending on which browser is being used to view them.

PDFs are a common format for eBooks and other written material. It's also a great format for transmitting material intended to be printed. PDFs can be searched for content, and you can even hyperlink content in a PDF you create. Agencies distribute PDF versions of forms that can be filled in and printed — no more messing around with typewriters! The other big advantage to using a PDF is that your content is protected; you control the format (the way it looks), and you ensure that the text can't be copied and pasted into another document. This protection provides a little bit of security for your text, making it a little harder for others to quickly make use of your text.

To open and view PDF documents, you need the Adobe Reader (www.adobe. com/products/acrobat/readstep2.html, available for free). To create PDF files, you need to purchase Adobe Standard (www.adobe.com/products/ acrobatstd, available for $299) or Acrobat Professional (www.adobe.com/ products/acrobatpro, available for $499). There is also a very reasonably priced Adobe PDF Online service (createpdf.adobe.com, available for a free trial).

HTML Files

Because BitTorrent is part of the Internet, you won't be surprised to come across Hypertext Markup Language files (.htm, .html). These versatile files are intended to be displayed in a Web browser, but you can also open and view them in any text or HTML editor.

Although you can use an editor to view HTML documents, they're intended to be viewed using a Web browser like Mozilla, Firefox, Opera, Netscape, or Internet Explorer.

These files frequently come in conjunction with other media — images, audio, video, and animation. If you have a folder of several HTML pages and other files, look for the one named index.htm or index.html. The index is often the starting point for any Web page presentation.

Flash Files

Macromedia Flash is the application used to create many Web animations, from pointless corporate promos to equally pointless (but snazzy) games. The file extension for these animations is .swf, and like PDF files, SWF documents play on any computer that is running the Macromedia Flash Player. Happily, SWF files always look and act the same way, no matter what kind of computer they are played on.

The exciting thing about Flash animation is its small file size, combined with graphics that permit a lot of scaling — watch the animation in a small-screen format, and then watch it at a bigger resolution; the file looks good both ways.

Even though Flash is designed to produce the smallest possible file size, the nature of animation files make them complicated, long and, consequently, perfectly suited for delivery with BitTorrent. Watch the animation by double-clicking it or by dragging it into a Web browser.

Get Macromedia Flash Player for free from www.macromedia.com/shockwave/ download/download.cgi?P1_Prod_Version=ShockwaveFlash.

Executable Files

An executable file has the `.exe` extension. These files run applications on your computer. For example, the program Microsoft Word opens when your computer accesses and runs the file `winword.exe`.

If you download an EXE file from the Internet or with BitTorrent, be cautious about running it. These are powerful programs, and can make changes at all levels of your operating system. Don't ever download or run an executable file if you aren't sure whether it is what it claims to be. Use common sense about where you download these files from. For example, if you download the Adobe Reader from the Adobe Web site, you can be fairly sure that the executable you are receiving is not malicious. On the other, hand if you intend to download an MP3 file, and you end up with an EXE file, be very suspicious. In Chapter 17, I share my tips for staying safe from viruses, which can be transmitted using BitTorrent.

Many software manufacturers offer downloadable executable files that are actually installers, programs that fetch and install the actual application. Malicious executable files may install spyware or viruses on your computer.

Macintosh software is installed by dragging files from a disc image, or DMG, onto the computer's hard drive. Exercise the same caution with DMGs that you do with EXE files on a PC.

Chapter 17

Ten (Or So) Things You Can Do to Stay Safe from Viruses

....

....

*N*o one who uses the Internet (much less downloads and shares files online) can afford to ignore the issues of spam, spyware, and viruses. Most computer users don't understand how viruses work and how computers can be compromised by even the smallest software bug. As users become more computer savvy and high-speed Internet connections grow in popularity, you see more computers being hacked more often. As a result, a good firewall is a file downloader's best friend.

Unfortunately, files downloaded via BitTorrent are as likely as any to contain harmful bits of computer code. All person-to-person file-sharing systems are plagued with viruses that love to hop along for the ride. Some viruses are distributed inadvertently by people who are unaware that their files are infected. Others are unleashed specifically because BitTorrent is a great technology for starting a viral plague.

Sadly, a lot of these attacks go unnoticed until the computer user notices something is wrong and addresses it. Days, even weeks, can pass before the user realizes what's happened, and by that time it's too late. Data may have been stolen, copied, deleted, or the computer itself may have been used for some other purpose. Certainly, the nature of the BitTorrent network means that the torrent has been shared back into the community, further spreading the virus.

How do you avoid this problem? Be diligent and attentive about the files you download and also pay attention to the files you share. In this chapter, I share some of my advice for maintaining a good relationship with BitTorrent, BitTorrent sharers, your friends, and — most importantly — your computer.

I don't want to scare you away from downloading and sharing files, but you shouldn't ignore these issues. Keeping a computer healthy is very important when you share files across the globe.

Install Antivirus Software

I can't stress enough the importance of having and using antivirus software. Antivirus software is made for all computer users, from the most to least savvy. New viruses appear all the time, so keeping up with all the changes can be a full-time job. That's why you need good software to monitor your computer 24 hours a day, 7 days a week.

Not only can antivirus software protect your computer, it can also protect *you*. All kinds of information gets shared across the Internet, including bank records and other personal data. Just about anything you can store on your home computer can be a target for those who wish to access it. Protecting that data and making sure to keep your protection up to date are critical.

Run your antivirus program regularly, both to obtain updates from the manufacturer and to check your data, even if you don't think you have a virus.

Many users want their antivirus software to just work. They want to install it and forget about, hoping against hope that their protection is occurring in the background. But makers of viruses have amply demonstrated in recent years that they can be just as creative as any painter, composer, or writer. Virus manufacturers express their creative side by exploiting weaknesses and security holes. The most significant security hole is the lack of proactive effort that many users make to run regular virus scans.

By keeping your antivirus software updated, and by running it at least once a week you can keep yourself from being the victim of these artists. If you're in the market for antivirus software, Table 17-1 lists a few software programs (from most expensive to least expensive) that you should consider.

Table 17-1	Good Antivirus Software Products	
Name	*Price*	*Web Site*
Symantec Norton AntiVirus	$50	www.symantec.com/nav
McAfee VirusScan	$40	www.mcafee.com
Grisoft AVG Anti-Virus	$33	www.grisoft.com
ClamAV	Free	www.clamav.net

Inform Yourself about New Virus Threats

Be aware of new virus threats even if you have antivirus software. It's a bit boring, I know, but if only a few people maintained even a small understanding about the computer threats out there, the spread of viruses could be greatly slowed.

Mac OS is not immune to virus attacks

One of the most common beliefs about Apple computers is that they're invincible, especially safe from viruses that usually plague PCs. The truth is that viruses *can* spread through Apple computers and, yes, some viruses target Mac OS X computers. If you're a Mac user, here are two concerns to keep in mind:

✔ Just because your machine doesn't show any symptoms of infection or isn't susceptible to a particular virus doesn't mean it's not capable of passing the virus on. In fact, if you accidentally download a Windows virus using BitTorrent, the virus won't infect your Apple machine, but it will be passed out again to the BitTorrent community by your computer.

✔ Some virus programs out there target Macs, and Macs are susceptible to Unix viruses (Apple's latest operating system is built on Unix).

Antivirus software is just as important for Apple users as it is for PC users, if only so that you don't commit the unforgivable sin of passing on a virus to others.

Many antivirus providers keep public records, solutions, and documents on their Web sites. For example, at the Symantec Web site, shown in Figure 17-1, you can access the newest threats, advisories, and downloads. By keeping customers current to new threats and potential problems, Symantec keeps its customers safer.

It takes time for a new threat to become public and for the antivirus software company to develop an antidote. Knowing that you're at risk enables you to take precautions during those times when your antivirus software can't protect you.

Scan Your BitTorrent Downloads

After you download a file with BitTorrent, scan it! If the scan is completed and nothing bad turns up, you're probably good to go. If, on the other hand, you get a virus warning, get rid of those files immediately and then run a scan on your whole computer.

Running scans on individual files is worth the occasional extra hassle. The alternative may be dealing with a crashed computer and reinstalling your system software! Pat yourself on the back each time you scan your downloads — the majority of users do not.

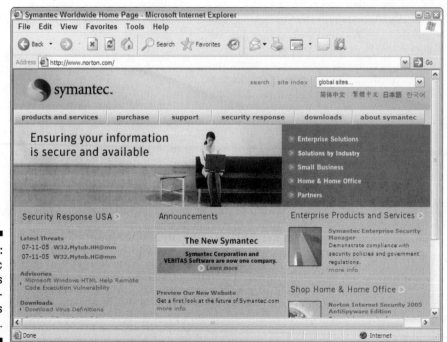

Figure 17-1:
Symantec posts alerts and warnings on its home page.

Pay Attention to Warnings and Messages

With antivirus software installed, you get occasional messages from that software that you need to pay attention to. The software is designed to warn you when your computer is about to take a risky action. Don't ignore them!

Look for a link in the message that gives you additional information and explanation. If you don't understand a message, query your antivirus software help desk.

If an application requests access to the Internet, make sure you understand which application is making the request before you approve it. Viruses frequently try to phone home or spread to other computers, so a warning that an application you don't recognize wants to access the Internet may be a warning sign of a virus — which is, of course, exactly why your antivirus software gives you the message.

Not every warning is an emergency; some may only be reminders to perform a scan on your computer, or to update your virus definitions.

Update. Update Again. And Again.

You should update your antivirus software often to ensure that your computer is protected with the latest virus definitions and not open to any known threats. In most packages, updates occur automatically, but don't rely solely on the automatic systems. If your computer wasn't connected to the Internet when the software attempted to update itself, or if you shut down the computer in the middle of an update, you may have interrupted or prevented an update.

Get in the habit of checking to make sure your antivirus software is frequently updated. If it has been more than a few days since the last automatic update, manually update the virus definitions yourself. If you have a high-speed Internet connection, you are more likely to be updated regularly. If you have dial-up access, make sure the first thing you do is update your protection when you connect to the Internet.

Scan Your Computer Regularly

Scanning your entire system on a regular basis is always a good idea. If you are a regular BitTorrent user you should be very conscientious about regular scans because you add foreign files to your computer quite often. Running frequent system scans is especially important if you forget to scan all of your downloaded files as they come onto your system. (Don't be lazy — run frequent system scans *and* scan individual files!)

Scan your system at least once a week. If you frequently share files and you share large numbers of files, you should scan files even more often.

Most antivirus software enables you to schedule scans that run automatically at a certain time of day on a certain day of the week. Pick a time when you're not usually using your computer, because a scan of every file on your system does slow down performance.

If you leave your computer on when you are not using it, set a time during the night when the computer can scan without interruption.

One of the major reasons computers get infected is because users cancel system scans and stop them from running. If you're in the middle of some project, like writing an essay, doing your taxes, or surfing the Web for the latest the antivirus updates, and your antivirus program decides to scan your machine, you should choose one of the following options:

- ✔ Pause the scan and continue it when you know you are done for the day.

- ✔ Reschedule the scan for later in the day.

- ✔ Set your project aside and let your antivirus software do its thing. (Go out for a latte or something.)

Most software enables you to run a scan whenever you want, so set a time when you won't need to cancel the scan.

Spread the Word

If you make a discovery or read something about protecting your computer against attack, let others know where you got the information. Keep everyone you know in the loop.

Be careful not to spread rumors. E-mails commonly flood the Internet warning about horrendous viruses that don't actually exist. When you see information about a virus that annihilates your whole address in milliseconds, check the Web site of your antivirus software. A simple query about whether the rumor is true could keep you from irritating everyone in your address book with the latest scam. It could also mean you're able to let all these people know about a real risk.

Look for references to hoaxes on your antivirus software company's Web site; each company commonly updates a list of hoax viruses to prevent false alarms.

Here are a few good sources of current virus information:

- ✔ **Symantec AntiVirus information:**

  `securityresponse.symantec.com/avcenter`

  For information about hoaxes, visit:

  `securityresponse.symantec.com/avcenter/hoax.html`

- ✔ **McAfee AntiVirus information:**

  `us.mcafee.com/virusInfo`

  For information about hoaxes, visit:

  `us.mcafee.com/virusInfo/default.asp?id=hoaxes`

- ✔ **Panda AntiVirus information:**

  `www.pandasoftware.com/virus_info`

  For information about hoaxes, visit:

  `www.pandasoftware.com/virus%5Finfo/hoaxes`

If you accidentally send a message about a hoax virus to your friends and contacts, make sure you follow up with a message letting them know there isn't actually a threat. Most people will understand that your mistake was honest and appreciate the intent behind your warning. If someone sends you false information about a threat that doesn't exist, politely let the person know.

Installing Spyware-Killing Software

One of the most common buzzwords floating around the Internet over the last year or two is the term *spyware*. A virus is software that's intended to destroy a computer and to propagate itself. Spyware is a small software package or a small bit of code that is designed to collect information about you, your computer, or your computer use.

The information collected by spyware is sometimes used to inform advertising networks about your interests. Other times it's collected by people who should definitely not have the password to your online banking account. In either case, spyware can be distributed via BitTorrent just as easily as legitimate files can. Usually spyware is identified as a different file or is packaged with a file you actually want.

To combat these spyware packages, you can install data-mining removal software. I list the most popular here.

> ✔ **Lavasoft Ad-Aware SE:**
>
> www.lavasoftusa.com/software/adaware
>
> ✔ **Spybot Search and Destroy:**
>
> www.safer-networking.org

Some antivirus software is set up to scan your system for spyware, too.

Update Your Operating System

One more important step in maintaining a healthy computer is to keep it up to date with system software updates and fixes. The Windows operating system automatically notifies you of new fixes, called *patches*. To see if your Windows computer is up to date, visit the Windows Update Web site (windowsupdate.microsoft.com).

If you don't want any direct involvement in choosing and installing updates, you can allow Windows to update your system for you. You tell the computer to download and install any updates that are released at a time when you're not using the computer, ensuring that you're always current and never miss an update. You can also set Windows Update to simply let you know when an update is available, rather than updating without asking. Some users prefer to know what is going on with their system rather than just letting Windows do its thing.

Apple computers have a similar system for staying current. By running the Apple Software Updates tool, you find out which downloads are available to keep your system running happily.

Follow Your Gut

You probably know something about the content you are trying to download. You may know the title, artist, or the media type, for example. Unfortunately, some people out there try to share files that seem like what you want — and definitely aren't.

To defeat these kinds of people who purposely spread bad code, you must be vigilant. If you download a file your computer doesn't understand or recognize, you should hear alarms go off. If you don't feel right about a file or just get a twinge of doubt about what you have downloaded, trust your gut and delete it.

An unknown file type isn't always spyware or a virus. Sometimes files get renamed and lose the appropriate file information. Or perhaps you don't have the right software to access the file.

Scan Files You Download through Instant Messengers and E-mail

Most instant messaging programs today permit users to transfer files, leaving your computer vulnerable if you happen to receive files during instant messaging sessions. Some instant messengers are scanned by antivirus software and firewalls, but not all. If you download a file across an instant messenger system, make sure to scan it before adding it to any torrent file you make. An unprotected messenger system can trade files back and forth all day long and never scan any of the files you exchange. Likewise, make sure that files that you send and receive via e-mail are scanned!

Chapter 18

Ten Fun BitTorrent Downloads

*W*hile doing the research for this book, I found many great media files to download with BitTorrent. In this chapter, I get to share my ten favorite pieces of content with you!

Everything I mention in this chapter is both free, and freely available. Each of the publishers featured in this chapter has set out to create content that can be freely downloaded and distributed via file-sharing technologies, so you don't have to worry about copyright infringement.

Whether you're a music lover, a video hound, or like to read, you can find something in this chapter to enjoy. I even include a game you can download and play. Enjoy!

WIRED Magazine's Creative Commons CD

This collection of music was given away with the November 2004 issue of *WIRED* magazine along with the directives: "Rip. Mash. Sample. Share." Songs by artists like the Beastie Boys, David Byrne, Spoon, and others are included among the 16 tracks. Most of the songs are available for non-commercial sharing and commercial sampling, but restrict advertising uses of the music.

The CD is a tribute to the idea that, for musicians, creative inspiration often comes from the works of other artists. It is the hope of all the editors and contributors at *WIRED* that you can use these songs to keep your own creative juices flowing.

Visit the Web site: `www.wired.com/wired/archive/12.11/sample.html`

Get the torrent: `www.legaltorrents.com/bit/wired-creative-commons-cd.torrent`

Panorama Ephemera

Rick Prelinger's documentary treatment of freely available industrial, advertising, educational, and amateur films has produced a strange and fascinating look at American history.

Prelinger produced *Panorama Ephemera* in 2004, and released it in several formats, including via BitTorrent. Pieces of the collage include footage from a meat-processing plant, American protests, and everyday objects seen through the camera lens. Over time, a curious story emerges.

Panorama Ephemera was released under a Creative Commons license, and may be freely shown, copied, or distributed with attribution and for non-commercial purposes. Prelinger even offers the Final Cut Pro project for use by other filmmakers who would like to remix the film themselves.

Visit the Web site: `www.archive.org/details/panorama_ephemera2004` (See Figure 18-1.)

Check out the torrent:
`www.legaltorrents.com/bit/panorama_ephemera.torrent`

Blue: A Short Film

Blue is an animated science fiction short featuring a likable computer graphics robot named Blue (see Figure 18-2). During Blue's adventures on a space station, he pushes buttons he shouldn't and gets into trouble.

The film was created by Christopher Mullins, Aaron Webster, and James Anderson, and was released in September 2003. It was entered and shown on the film festival circuit and took prizes at several festivals. The creators of *Blue* went on to start Xenobi Studios together.

Blue is 23 minutes long. This animated film is suitable for children. The makers have released the film with a Creative Commons license.

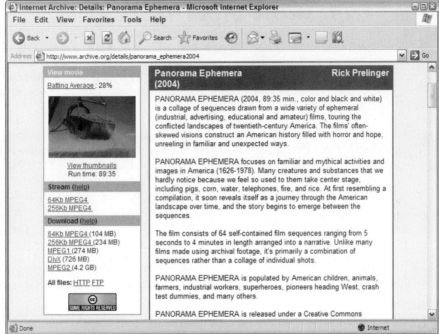

Visit the Web site: www.blueshortfilm.com

Get the torrent: www.legaltorrents.com/bit/blue-a-short-film.
torrent

Figure 18-2:
Meet
Blue, the
inquisitive
robot
featured
in this
animated
short film.

Field Trip: West Siberia

Ever wondered what Siberia looks like? You find out in *Field Trip: West Siberia,* a 55-minute movie that follows a group of ornithologists across the Siberian landscape. The movie is beautifully produced — and unless you've got pretty different ideas about vacation destinations, is probably as close to Siberia as you are likely to get.

Wildlife abounds, from owls to hedgehogs. You also see fascinating local cultures. *Field Trip: Siberia* was produced by Hanawey Studios, and is the studio's first film targeted to Western viewers. Hanawey specializes in documentaries. *Field Trip: West Siberia* is available for free distribution for non-profit and non-commercial viewing, under a Creative Commons license. The film is in Russian, and has English subtitles.

Visit the Web site: `mirror.mricon.com/fieldtrip`

Get the torrent: `www.legaltorrents.com/bit/field-trip-west-siberia-avi.torrent`

The Scene

Here's the setup: "NYU student Brian Sandro has a secret: He and his friends pirate hundreds of millions of dollars of illicit Hollywood movies in their spare time. They are revered, reviled, hunted, and admired. No one knows who they are — at least, not as far as they know."

The Scene is a dramatic TV series created by Jun Group Entertainment, and free to all file sharers. *The Scene* explores where digital piracy begins, as movies, songs, and video games are made available on peer-to-peer file-sharing networks.

This archive contains the first nine episodes, but expect more.

Visit the Web site: `www.welcometothescene.com` (See Figure 18-3.)

Get the torrent: `www.legaltorrents.com/bit/welcome-to-the-scene-vol-1.torrent`

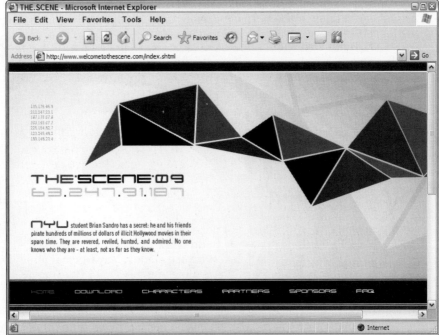

Figure 18-3:
Find out
more about
the char-
acters in
The Scene
at the
show's
Web site.

Free Culture

Free Culture, written by Lawrence Lessig, is a book that's available in two formats via BitTorrent: You can get a PDF version of the book's text, or you can
access it as an audio book. The audio book, read by volunteers who each
took on a chapter, is the direct result of the Creative Commons license used
by Lessig to permit derivative works based on the book's text.

Free Culture is an exploration of the social aspects of creativity. Lessig looks
at how creativity in one form can inspire and inform new works, paying particular attention to how society's laws and technologies permit and inhibit
the creation of derivative works. Ultimately, Lessig argues, current structures
are actively damaging the future of creative innovation — and, Lessig says,
our creative freedom. Lessig is no stranger to the changes digital technology
has created in how copyrighted works are handled.

Lessig's Creative Commons license for the work permits redistribution, copying, and reusing the book for non-commercial purposes as long as he is credited.

Visit the Web site: `free-culture.cc` (See Figure 18-4.)

Get the torrent of the PDF: `www.legaltorrents.com/bit/freeculture.zip.torrent`

Get the torrent for the audio book: `www.legaltorrents.com/bit/freeculture-audiobook.zip.torrent`

Piracy Is Good?

In May 2005, the online magazine *Mindjack* published a two-part article by Mark Pesce titled "Piracy Is Good? How *Battlestar Galactica* Killed Broadcast TV." Along with the articles, *Mindjack* made a May 6 digital piracy presentation done by Pesce available as a high-quality QuickTime movie, and downloadable via BitTorrent.

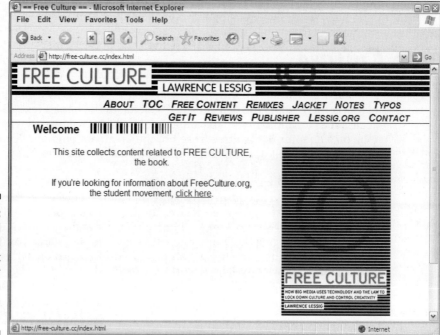

Figure 18-4:
Read reviews and more about the author at the Free Culture Web site.

Pesce discusses "the day that television died," which he identifies as October 18, 2004. On October 18, British broadcaster SkyOne ran the premiere of *Battlestar Galactica.* Not long after the episode aired, it was available on the Internet for download. Although *Battlestar Galactica* wasn't slated for broadcast in the United States until January 2005, U.S. viewers didn't have to wait (although, of course, these files weren't available legally). Pesce discusses the effect of digital piracy on broadcasters, and talks about how peer-to-peer file-sharing must change the entire distribution industry.

Mark Pesce is the co-creator of VRML (Virtual Reality Modeling Language), author of *The Playful World: How Technology Is Transforming Our Imagination* and is redesigning the curriculum of the Australian Film Television and Radio School.

Read Pesce's article on the *Mindjack* Web site: `www.mindjack.com/feature/piracy051305.html` (See Figure 18-5.)

Access the torrent: `interactive.edu.au/PiracyIsGood-small.mov.torrent`

Figure 18-5:
Mindjack magazine's "Piracy Is Good?" by Mark Pesce includes a torrent of a BitTorrent presentation by Pesce.

South by Southwest Showcasing Artist MP3s

At the South by Southwest Music and Media Conference held in 2005, festival organizers worked with CitizenPod to produce a torrent of tracks from many of the festival's performers. More than 1,200 artists were part of the festival, and many musical acts permitted SXSW to included their songs in the SXSW 2005 Showcasing Artist MP3 library in full, or in 30-second clips — all downloadable via BitTorrent.

You can find more than 750 CD-quality MP3 files to download. You need 2.6GB of space on your computer to hold all this music, and another 85MB for the additional songs added later.

See which artists are involved in the SXSW Music and Media conference at this Web site: 2005.sxsw.com/music/showcases/date/2005-03-16.html.

Get the torrent: 2005.sxsw.com/geekout/fest4pod/

8BitPeoples Archives

8BitPeoples is a collective of musicians producing music inspired by a love of classic video games. The tracks reflect the frenetic energy of most video games. 8BitPeoples distributes its music for free, and even provides artwork and liner notes for those who want to burn CDs. (You can also purchase higher-quality files if you prefer them to the freely available MP3s.)

You can download individual MP3s from the 8BitPeoples Web site or download an archive compilation from LegalTorrents.com. The LegalTorrents archive includes 196 songs.

Visit the Web site: www.8bitpeoples.com (See Figure 18-6.)

Get the torrent: www.legaltorrents.com/bit/8bitpeoples-archives-vol-1.torrent

Figure 18-6:
Get a full discography of 8BitPeoples' work at this Web site.

Façade

Feel like playing a game? You're in luck! Façade, created by Procedural Arts, is an artificial intelligence–based game. The game sets you up as the visitor of married couple Grace and Trip. During your visit, their marriage starts to disintegrate before your eyes, and what you say to the two of them determines how the game plays out.

Procedural Arts calls the game "an attempt to move beyond traditional branching or hyper-linked narrative to create a fully-realized, one-act interactive drama." Because playing with artificial intelligence isn't something you get to do every day, you will no doubt have a good time in this 3D virtual environment. Façade was publicly released as a freeware download in July 2005. You can also purchase a CD of the game on the Web site. You can see a screenshot from the game in Figure 18-7. Don't let the graphics fool you — this game is a sophisticated experience!

Make sure you have the hard drive space to handle the game before you get started: This is an 800MB download.

Visit the Web site: www.interactivestory.net

Get the torrent: www.interactivestory.net/bittorrent

Figure 18-7:
The interactive game Façade is available for download via BitTorrent.

Index

• G •

• *O* •

SINESS, CAREERS & PERSONAL FINANCE

Grant Writing FOR DUMMIES

0-7645-5307-0

Home Buying FOR DUMMIES

0-7645-5331-3 *†

Also available:
- Accounting For Dummies †
  0-7645-5314-3
- Business Plans Kit For Dummies †
  0-7645-5365-8
- Cover Letters For Dummies
  0-7645-5224-4
- Frugal Living For Dummies
  0-7645-5403-4
- Leadership For Dummies
  0-7645-5176-0
- Managing For Dummies
  0-7645-1771-6

- Marketing For Dummies
  0-7645-5600-2
- Personal Finance For Dummies *
  0-7645-2590-5
- Project Management For Dummies
  0-7645-5283-X
- Resumes For Dummies †
  0-7645-5471-9
- Selling For Dummies
  0-7645-5363-1
- Small Business Kit For Dummies *†
  0-7645-5093-4

ME & BUSINESS COMPUTER BASICS

Windows XP FOR DUMMIES

0-7645-4074-2

Excel 2003 ALL-IN-ONE DESK REFERENCE FOR DUMMIES

0-7645-3758-X

Also available:
- ACT! 6 For Dummies
  0-7645-2645-6
- iLife '04 All-in-One Desk Reference
  For Dummies
  0-7645-7347-0
- iPAQ For Dummies
  0-7645-6769-1
- Mac OS X Panther Timesaving
  Techniques For Dummies
  0-7645-5812-9
- Macs For Dummies
  0-7645-5656-8

- Microsoft Money 2004 For Dummies
  0-7645-4195-1
- Office 2003 All-in-One Desk Reference
  For Dummies
  0-7645-3883-7
- Outlook 2003 For Dummies
  0-7645-3759-8
- PCs For Dummies
  0-7645-4074-2
- TiVo For Dummies
  0-7645-6923-6
- Upgrading and Fixing PCs For Dummies
  0-7645-1665-5
- Windows XP Timesaving Techniques
  For Dummies
  0-7645-3748-2

OD, HOME, GARDEN, HOBBIES, MUSIC & PETS

Feng Shui FOR DUMMIES

0-7645-5295-3

Poker FOR DUMMIES

0-7645-5232-5

Also available:
- Bass Guitar For Dummies
  0-7645-2487-9
- Diabetes Cookbook For Dummies
  0-7645-5230-9
- Gardening For Dummies *
  0-7645-5130-2
- Guitar For Dummies
  0-7645-5106-X
- Holiday Decorating For Dummies
  0-7645-2570-0
- Home Improvement All-in-One
  For Dummies
  0-7645-5680-0

- Knitting For Dummies
  0-7645-5395-X
- Piano For Dummies
  0-7645-5105-1
- Puppies For Dummies
  0-7645-5255-4
- Scrapbooking For Dummies
  0-7645-7208-3
- Senior Dogs For Dummies
  0-7645-5818-8
- Singing For Dummies
  0-7645-2475-5
- 30-Minute Meals For Dummies
  0-7645-2589-1

TERNET & DIGITAL MEDIA

Digital Photography FOR DUMMIES

0-7645-1664-7

Starting an eBay Business FOR DUMMIES

0-7645-6924-4

Also available:
- 2005 Online Shopping Directory
  For Dummies
  0-7645-7495-7
- CD & DVD Recording For Dummies
  0-7645-5956-7
- eBay For Dummies
  0-7645-5654-1
- Fighting Spam For Dummies
  0-7645-5965-6
- Genealogy Online For Dummies
  0-7645-5964-8
- Google For Dummies
  0-7645-4420-9

- Home Recording For Musicians
  For Dummies
  0-7645-1634-5
- The Internet For Dummies
  0-7645-4173-0
- iPod & iTunes For Dummies
  0-7645-7772-7
- Preventing Identity Theft For Dummies
  0-7645-7336-5
- Pro Tools All-in-One Desk Reference
  For Dummies
  0-7645-5714-9
- Roxio Easy Media Creator For Dummies
  0-7645-7131-1

 **WILEY**

SPORTS, FITNESS, PARENTING, RELIGION & SPIRITUALITY

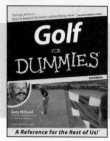

0-7645-5146-9

0-7645-5418-2

Also available:

- Adoption For Dummies
  0-7645-5488-3
- Basketball For Dummies
  0-7645-5248-1
- The Bible For Dummies
  0-7645-5296-1
- Buddhism For Dummies
  0-7645-5359-3
- Catholicism For Dummies
  0-7645-5391-7
- Hockey For Dummies
  0-7645-5228-7

- Judaism For Dummies
  0-7645-5299-6
- Martial Arts For Dummies
  0-7645-5358-5
- Pilates For Dummies
  0-7645-5397-6
- Religion For Dummies
  0-7645-5264-3
- Teaching Kids to Read For Dummies
  0-7645-4043-2
- Weight Training For Dummies
  0-7645-5168-X
- Yoga For Dummies
  0-7645-5117-5

TRAVEL

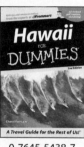

0-7645-5438-7

0-7645-5453-0

Also available:

- Alaska For Dummies
  0-7645-1761-9
- Arizona For Dummies
  0-7645-6938-4
- Cancún and the Yucatán For Dummies
  0-7645-2437-2
- Cruise Vacations For Dummies
  0-7645-6941-4
- Europe For Dummies
  0-7645-5456-5
- Ireland For Dummies
  0-7645-5455-7

- Las Vegas For Dummies
  0-7645-5448-4
- London For Dummies
  0-7645-4277-X
- New York City For Dummies
  0-7645-6945-7
- Paris For Dummies
  0-7645-5494-8
- RV Vacations For Dummies
  0-7645-5443-3
- Walt Disney World & Orlando For Dummies
  0-7645-6943-0

GRAPHICS, DESIGN & WEB DEVELOPMENT

0-7645-4345-8

0-7645-5589-8

Also available:

- Adobe Acrobat 6 PDF For Dummies
  0-7645-3760-1
- Building a Web Site For Dummies
  0-7645-7144-3
- Dreamweaver MX 2004 For Dummies
  0-7645-4342-3
- FrontPage 2003 For Dummies
  0-7645-3882-9
- HTML 4 For Dummies
  0-7645-1995-6
- Illustrator CS For Dummies
  0-7645-4084-X

- Macromedia Flash MX 2004 For Dummies
  0-7645-4358-X
- Photoshop 7 All-in-One Desk Reference For Dummies
  0-7645-1667-1
- Photoshop CS Timesaving Techniques For Dummies
  0-7645-6782-9
- PHP 5 For Dummies
  0-7645-4166-8
- PowerPoint 2003 For Dummies
  0-7645-3908-6
- QuarkXPress 6 For Dummies
  0-7645-2593-X

NETWORKING, SECURITY, PROGRAMMING & DATABASES

0-7645-6852-3

0-7645-5784-X

Also available:

- A+ Certification For Dummies
  0-7645-4187-0
- Access 2003 All-in-One Desk Reference For Dummies
  0-7645-3988-4
- Beginning Programming For Dummies
  0-7645-4997-9
- C For Dummies
  0-7645-7068-4
- Firewalls For Dummies
  0-7645-4048-3
- Home Networking For Dummies
  0-7645-42796

- Network Security For Dummies
  0-7645-1679-5
- Networking For Dummies
  0-7645-1677-9
- TCP/IP For Dummies
  0-7645-1760-0
- VBA For Dummies
  0-7645-3989-2
- Wireless All In-One Desk Reference For Dummies
  0-7645-7496-5
- Wireless Home Networking For Dummies
  0-7645-3910-8

ALTH & SELF-HELP

0-7645-6820-5 *†

0-7645-2566-2

Also available:

Alzheimer's For Dummies
0-7645-3899-3

Asthma For Dummies
0-7645-4233-8

Controlling Cholesterol For Dummies
0-7645-5440-9

Depression For Dummies
0-7645-3900-0

Dieting For Dummies
0-7645-4149-8

Fertility For Dummies
0-7645-2549-2

Fibromyalgia For Dummies
0-7645-5441-7

Improving Your Memory For Dummies
0-7645-5435-2

Pregnancy For Dummies †
0-7645-4483-7

Quitting Smoking For Dummies
0-7645-2629-4

Relationships For Dummies
0-7645-5384-4

Thyroid For Dummies
0-7645-5385-2

JCATION, HISTORY, REFERENCE & TEST PREPARATION

0-7645-5194-9

0-7645-4186-2

Also available:

Algebra For Dummies
0-7645-5325-9

British History For Dummies
0-7645-7021-8

Calculus For Dummies
0-7645-2498-4

English Grammar For Dummies
0-7645-5322-4

Forensics For Dummies
0-7645-5580-4

The GMAT For Dummies
0-7645-5251-1

Inglés Para Dummies
0-7645-5427-1

Italian For Dummies
0-7645-5196-5

Latin For Dummies
0-7645-5431-X

Lewis & Clark For Dummies
0-7645-2545-X

Research Papers For Dummies
0-7645-5426-3

The SAT I For Dummies
0-7645-7193-1

Science Fair Projects For Dummies
0-7645-5460-3

U.S. History For Dummies
0-7645-5249-X

Get smart @ dummies.com®

- **Find a full list of Dummies titles**

- **Look into loads of FREE on-site articles**

- **Sign up for FREE eTips e-mailed to you weekly**

- **See what other products carry the Dummies name**

- **Shop directly from the Dummies bookstore**

- **Enter to win new prizes every month!**

arate Canadian edition also available

arate U.K. edition also available

ble wherever books are sold. For more information or to order direct: U.S. customers visit www.dummies.com or call 1-877-762-2974.
ustomers visit www.wileyeurope.com or call 0800 243407. Canadian customers visit www.wiley.ca or call 1-800-567-4797.